CHINA'S
TRUMP CARD

CHINA'S TRUMP CARD

CRYPTOCURRENCY AND ITS GAME-CHANGING ROLE IN SINO-US TRADE

RAYMOND YEUNG

WILEY

Registered Office(s)

John Wiley & Sons, Ltd.,

Editorial Office

111 River Street, Hoboken, NJ 07030, USA

For details of our global editorial offices, customer services, and more information about Wiley products visit us at www.wiley.com.

Wiley also publishes its books in a variety of electronic formats and by print-on-demand. Some content that appears in standard print versions of this book may not be available in other formats.

Library of Congress Cataloging-in-Publication Data

Names: Yeung, Raymond Y. T., author.
Title: China's Trump card : cryptocurrency and its game-changing role in
  Sino-US trade / Raymond Yeung.
Description: First edition. | Hoboken : Wiley, 2020. | Includes
  bibliographical references and index.
Identifiers: LCCN 2020025712 (print) | LCCN 2020025713 (ebook) | ISBN
  9781119699125 (hardback) | ISBN 9781119699149 (adobe pdf) | ISBN
  9781119699156 (epub)
Subjects: LCSH: China—Commerce—United States. | United
  States—Commerce—China. | Tariff—China. | Tariff—United States. |
  China—Foreign economic relations—United States. | United
  States—Foreign economic relations—China. | Trump, Donald, 1946-
Classification: LCC HF3838.U6 Y46 2020 (print) | LCC HF3838.U6 (ebook) |
  DDC 382.0951/073—dc23
LC record available at https://lccn.loc.gov/2020025712
LC ebook record available at https://lccn.loc.gov/2020025713

Cover Design: Wiley
Cover Images: Dragon © ly86/Getty Images,
Cryptocurrency icon © Puwadol Jaturawutthichai/Shutterstock, Cardboard paper © koosen/Shutterstock

Set in 11.5/14pt BemboStd by SPi Global, Chennai, India

Printed and bound by CPI Group (UK) Ltd, Croydon, CR0 4YY

10 9 8 7 6 5 4 3 2 1

To all the victims who have suffered from the deadly coronavirus. To all the medical heroes who fought selflessly in the front line.

Contents

Acknowledgments

This book could not have been completed without the help of many awesome individuals. My beloved wife Theresa read the first draft of the manuscript while serving me a bowl of noodles when I was burning the midnight oil. A special appreciation to my niece Tiffany Kwok, a smart, passionate student in political science at the University of Toronto who served as my secret "reviewer" and offered me helpful comments.

Thanks to everyone on the Wiley team, notably Gladys (Syd) Ganaden, Purvi Patel, and Karen Weller, who helped me so much in the publication process.

I thank my employer, Australia and New Zealand Banking Group Limited (ANZ) for approving this external engagement with Wiley. I am indebted to Richard Yetsenga, ANZ's Chief Economist, for supporting this endeavor and my personal development. Richard and many colleagues I've collaborated with closely during the past decade are an integral part of my career development.

This book covers a very complicated subject. I have benefited from many knowledgeable individuals in the business community, institutional investors, and policymakers. Many of them have significant stakes in the Sino–US economic relationship. They've offered me many different perspectives in analyzing this trillion-dollar question. I can only express my gratitude to them anonymously.

Last, but not least, without God's provision I wouldn't be able to do any of this when the world is beset by pandemic and other socio-chaotic woes.

All views expressed in this book are neither my employer's nor the aforementioned parties. All errors are solely my responsibility.

About the Author

Raymond Yeung graduated with a PhD in Economics from Queen's University in Canada and is a holder of the Financial Risk Manager (FRM) certification. He began his economist career one week prior to the Asian Financial Crisis in 1997. He is currently Chief Economist Greater China at Australia and New Zealand Banking Group Limited (ANZ), leading an award-winning team covering the region's macroeconomic and financial market research. His insights have received strong following, including institutional investors, corporate treasurers, and central banks. He speaks frequently in industry conferences and shares his views on Bloomberg, Financial Times, CNBC, Di Yi Cai Jin, and Caixin. Prior to joining ANZ, Raymond was Deputy Head of Economic Research Asia at Swiss Re. He is a Council member of China Chief Economist Forum and a columnist in the Chinese media.

Preface

When I submitted the manuscript to the Wiley team, China and the rest of the world were battling against the COVID-19 pandemic. To prevent the virus from spreading, the Chinese government imposed a lockdown policy unprecedentedly. Economic activity was weighed down acutely. Supply chains were interrupted. The global situation was also alarming as the virus cases soared in other countries, including the US. In response to the negative economic impact, the Federal Reserve reduced policy interest rate to zero and restarted quantitative easing. Other central banks also followed the Fed and eased their monetary policy.

The virus shock represented an unpredictable "Black Swan" event in a fashion similar to Trump's initiated trade war. When the 45th US president took over the White House in early 2017, not too many people treated his "America First" claim seriously. His tweets, his tariff, and his "friendship" with president Xi Jinping stirred up market volatility. When he started the trade war in 2018 shortly after hosting Xi in Florida, exporters were caught off guard. Many people in the financial markets regarded the trade war as the "black swan" of the year.

In this book, however, I argue that this US–China trade war is not a black swan. Unlike coronavirus, the trade tension is predictable. When the trade war was looming in July 2017, a high-profile editorial in *People's Daily* warned that China should be on guard against not only the black swan but also the "grey rhino." The Chinese government was pointing the latter to the lingering concern of a financial bubble, equivalent to a national security issue as I interpreted in a Bloomberg interview on July 19, 2017.

"Grey rhino," a concept coined by Michele Wucker in light of the Global Financial Crisis (GFC), refers to event risks that are impactful, obvious, and predictable. To Wucker, the US housing bubble in 2008 should have been foreseeable. The crisis was due to policymakers' lack of guts to right the wrong. When the GFC broke out, the market thought it was random and unpredictable. In hindsight, the policymakers should have noticed the danger and fixed it.

Likewise, the tension between the US and China was so obvious. The trade war was a "grey rhino." Three years prior to the GFC, Ben Bernanke agreed that the rising US current account deficit stemmed from a global saving glut. What he did not admit was that the only way to stop it was to take away the "exorbitant privilege" of the dollar. The then chairman of the US Fed printed money seemingly unlimitedly to save the US financial markets. China stocked up the US government debts and funded the ever-widening US–China trade gap. Trade imbalance was actually a monetary phenomenon. People said the trade war was a "black swan." Beneath the swan's feathers was actually a "grey rhino."

This book proposes a way to break the tie between the China–US trade imbalance and the global addiction to the US dollar, i.e. an outcome of the Triffin Dilemma. As the trade war is the onset of deglobalization, de-dollarization inevitably becomes a natural consequence. Cryptocurrency signals the need to reform the global monetary system. Just when China and the US are competing in the technological realm, Blockchain provides a perfect alternative to the current system of global foreign reserve. In 2009, Zhou Xiaochuan requested a reform of the dollar-based regime. In 2019, Mark Carney responded to his question and agreed to develop a "synthetic hegemonic currency."

In the first chapter, I review the causes, the impact, and the outlook of the trade war. On the surface, the US was frustrated with China's

track record of intellectual property rights and forced technology transfer, offering an excuse for the US to act. However, behind the conflict seemed to be the crash between the ideologies of "China Dream"
and "America First." Import tariff is just smoke and mirrors. The US
administration decided to attack the global supply chains. Prohibiting
US companies from business transactions with some Chinese companies
could paralyze their production line. It was an alternative way to drag
China's exports to the US. This trade war is unconventional.

In **Chapter 2**, I argue that, no matter how unconventional they are,
the trade measures and even trade agreements cannot reduce US current account deficits. Due to the "exorbitant privilege" of the US dollar, the US lacks an incentive to manage its fiscal and external balances.
China, a country having USD 3 trillion of savings in foreign currency,
has recycled its export surplus into US dollar assets. This loop, I call it
"factory dollar recycling," resembles what oil-exporting countries have
been doing after the Nixon shock. Even without gold backing, the US
dollar continues to secure the advantage of network externalities. The
problem of trade imbalance is chronic. Neither import tariff nor currency revaluation can fix it.

Is the leading position of the US dollar unshakable? **Chapter 3**
searches for an answer from history. The interchanging position between
pound sterling and the dollar in the Interwar Period offered many
important insights. In my discussion, I stress that globalization, financial integration, and dollarization are interlinked. When deglobalization
begins, as the trade war is signaling, populism and protectionism also
question the role of financial integration, especially after a financial crisis.
As the global market is divided, the dollar's monopolistic position is not
invincible.

Naturally, the protagonist in the trade war is the one eager to de-
dollarize, as I explain in **Chapter 4**. In 2005, China began to unpeg the
renminbi from the greenback. In 2009, the authorities kicked off a high-
profile campaign of currency internationalization. By Mundell's impossible trinity, a more flexible exchange rate regime will allow China to
hold less foreign reserve. Using the yuan as a trade currency also allows
China to distance itself from the US dollar. This policy preference may
also be revealed by the currency allocation of China's sovereign wealth
funds. Contrary to the topic of RMB internationalization, China's

reserve management has not received much coverage in the existing literature. But it is a critical part of reforming the global monetary regime.

After the Nixon shock, the US secured the fate of its currency
through semi-pegging with Saudi Arabia's oil reserve. In the twenty-
first century, what kind of tie should the Chinese yuan develop? In
Chapter 5, I argue that technological development is the only way for
the country to beat the middle-income trap. "Go digital" is a development strategy many countries have adopted in order to stay competitive.
China has already held a leading position in e-commerce and internet
connectivity. Belt and Road (supposedly) has become an opportunity to
extend this connectivity globally. In the last few decades, petroleum was
backing the global influence of the US dollar. In digital times, 5G will
very likely support China's total factor productivity. In this century, China's position in the digital economy defines the value of the renminbi.

Can the Chinese yuan replace the US dollar in the digital economy?
The answer is "possibly." The pound lost its global position after a series
of shocks during the Interwar Period. Similarly, another shock is required
to trigger a reform in the international monetary system. In my view,
blockchain is the trigger. In **Chapter 6**, I offer my two cents on cryptocurrency from an outsider's point of view. My wish is for the readers to
appreciate that, based on blockchain, cryptocurrency is technically capable of being a secured form of payment. My discussion in this chapter
focuses on the micro foundation of cryptocurrency. In contrast to our
money-and-banking system, distributed ledger technology is disinterme-
diating. The architecture is completely different from sovereign money, be
it the yuan or the US dollar. However, distributing the trust across participating members does not disqualify its legitimacy as a form of money.

In **Chapter 7**, I lift the discussion of cryptocurrency to the macro
level. The international monetary system is sovereign-based. The system is rule-based, as the Balance of Payment Manual states the foreign
reserves have to be denominated in currency of the legal tender. Well,
gold is exceptional. But, in my view, there is no reason not to expand
the list of exceptions. Facebook's introduction of Libra has prompted
regulators to quicken the development of central bank digital currency.
Zhou's request was met with a cold shoulder. Satoshi Nakamoto's invention was regarded as a cult. Eventually, Carney's call for going digital will
likely receive a red-carpet treatment.

In the **final chapter**, I propose a practical solution that takes Carney's idea one step forward. The digital currencies issued by different central banks are largely an electronic version of M0. They are still fiat money. To preserve the spirit of blockchain, global policymakers should develop an official cryptocurrency that can also overcome some operational issues of private coins, such as governance of reserve or AML/CTF. I name this coin the World Crypto Currency (WCC). Given its official status, the WCC could also be a reserve currency for China to consider. Don't be afraid, China. The new system will facilitate your reserve diversification. The WCC is not a yuan competitor. It is a venue to support the value of the renminbi.

Lastly, I definitely need to underscore certain caveats here. This book is perhaps the first attempt to integrate several seemingly unrelated economic topics into a single coherent theme: the US–China trade war, the economic history of globalization, digital economy, cryptocurrency, and monetary economics. My broad and superficial knowledge does not qualify me an expert in any of them. The thoughts presented in this book do not form any base for an investment recommendation. I do not have personal holdings in cryptocurrency (as of March 2020). My hope is for this book to offer some food for thought in the era when the new international economic order begins.

Chapter 1

An Unconventional Trade Feud

1.1 Thanos and Trump

Beware readers, spoiler alert ahead.

> *"I thought by eliminating half of life, the other half would thrive . . . with the stones you've collected for me, create a new one teeming with life that knows not what it has lost but only what it has been given. A grateful universe. . . . I am inevitable."*

> *Thanos,* Avengers: Endgame.

On June 20, 2018, I came across an interesting headline, "Avengers star Josh Brolin explains how Trump is similar to his 'Infinity War' villain Thanos," on an online business magazine.[1] In his interview with

---

[1] *Insider.* "Avengers" star Josh Brolin explains how Trump is similar to his "Infinity War" villain Thanos. *Insider* (June 20, 2018). (https://www.insider.com/josh-brolin-avengers-infinity-war-thanos-donald-trump-stephen-colbert-video-2018-6).

Stephen Colbert, Brolin hilariously read Trump's tweet in Thanos's tone. The Hollywood star, whose character erased half of the galaxy's population to fulfill his own political belief, said Trump's public policies were akin to what Thanos did in the Marvel trilogy. His own planet, Titan, ran out of resources due to overpopulation. In response, Thanos thought the resource imbalance problem facing the universe could be addressed through massacring half of the creatures. He was addressing an economic problem. He tried to search for an equilibrium, and he called it "balance." "When I'm done, half of humanity will still exist. Perfectly balanced, as all things should be."

What was Thanos's plan? The *Avengers* villain offered "a peaceful way" to finish people's lives painlessly and indiscriminately. He collected six Infinity Stones, snapped his fingers, and turned many superheroes into ashes—a very sad ending, surprising the audience that walked out of the cinema. Handling the Infinity Stones was not an easy task. The gems were full of gamma rays. Anyone who held the stones needed a strong will to do so. Thanos believed he was the chosen one to fulfill his "destiny." He said, "I'm the only one who knows that. At least I'm the only who has the will to act on it." He even sacrificed his beloved daughter Gamora in exchange for the soul stone. "The hardest choice requires the strongest will." Do Thanos's words sound like a president who claimed he was the designated one to lead his country to greatness again?

Donald Trump thought flagging a trade war could restore the trade balance of the US. He could order his administration to severely penalize China. Lifting import tariff rates from 0% to 25% on Chinese goods in a flash caught the world off guard. Half a million factory workers were affected. China was labeled a currency manipulator even though everyone knew the country actually wanted a stronger rather than weaker currency. Trump's trade measures hurt many American companies and US consumers. But he did not care. He had a strong will like Thanos and he decisively went his own way. "We reject globalism and embrace the doctrine of patriotism," he said, delivering his second address to the United Nations in November 2018.[2]

---

[2]Trump, D. (2018). Speech presented at the 73th regular session of the United Nations General Assembly (September 25). (https://www.whitehouse.gov/briefings-statements/remarks-president-trump-73rd-session-united-nations-general-assembly-new-york-ny/).

At the same time, there are still believers in free trade. Germany, Canada, Mexico, Korea, Japan, and other countries have risen to prosperity in the past few decades. They prefer globalization of some sort. The G20 Summit in Hamburg 2017 issued a heroic declaration to defend the prevailing international arrangement: "Globalization and technological change have contributed significantly to driving economic growth and raising living standards across the globe. However, the gains from globalization have not been shared widely enough. By bringing together developed and emerging market economies, the G20 is determined to shape globalization to benefit all people. Most importantly, we need to better enable our people to seize its opportunities."[3]

China was the top winner in globalization. In 1979, the Middle Kingdom decided to open up, fueling the world with a massive supply of labor. After 40 years of strong growth, the country became the production line for the world, receiving orders from the US, Japan, and Europe. Its ability for mass production was unchallengeable. The quality and technological content of Chinese products improved rapidly in the past few years. It began to develop its own brand. China became a prime target of Trump's new trade policy.

Meanwhile, China was also faced with many structural economic issues, namely a notably aging population and debt pileup. President Xi Jinping saw the urgency to upgrade the economy. He wanted China to become a tech-driven economy by the middle of this century. His "China Dream" was seen as a threat to the Western-centric world. Xi vowed to bring prosperity to Eurasia via his Belt and Road campaign. He played as a champion for globalization. He wanted more countries to use the renminbi (RMB). Perhaps Trump thought if he didn't stop China now, it would be too late. Maybe the trade war was meant to safeguard the global dominance of the US. Whatever his initial motivation, the battle has begun. A new economic order is evolving.

This chapter reviews the causes, the impact, and the outlook of the trade war. In Section 1.2, I discuss several possible reasons for the trade war. Trump's policy stance clearly showed a discontent with globalization. All the disputes he created with other countries pointed to a rising era of unilateralism and neo-nationalism. Since China represented almost

---

[3]G20 (2017). Leaders' Declaration: Shaping an Interconnected World (July 8). (http://www.g20.utoronto.ca/2017/2017-G20-leaders-declaration.html).

two-thirds of the US total trade imbalance, treating China harshly was tactical. The US was frustrated with China's track record of intellectual property rights and forced technology transfer. This seemed to offer a legitimate reason for the US to act. However, underlying the trade tension appeared to be a rivalry between the China Dream and America First. China threat theory has become increasingly popular under the current political climate.[4] In a nutshell, the trade war is not an issue of trade imbalance.

Section 1.3 identifies the features of this conflict. Compared with other trade disputes, this US–China trade war is unconventional. An import tariff only serves as an appetizer but is not the main course itself. The US administration clearly understands how globalization works and decides to attack the global supply chains. Prohibiting US companies from business transactions with some Chinese companies can paralyze their production line. China can also retaliate by limiting the supply of rare earth. The tit-for-tat actions of both countries are strategic, calculative, and innovative.

In Section 1.4, I propose the possible outcomes of this trade war. The central theme of this book is that trade measures will not address the fundamental causes of the US trade imbalance. Import tariffs and investment restriction will hurt the economic interest of the US as importers will probably pass the cost to consumers. China will hedge the risk of excessive trade exposure and focus on developing its domestic economy. Europe and Japan would benefit from a closer economic tie with China. Trump's policy, which aims to make "America great again," would probably backfire on his country.

1.2 What Causes the Trade War?

1.2.1 Trump's Unilateralism

We have probably reached an inflection point in modern economic history. As the world's economic superpower, the US decided to change its

---

[4]Ciovacco, C. (2018). Understanding China threat. *The National Interest* (November 29).

course. After President Donald Trump took over the White House, his administration changed its approach to dealing with global economic affairs. The 45th president of the US paid no respect to the prevailing international order that seemed to have functioned well. Immediately taking over the White House, the US was pressing Mexico and Canada to renegotiate the North American Free Trade Agreement, one of the most significant trade bloc agreements in the world since 1994. Stepping into the second year of his tenure, his administration embarked on a trade war with China. By citing that China had stolen American jobs, the populist president posed a serious challenge not only to the trade partners of the US but also the long-held belief in globalization of other countries.

With hindsight, Trump's trade policy shouldn't have surprised anyone. In the early days of his election campaign, the Republican candidate had already revealed his controversial plan to build a "great wall" along the US–Mexico border. He wrote a two-page memo to the *Washington Post* in March 2016 and vowed to execute his plan to build a 1,000-mile border fence.[5] He threatened to halt remittance transfers to Mexico, sent by Mexican immigrants in the US, which amounted to nearly USD 25 billion a year. Trump said the border wall that would cost USD 8 billion should be paid for by the Mexican government. In addition, he also planned to restrict Mexican imports, halt legal immigration, and increase fees for visas and green cards. On the issue of illegal immigrants he said, "We have the moral high ground here, and all the leverage."

In the past few years, the world has witnessed his unconventional approach to managing economic affairs by the populist ideology. He evaluated the positions of his counterparty and his own in a holistic manner. The bilateral issues under his radar were not necessarily confined within trade and investment. In his game, everything, such as climate change and international security, could be monetized and bargained. Typically, American politicians saw North Korea as a national security issue. But Trump said he would consider withdrawing US military stationed in South Korea unless the latter paid for the defensive support. In his campaign, he described the US–Korea Free Trade Agreement that

---

[5] *Washington Post.* Trump reveals how he would force Mexico to pay for border wall. (April 5, 2016). (https://www.washingtonpost.com/politics/trump-would-seek-to-block-money-transfers-to-force-mexico-to-fund-border-wall/2016/04/05/c0196314-fa7c-11e5-80e4-c381214de1a3_story.html).

was launched in 2007 as a "job-killing trade deal." He began to renegotiate this shortly after his arrival at the White House.

Many political scholars suggested that Trump's "America First"
could be inherited from the unilateralist–isolationist tradition dating
back to the 19th century. Trump's presidential election might mirror the
surge of a "Jacksonian," or populist, view of world politics (Mead 1999).
The Jacksonian approach combined elements of ethno-nationalism, anti-
elitism, and strong commitment to the values of the American "folk
community." This approach tended to see the US as a loser in opening
the economy to the world.[6] Nonetheless, the development in the past
few years indicated that unilateralism had been increasingly adopted by
some governments in dealing with global affairs. Hirsh (2016) warned
that the global trend of neo-nationalism would continue to last, as there
was a parallel development not only in Trump's trade policy but also
Boris Johnson's attitude in Brexit.

The Jacksonian stance was well reflected by the list of international agreements withdrawn by the US (Fehl and Thimm 2019). They
included the Paris Agreement on Climate Change, the UN Human Rights
Council, and the UN Educational, Scientific and Cultural Organization
(UNESCO) to more obscure treaties such as the Universal Postal Union.
In his 2017 and 2018 speeches at the UN General Assembly, Trump
announced his unrelenting position to "defend America's interests above
all else"[7] and "choose independence and cooperation over global governance, control, and domination."[8] This was probably one of the most
undiplomatic expressions ever voiced from any US president. Trump
also threatened to withdraw the US from the World Trade Organization
(WTO), stating that "If they don't shape up, I would withdraw from the

---

[6]Spatafora, G. (2018). The Jacksonian Foundations of Trump's American Foreign
Policy. The Oxford University Politics Blog (January 12).

[7]Trump, D. (2017). Speech presented at the 72nd regular session of the United
Nations General Assembly (September 19). (https://gadebate.un.org/sites/default/
files/gastatements/72/us_en.pdf).

[8]Trump, D. (2018). Speech presented at the 73th regular session of the United
Nations General Assembly (September 25). (https://www.whitehouse.gov/
briefings-statements/remarks-president-trump-73rd-session-united-nations-
general-assembly-new-york-ny/).

WTO" and claimed that "[the US] lose the lawsuits, almost all the lawsuits in the WTO."[9]

Trump's anti-multilateral approach shocked his US allies in Asia-Pacific. He walked away from the Trans-Pacific Partnership (TPP) trade agreement. The trade pact, originally proposed by a group of Pacific countries back in 2016, was considered a move to counter China's growing influence in the region.[10] Australia, Brunei, Canada, Chile, Japan, Malaysia, Mexico, New Zealand, Peru, Singapore, Vietnam, and the US (President Barack Obama) signed the deal on February 4, 2016. After Trump's withdrawal, the agreement could not enter into force. In December 2018, the remaining signatories renamed the new deal as the Comprehensive and Progressive Agreement for Trans-Pacific Partnership, forming a trade pact of much smaller scale without the participation of the US and China.

As a unilateralist, Trump believed the US could gain more from squeezing the last penny from other countries' wallets. He dealt with every country individually. Sachs (2018) pointed out that Trump's policies were based on a mindset of zero-sum game. Even though free trade helped the world reach another equilibrium at which the US has gained more, the unilateral approach might have held appeal to politicians who focused narrowly on the second-best outcomes under a political cycle. Indeed, political analysts proposed that unilateralism could be a rational course of action for the major powers and was often a preferred approach of the hegemonic state. Tago (2017) wrote, "A powerful state that can achieve its policy goals using its own resources without the need of international support can pursue a foreign policy that would not follow accepted international norms."

1.2.2 A Stubbornly Large China Deficit

Back in 2009, former US president Barack Obama and former Chinese president Hu Jintao established the US–China Economic and Strategic Dialogue at the G20 Summit in London. There was an Economic Track in

---

[9]BBC News. Trump threatens to pull US out of World Trade Organization (August 31, 2018). (https://www.bbc.com/news/world-us-canada-45364150).

[10]Naughton, B., Kroeber, K., Jonquières, G.D., Webster, G. (2015). What Will the TPP Mean for China? Foreign Policy (October 7).

the dialogue for bilateral economic issues. Even though the two countries had agreed with the US–China Comprehensive Framework for Promoting Strong, Sustainable and Balanced Growth and Economic Cooperation in 2011,[11] the annual meetings could not reduce the trade imbalance. Trump said, "And I blame us, I don't blame them. I don't blame President Xi. I blame all of our presidents, and not just President Obama. You go back a long way. You look at president Clinton, Bush—everybody. They allowed this to happen, they created a monster. . . . We rebuilt China because they get so much money."[12]

Of all the US trading partners, China was the most visible one. Their trade flow represented the largest factory and largest buyer in the world. After China's opening up to the US and other investors, the two countries were deeply integrated. "Doing business in China" was the popular theme in MBA programs specializing in International Business. Excluding intra-EU trade, China represented 16.2% of the world's total exports and the US accounted for 16.6% of the world's total imports in 2018, according to data from the WTO. The bilateral goods and services trade was worth USD 737 billion in 2018 (see Table 1.1). It was the largest country–country trade flow in the world, more than the size of the Switzerland economy (the 20th largest economy in the world).

Of all countries registering trade surplus with the US trade, China stood out. In 2018, the US reported a trade deficit in goods of USD 880.3 billion. China alone accounted for 48% of the total, which was USD 419.6 billion (see Figure 1.1). If trade in services was included, the deficit with China was USD 380.0 billion or 66% of the total. The trade deficit on goods and services with China was three times the combined amount of Germany and Japan. If Trump could reduce the US trade deficit with China by 20%, the size could offset the entire trade deficit with Mexico. Closing the trade gap with China could have improved the overall trade balance of the US materially.

---

[11]U.S. Department of the Treasury (2011). U.S.-China Comprehensive Framework for Promoting Strong, Sustainable and Balanced Growth and Economic Cooperation. Press release (May 10). (https://www.treasury.gov/press-center/press-releases/Pages/TG1171.aspx).

[12]*Newsweek*. Donald Trump blames Obama, Bush, Clinton for China deficit. (May 20, 2019).

Table 1.1 Economic tie between the US and China.

Items at Stake	Activities in/from China	Activities in/from the US
Goods trade, 2018	Chinese exports to US: USD 540 billion	US exports to China: USD 120 billion
Services trade, 2018	Chinese exports to US: USD 18 billion	US export to China: USD 59 billion
Major items (USD billion)	Electrical machinery (152), machinery (117), furniture and bedding (35), toys and sports (27), plastics (19)	Aircraft (18), machinery (14), electrical machinery (13), optical and medical instruments (10), vehicles (9), agricultural (9)
FDI stock, 2017	US FDI in China: USD 108 billion	China's FDI in US: USD 40 billion
MNC foreign affiliates, 2016	US companies in China: Sales USD 55 billion	China companies in US: Sales USD 8 billion
Financial claims	China's holding of US government securities: USD 1.1 trillion (November 2019)	US banks' claims in China: Immediate counterparty basis: USD 87 billion (Q4 2018) Ultimate risks basis: USD 96 billion (Q4 2018)

Sources: USTR, US Treasury, BIS

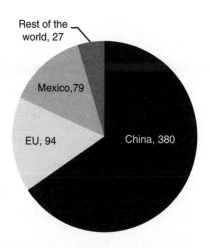

Figure 1.1 US trade deficit in 2018 in USD billion.
Source: US Bureau of Economic Analysis (US BEA)

Rather worryingly, the US trade deficit with China showed no sign of slowing. China was already an offshore production base of US companies. This relationship was irreversible. When China was admitted to the WTO in 2001, the trade deficit was USD 81.3 billion. In less than two decades, the gap had expanded more than four times to USD 380 billion in 2018 (see Figure 1.2). In the same period, the size of US GDP had only doubled from USD 10.6 trillion to USD 20.5 trillion in 2018, while China's GDP was 10 times larger than its original position (2001: USD 13.4 trillion). China's faster pace of economic expansion was perceived to have been a result of an unfair advantage over the US.

The reality is that the Sino-US economic tie goes beyond trade. The bilateral economic tie comprises both current account and financial/capital account transactions. Underlying the goods flows have been the massive investments by American companies in China. The US is a net foreign direct investor in China. American companies profit from their offshore operations in China. The US also receives net earnings from its service exports (2018: USD 38.8 billion), including spending by Chinese tourists and overseas students. On the financial side, China is the second-largest foreign holder of US government debts (November 2019: USD 1.1 trillion), almost three times the annual trade surplus China earned from the US.

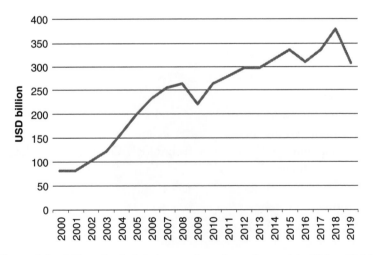

Figure 1.2   US trade deficit in goods and services with China 2000–2018.
Source: US BEA

1.2.3 Unfair Trade Practices

What frustrates the US is not only the size of the trade balance but also China's trade practice. Even though China's accession to the WTO has contributed to the global economy, there have been many complaints about China's commitment to free trade and market liberalization. The US accused China of several issues:

- Higher import tariff: China generally imposes an import tariff at higher rates than many countries. For instance, tariff rates on automobiles had been 25% since 2005. In 2017, China reduced the tariff rates to 15%, possibly due to pressure from the US and other countries. One issue is China's status as a developing country at the WTO, which allows it to maintain some trade barriers to nurture industrial development. As China is now the world's second-largest economy, it is reasonable for the US to question China's special status.

- Market accession: Foreign investors often complain about market access in China. The government has maintained some implicit and explicit entry barriers. For instance, foreign ownership in life insurance was capped at 51% (to be relaxed in 2020). Banks were required to obtain additional licensing approval by the financial regulator if they wanted to expand their scope of operations or geographical location of branches. It was only in 2018 that the government announced a large degree of financial liberalization. This policy was perceived to be a measure to stabilize the yuan's exchange rate, in addition to the pressure from the US.

- Protection of intellectual property rights (IPR) and forced technology transfers: There has been a general impression that China is a copycat. E-commerce operators are accused of selling counterfeit goods. Worst of all, the joint venture arrangement is believed to be a platform for China to tap into and learn US technology. There are anecdotes claiming that Chinese scientists are stealing trade secrets from the US.

- Competitive devaluation: Since 2005, China has gradually shifted from pegging its currency with the dollar to a floating exchange rate regime. On August 11, 2015, the People's Bank of China (PBOC) implemented a market reform, involving a one-off alignment of the daily fixing rate against the prevailing market rates. However, the perception remains that the Chinese central bank continues to actively intervene in the market (although the PBOC's objective is to push for a stronger yuan). When the yuan weakened and USD/CNY rose above 7.0 in 2019, the US designated China as a currency manipulating country. When it dropped below 7.0 in January 2020, the designation was removed.

Section 301 of the Trade Act 1974 is a principal tool for the US administration to handle unfair trade practices. According to Congressional Research Services, Section 301 procedures apply to foreign acts, policies, and practices that the United States Trade Representative (USTR) determines either (1) violate, or are inconsistent with, a trade agreement; or (2) are unjustifiable and burden or restrict US commerce. In the past, the USTR used to bring all trade disputes to the WTO for adjudication. Because Trump does not believe in the WTO, Section 301 offers a handy way for his administration to tackle China unilaterally.

In March 2018, Trump ordered the Section 301 Investigation into China's trade practices.[13] The investigation concluded that:

- First, China uses foreign ownership restrictions, including joint venture requirements, equity limitations, and other investment restrictions, to require or pressure technology transfer from US companies to Chinese entities. China also uses administrative review and licensing procedures to require or pressure technology transfer, which, inter alia, undermines the value of US investments and technology and weakens the global competitiveness of US firms.
- Second, China imposes substantial restrictions on, and intervenes in, US firms' investments and activities, including through restrictions on technology licensing terms. These restrictions deprive US technology owners of the ability to bargain and set market-based terms for technology transfer. As a result, US companies seeking to license technologies must do so on terms that unfairly favor Chinese recipients.

---

[13]The White House, United States Government (2018). Presidential Memorandum on the Actions by the United States Related to the Section 301 Investigation. Presidential Memorandum (March 22). (https://www.whitehouse.gov/presidential-actions/presidential-memorandum-actions-united-states-related-section-301-investigation/).

- Third, China directs and facilitates the systematic investment in, and acquisition of, US companies and assets by Chinese companies to obtain cutting-edge technologies and intellectual property and to generate large-scale technology transfer in industries deemed important by Chinese government industrial plans.
- Fourth, China conducts and supports unauthorized intrusions into, and theft from, the computer networks of US companies. These actions provide the Chinese government with unauthorized access to intellectual property, trade secrets, or confidential business information, including technical data, negotiating positions, and sensitive and proprietary internal business communications, and they also support China's strategic development goals, including its science and technology advancement, military modernization, and economic development.

Following the Section 301 investigation, the USTR announced a list of Chinese goods to be covered by import tariffs. The initial tariff rates on Chinese products on Lists 1–3 were imposed in May 2019. Since July 2018, bilateral negotiations between the two countries were held in Beijing and Washington, DC several times. These talks were largely unsuccessful and could not prevent the tension from escalating. Instead, Trump and Xi met several times at the G20 Summit, leading to some delays in tariff implementation. In January 2020, the two countries agreed on a truce while Trump was under political pressure domestically due to an impeachment.[14] In the Phase One agreement, China pledged to improve the standard of IPR protection and prohibit Chinese enterprises from forced technology transfer.

1.2.4 "China Dream" vs. "America First"

The US has been the leader amongst the advanced countries, while China often considers itself as representing the voice of the developing world. What is interesting is that while the US questions the international order it helped to establish, China is exerting a larger influence on global economic affairs. This conflict is also the result of tension between

---

[14]Bloomberg. January 19, 2020. (https://www.bloomberg.com/news/articles/2020-01-19/trump-s-china-deal-is-his-hedge-against-impeachment-damage).

a Western country that has awkwardly adopted a unilateralist approach and a Communist country that is striving for a bigger role in globalization. In terms of purchasing power parity (PPP), the size of China's economy surpassed the US in 2014 (see Figure 1.3). There has been a concern that the rise of China will eventually overtake the US.[15] The "China threat theory" has a big market in the circle of foreign affairs.

Back in March 2013, President Xi Jinping delivered his first national address, stating that "we must make persistent efforts, press ahead with indomitable will, continue to push forward the great cause of socialism with Chinese characteristics, and strive to achieve the Chinese dream of great rejuvenation of the Chinese nation." Over the past several years, the Chinese government launched a package of policies to transform the economy, including supply-side reforms, environmental protection, and technological innovation. The old economic model that was labor and credit intensive was no longer applicable. After a period of high-speed growth after the Global Financial Crisis (GFC), the country needed to address many economic concerns including debt pileup,

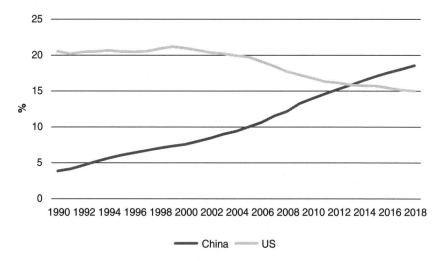

Figure 1.3   Share of World GDP in PPP terms.
Source: World Bank

[15]Whalen, C. (2019). A (Trade) war with China is inevitable. *The National Interest* (May 20).

property bubbles, corruptions, and air pollution. Xi called for a massive policy shift to focus on quality of growth instead of the speed of growth. This policy shift was thought to be less resource demanding and more sustainable.

China's economic reform involves the structural rebalancing of the economy (Zhang 2016). In essence, net export contribution to growth is trending down. A faster increase in imports than exports will be consistent with the structural shift from an investment-led to a consumption-led model. China is willing to buy more from the rest of the world, including the US. The era of persistently high current account surplus is almost over. As the national savings rate declines, the current account balance also falls (see Figure 1.4). The rising middle class has seen a sharp spike in outbound tourism. In 2018, China registered a net deficit of the service account of around 2% of GDP, offsetting two-thirds of the goods account surplus. China's economic profile will be less export-dependent.

However, shifting towards a domestically driven economic model does not mean an inward-looking approach. Xi wants to take the open door policy of Deng Xiaoping one step forward. He looks for the further

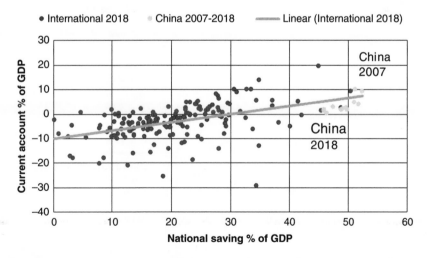

Figure 1.4 Current account balances and national savings rates of different countries.

Sources: IMF, author analysis

integration of China into the global economy beyond the goods trade. At the Party Congress in October 2017, Xi Jinping said that "openness brings progress, while self-seclusion leaves one behind." He pledged to "expand foreign trade, develop new models and new forms of trade and turn China into a trader of quality." A month later, China cut import tariffs on 187 items, ranging from milk powder to red wine. The appointment of a non-Chinese bank (JPMorgan) as a yuan clearing bank in the US in February 2018, also contrasted the previous practices of appointing only Chinese banks in other countries. China also held the International Import Expo in Shanghai in 2019. China seems to have accepted that trade liberalization is a natural outcome of rising economic status as measured in GDP per capita (see Figure 1.5).

A few years prior to the trade war, the Chinese government decided to adopt a list of recommendations in *China 2030: Building a Modern, Harmonious, and Creative Society*, a report jointly issued by Development Research Centre of China's State Council and the World Bank.[16] The theme of this report covers how China can avoid falling into the middle

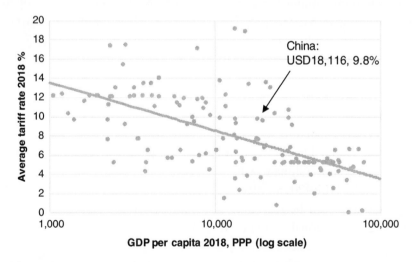

Figure 1.5   Import tariffs and GDP per capita 2018.

Sources: WTO, IMF, author analysis

[16]The World Bank. The Development and Research Centre of the State Council of the PRC. (2012). *China 2030: Building a Modern, Harmonious and Creative Society* (February 27).

income trap. Many recommendations of this report were adopted by the Chinese government. Specifically, one recommendation is to "seek mutually beneficial relations with the world by becoming a proactive stakeholder in the global economy, actively using multilateral institutions and frameworks, and shaping the global governance agenda." This stands as one of the explanations as to why China has adopted a high-profile approach in global trade affairs.

Xi's activism in multilateralism contrasted Trump's unilateral approach. After World War II, the Western world began to promote free trade. The Allies established the General Agreement on Tariffs and Trade (GATT) in 1947, three years after the Bretton Woods agreement on the international monetary system as well as the creation of the IMF and the World Bank, with headquarters in Washington, DC. In recent years, China has marketed an oriental version. In 2013, Xi kicked off with his Belt and Road Initiative (BRI) (see Annex A). Officially, the objectives were "to construct a unified large market and make full use of both international and domestic markets, through cultural exchange and integration, to enhance mutual understanding and trust of member nations, ending up in an innovative pattern with capital inflows, talent pool, and technology database." Following the launch of Belt and Road, China led the establishment of the Asian Infrastructure Investment Bank, headquartered in Beijing. In addition, Shanghai hosted the headquarters of New Development Bank, formerly known as the BRICS Bank, with Brazil, Russia, India, China, and South Africa. Multilateral organizations were not necessarily based in Washington, DC or Geneva.

The "China Dream" is regarded by some scholars as "a national strategy to restore China to its historical glory and take the US' place as world leader" (Liu 2015). Naturally, the China hawk policy of Trump's administration can be read as the US pre-emptive response to China's growing international influence. In the 19th Communist Party Congress in 2017, Xi pronounced his vision of the New Era, pushing China into a great modern socialist country that is "prosperous, powerful, democratic, culturally advanced, harmonious and beautiful. . . . [By the middle of the twenty-first century] China will become a global leader in terms of composite national strength and international influence." [17]

---

[17]http://www.xinhuanet.com/english/2017-10/18/c_136688933.htm.

This announcement was viewed by many as a direct confrontation to the global dominance of the US, despite Xi's repeated reiterations, publicly assuring other countries to abandon the "cold war mindset" and accept China's expansion as a "peaceful rise."

1.3 The Novelty of This Trade War

1.3.1 The Art of Being Unpredictable

Throughout the economic history, there have been numerous trade conflicts in the world. Typically, previous disputes involved conventional instruments such as import tariffs, quotas, subsidies, and other anti-dumping measures, aiming to penalize the counterparties or to support the affected industries. However, the trade war between the US and China is unconventional. It features many new and unique behaviors, enriching our understanding of international economics in the twenty-first century.

Trump represents a drastic change in personality of the US presidency. Of the 44 past presidents in US history, 26 were previously lawyers and 22 had military experience. Trump, a businessman, never held any public office nor military position. His approach to managing foreign affairs is unconventional. Other countries have difficulty coping with his "unpredictable character." As an active user of Twitter, Trump seems to deliberately desire to create some uncertainties so that the counterparties cannot fully grasp his actual position. In a foreign speech in April 2016, he admitted that "we have to be unpredictable."[18] Trump believes that he can leverage this approach in bargaining.

This special character was clearly illustrated in his China policy. On April 6, 2017, Trump hosted President Xi Jinping under luxurious/first-class-style circumstances. They spent time together with their wives in Florida. "Xi and his wife Peng Liyuan drove down a palm-lined driveway past a military honor guard to Mr. Trump's Spanish-style Mar-a-Lago resort in Palm Beach, Florida, welcomed by Mr. Trump and his wife Melania before going inside," reported by Reuters. He also

---

[18] *Washington Post.* A transcript of Donald Trump's meeting with the *Washington Post* editorial board (March 21, 2016).

claimed, "We [Xi and him] have a great chemistry together. We like each other. I like him a lot. I think his wife is terrific." A year later, Trump tweeted "[we] will always be friends, no matter what happens with our dispute on trade." (@realDonaldTrump, April 8, 2018). In early 2017, many people believed the two countries could settle their trade disputes easily. This optimism was also shared by the Chinese trade negotiators.

In early 2018, it was reported that Trump wanted China to import more cars, aircraft, soybeans, and natural gas with a total worth of USD 100 billion. China was prepared to accept the terms. When China's Vice Premier Liu He held a formal trade talk in Washington, DC, even the US government agreed to issue a communiqué stating, "There was a consensus on taking effective measures to substantially reduce the US trade deficit in goods with China. To meet the growing consumption needs of the Chinese people and the need for high-quality economic development, China will significantly increase purchases of US goods and services. This will help support growth and employment in the US."[19] Yet, a month later, the US decided to impose a 25% tariff on USD 50 billion of Chinese goods.

A year later, the US and China held a trade negotiation in Beijing on April 30–May 1, 2019. The US Secretary of Treasury Steven Mnuchin described the negotiation as "productive." However, despite Mnuchin's promising description of the negotiation, the US president Donald refused to sign an agreement at the very last minute. In response, the Chinese government issued a white paper to state China's stance in the trade war, accusing the US of backtracking three times in the negotiation process.[20] In contrast, China's reaction had been very predictable. When the US president Donald imposed additional tariffs, China retaliated accordingly. In the past two years, positive progress in the trade talks

---

[19]The White House, United States Government (2018). Joint Statement of the United States and China Regarding Trade Consultations. Press release (May 19). (https://www.whitehouse.gov/briefings-statements/joint-statement-united-states-china-regarding-trade-consultations/).

[20]The white paper stated, "Since they were launched in February 2018, the economic and trade consultations have come a long way with the two sides agreeing on most parts of the deal. But the consultations have not been free of setbacks, each of them being the result of a US breach of consensus and commitments, and backtracking."

often ended with yet another round of escalation. The "flip-flop" behavior of Trump's administration had dampened the market confidence in the China–US long-term economic tie.

1.3.2 Breaking the Bulk in Tranches

The US administration did not impose import tariffs on all Chinese goods at once but introduced the trade measures in tranches. The strategy was to put China into a difficult situation and observe its response before deciding on further actions. The trade war began with USD 50 billion of Chinese goods in April 2018, followed by the second batch of USD 200 billion in September 2018 (see Table 1.2). The market was also nervous because a big bulk of the USD 325 billion was about to come due on December 15, 2019, right before the conclusion of the Phase One agreement. Likewise, China also passively reacted to the US tariff schedule and retaliated with several tariff lists. Trump's stepwise approach in trade negotiation resulted in a prolonged period of uncertainty that was harmful to global economic growth.

From the US' perspective, this tactical approach could reserve a "trump card" on hand. The unpredictable character of Trump's administration never committed to a once-and-for-all deal. At the G20 meeting in Osaka in June 2019, Xi Jinping and Donald Trump held a closed-door meeting. Prior to the meeting, the Chinese side had already unveiled

Table 1.2   Tariff action after Section 301 Investigation on China in 2018.

Phase	Tariff Rate	Value of Goods	Dates Implemented
List 1	25%	USD 34 billion	July 6, 2018
List 2	25%	USD 16 billion	August 23, 2018
List 3	10%, then 25%	USD 200 billion	10% hike effective on September 24, 2018; raise to 25% on May 10, 2019
List 4a	15%, then 7.5%	USD 112 billion	September 1, 2019; rate cut in January 2020 on Phase One deal
List 4b	15%	USD 160 billion	Halted on Phase One deal

Source: USTR

their bottom line via a white paper, stating that China was unwilling to negotiate further unless the US promised not to impose new import tariffs. Both sides agreed on a truce following the leadership meeting. Xinhua, the Chinese media, expressed a Panglossian outlook by stating "The US agrees not to impose new tariffs." However, in his press conference, Trump attached the words: "[not to escalate] at least for the time being . . . [but] I have the ability to put on [the tariff] if I want to."

In January 2020, the US and China signed the Phase One agreement in Washington, DC. Under the deal, China promised to increase imports from the US. The 96-page document also detailed mostly China's commitments to open up market access and non-discriminating trade practices, including protection of IPR and technology transfer.[21] Political leaders of the two sides hailed the effort of negotiators. During the signing ceremony, Trump said, "We are righting the wrongs of the past . . . and delivering a future of economic justice and security for American workers, farmers and families." *China Daily* commented that "Reaching the agreement will serve the fundamental interests of the people of the two countries and the world, and is expected to bring positive influences on areas including economy, trade, investment and the financial market."[22]

This Phase One deal stated that China should make additional purchases of US goods totaling USD 200 billion across 2020 and 2021 from the 2017 pre-trade war baseline level of USD 134.2 billion (see Table 1.3). The increase in imports would be USD 76.7 billion in 2020 and USD 123.3 billion in 2021. As China's domestic demand is actually slowing, these targets are generally believed to be unrealistic.[23] But the US has reserved the right to fire again if China cannot fulfill the promise. In fact, the two sides continued to maintain a high level of import tariff

---

[21]Economic and Trade Agreement between the Government of the United States and the government of the People's Republic of China (January 15, 2020). (https://ustr. gov/sites/default/files/files/agreements/phase%20one%20agreement/Economic_ And_Trade_Agreement_Between_The_United_States_And_China_Text.pdf).

[22]Xinhua, US agree on text of phase one trade deal. (December 13, 2019). (https:// www.chinadaily.com.cn/a/201912/13/WS5df3a9d7a310cf3e3557e128.html).

[23]Bown, C. (2020). Unappreciated hazards of the US–China phase one deal. PIIE (January 21).

rates. After signing the deal, average US tariff on Chinese goods was still 19% compared to 3% before the trade war (see Figure 1.6).

Besides the tariff, this stepwise approach was also reflected in the US' description of China's exchange rate policy. In August 2019, the US Treasury labeled China as a currency manipulator. However, it reversed the decision in January 2020, as China pledged not to push for competitive devaluation when signing the Phase One agreement. The reality was

Table 1.3 Increase in US exports to China 2020–21 under Phase One Agreement.

USD billion	2020	2021	Total
Manufacturing	32.9	44.8	77.7
Agriculture	12.5	19.5	32.0
Energy	18.5	33.9	52.4
Services	12.8	25.1	37.9
Total	76.7	123.3	200.0

Source: USTR

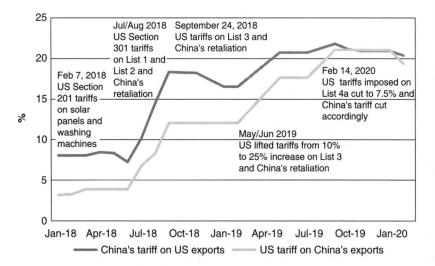

Figure 1.6 Tariff rates the US imposed on Chinese goods.

Sources: Narrative by the author. Data from Peterson Institute for International Economics (PIIE)

that China had reiterated its stance several times during trade negotiations in the past two years. The market also believed that the People's Bank of China (PBOC) did not weaken the currency. Nonetheless, this agreement was similar to the Plaza Accord when the US pressed Japan and West Germany not to weaken the currency. The Phase One deal here also wanted to guide exchange rate movement administratively. Its effectiveness is yet to be seen.

1.3.3 A Battle for Technology

Another feature of this trade war is the involvement of critical technology and the electronic supply chain. China and the US are widely believed to have undergone a technology race. China has an ambitious plan to roll out 5G transmission covering the whole country over the next few years. Technology giants such as Huawei are leaders in manufacturing 5G equipment. This new generation of data transmission technology is perceived to be a catalyst of digital transformation. First movers are expected to enhance their national competitiveness. However, China is also relying on the US supply of semiconductors. Besides import tariffs, the US also deploys export restrictions in the trade war.

On December 1, 2018, Huawei's CFO Meng Wanzhou was arrested in Vancouver by the Royal Canadian Mounted Police, at the request of the US, for allegedly defrauding multiple financial institutions in breach of US sanctions on Iran.[24] On May 17, 2019, the US Department of Commerce announced that it had included Huawei in the Entity List, warning that Huawei's telecommunication equipment could aid espionage and surveillance by the Chinese government. Under this measure, the sale or transfer of American technology to the companies on the list required a license issued by the Bureau of Industry and Security. It was unusual to see a trade dispute that involved high-profile action directed at a specific company.

To retaliate, China's Ministry of Commerce came up with its own "Unreliable Entity List" of foreign companies considered to have damaged the interests of China. Additionally, China could also limit the

---

[24]BBC. Huawei finance chief Meng Wanzhou arrested in Canada (December 6, 2018). (https://www.bbc.com/news/business-46462858).

export of rare earths, which are critical ingredients in the production of electronic components, including rechargeable batteries, superconductors, and even military equipment. Reportedly, China was supplying as much as 80% of the US demand.[25] If China were to turn off the tap, many production lines in the US could also be deactivated.

Indeed, the export control measures of this trade war has caused major interruptions to the global supply chain. This is very different from conventional tools that only aim to increase import prices. By imposing a barrier in the upstream of the production process, the US can paralyze the entire supply chain activities. Shocking the global supply chain is lethal. The impact not only restricts the shipments from China to the US but also affects China's supply to the rest of the world. This presents massive operational risks to manufacturing facilities based in China. To China, the economic damage of the US export control is more severe than the import tariff.

Many Chinese exporters are contracted manufacturers (see Figure 1.7). They are world-renowned suppliers famous in original equipment manufacturing (OEM). They receive orders from foreign brands from sport

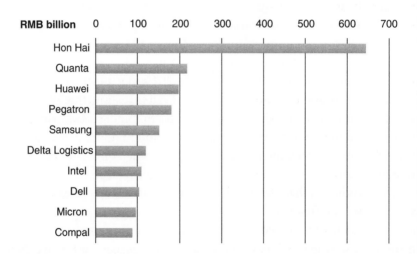

Figure 1.7 Top exporters in China 2018.
Source: National Bureau of Statistics, China Customs

---

[25]Reuters. U.S. dependence on China's rare earth: Trade war vulnerability (June 28, 2019). (https://www.reuters.com/article/us-usa-trade-china-rareearth-explainer/u-s-dependence-on-chinas-rare-earth-trade-war-vulnerability-idUSKCN1TS3AQ).

shoes to smartphones; import from other Asian economies; and organize the production logistics in different cities in mainland China. Hon Hai, also named Foxconn, has been the largest exporter in China for many years, as it is the contractor for Apple Inc. Another Taiwan OEM company, Quanta, is the world's largest contracted manufacturer in notebook computers and tablets. These electronic giants assemble electronic components from Asia, and even the US, via highly established and increasingly automated production lines. If export control becomes a regular trade measure, many companies will relocate their production facilities away from China.

1.3.4 Leverage Geopolitical Issues

When Trump first imposed import tariffs on steel and aluminium imports, Canada and Mexico were granted exemptions. Subsequently, many countries attempted to seek similar treatments. Trump said, "We'll be making a decision as to who they are. . . . We're going to be very flexible." On August 29, 2018, Trump tweeted "President Donald J Trump feels strongly that North Korea is under tremendous pressure from China because of our major trade disputes with the Chinese Government." Ahead of the Osaka G20 meeting in June 2019, the US heated up both the trade tension with China and the diplomatic affairs with North Korea. Political observers suggested the trade issue might prompt China to cooperate more closely with the US on North Korea to get Washington to stop the trade war.[26] Indeed, after the meeting with Xi in Osaka, Trump decided not to escalate the tariff plan and he became the first US president to shake hands with Kim Jong Un on North Korean soil a day later. Leveraging political issues in such an explicit manner was unconventional.

The reality is that the US is used to politicizing economic issues subtly. The US Treasury has an explicit scheme to enforce economic and trade sanctions "based on US foreign policy and national security goals against targeted foreign countries and regimes, terrorists, international narcotics traffickers, those engaged in activities related to the

---

[26] *South China Morning Post*. Xi-Trump at G20: Why North Korea is both common ground and trade war battleground. (November 27, 2018). (https://www.scmp.com/news/china/diplomacy/article/2175229/xi-trump-g20-why-north-korea-both-common-ground-and-trade-war).

proliferation of weapons of mass destruction, and other threats to the national security, foreign policy or economy of the US" (Office of Foreign Assets Control).[27] Countries and companies need to comply with the sanction list based on the US' political consideration. In this trade war, we also saw some sanctioned cases related to Chinese tech and mobile phone makers. Since China and the US differ in their ideological and political stance on many fronts, Trump's approach represents a significant event risk in global economic affairs.

In the last few decades, globalization has been largely based on a set of economic principles (at least on paper), notably most favored nation (MFN) and national treatment. Trade negotiations have been largely based on commercial terms and seldom looped into political consideration. Instead, Trump seems to run a portfolio of economic and political relationships. Trade negotiators have difficulty evaluating political demand. Officials at the ministerial rank should have limited authority in deciding on diplomatic relationships. If this approach becomes a global norm, the international economic order will face increasing complications. Multilateral economic platforms such as the WTO will be at high risk.

1.4 Economic Impacts and Consequences

1.4.1 Slowdown in Trade and Investment

Free trade has been the foundation of postwar economic prosperity, and vice versa. Yueh (2018) reminds us of the success of Great Britain in the nineteenth century. He wrote, "Using tariffs to improve a country's trade position was essentially what Britain rejected over a century ago. The argument was won due to the work of two great economists, Adam Smith, the father of economics, and David Ricardo, the father of international trade theory. When the United Kingdom repealed the Corn Laws, a piece of protectionist legislation, in 1846, it marked an era of greater opening for Britain, then the dominant trader in the world." Undoubtedly, free trade has its distributional aspect. But it is inevitable that trade barriers always hurt total growth.

---

[27]The US Treasury (https://www.treasury.gov/resource-center/sanctions/Pages/default.aspx).

There have been many studies on the impact of trade war. Almost all of them pointed to negative growth. The IMF provided a quantitative assessment on Trump's tariff plan and offered a range of estimates for China, the US, and the rest of the world. The study assumed a hypothetical scenario in which tariffs on all US–China goods trade increased by 25%. Using a dynamic stochastic general equilibrium model of the global economy, the study estimated that annual GDP would contract from 0.3% to 0.6% for the US and from 0.5% to 1.5% for China.[28] This GDP impact excluded the negative impact of economic uncertainty on capital expenditure by American corporates, another drag highlighted in an earlier study by the IMF.[29] As the estimates varied significantly under different model assumptions (see Figure 1.8), the results should be regarded as indicative only.

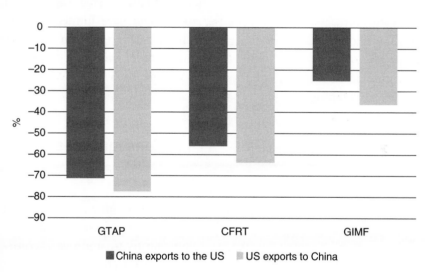

Figure 1.8 Effects of a 25% increase in tariffs on US–China bilateral trade.

Note: CFRT = Caliendo et al. (2017); GIMF = Global Integrated Monetary and Fiscal Model; GTAP = Global Trade Analysis Project
Sources: Data from IMF (2019)

[28]IMF (2019). *World Economic Outlook*. Washington, DC, International Monetary Fund. April 2019.

[29]IMF (2018). *World Economic Outlook*. Washington, DC, International Monetary Fund. October 2018.

The impact of the trade war was most apparent in China–US bilateral trade. But the changes were not the pattern predicted by simple trade theory. The US administration started Section 301 Investigation in mid-2017 and threatened to impose import tariffs. In most of 2017 and 2018, China's exports to the US were very strong, reaching, at one point, close to 20% year-on-year. The US buyers or the Chinese exporters appeared to act pre-emptively ahead of tariff implementation.

However, total shipments began to contract in the second half of 2018 as the second batch of tariffs were imposed and continued to drop in 2019 (see Figure 1.9). Because the outcome of the trade talks were uncertain, exporters tended to frontload the shipments in order to hedge the risk, regardless of whether their products were ultimately included on the tariff list. Therefore, the trade data could not reveal a noticeable difference in the pattern between tariffed and non-tariffed items.

Despite the decrease in imports, the US trade deficits with China actually widened during the trade war. In 2018, US Customs reported record-high trade deficits with China of USD 419 billion, 12% more than the previous year. Even though the US imposed import tariffs on a portion of Chinese goods, exporters had actually shipped more goods

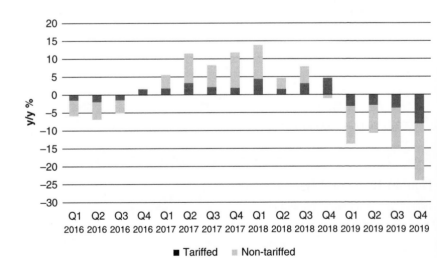

Figure 1.9   Exports from China to the US.

Source: USTR, ANZ Research

to the US ahead of time. In retaliation, China also reduced its imports of the US goods significantly. Import tariff measures did not improve US trade at all.

Besides the direct impact on exports, the highly uncertain business outlook was detrimental to the investment appetite of the corporate sector. Ahir, Bloom, and Furceri (2019) tracked the sentiment impact of the trade war using their World Trade Uncertainty Index (see Figure 1.10). They estimated that the increase in trade uncertainty observed in the first quarter of 2019 could be enough to reduce global growth by up to 0.75% in 2019. Similarly, Bloomberg Economics estimated that, relative to the scenario with no trade war, the uncertainty could lower the world's GDP by 0.6% in 2021, equivalent of USD 585 billion.[30] A US importer told Reuters, "The uncertainty makes it nearly impossible to make mid- to long-term business decisions. . . . We have

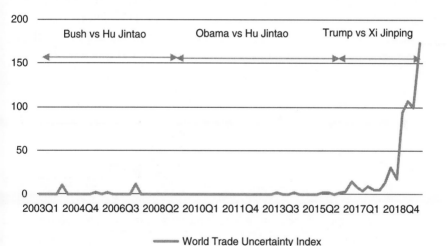

Figure 1.10   World Trade Uncertainty Index.

Source: Ahir, H., Bloom, N., and Furceri, D. (2018), "World Uncertainty Index," Stanford mimeo.

---

[30]Bloomberg. The price tag for global trade war uncertainty (August 19, 2019) (https://www.bloomberg.com/news/articles/2019-08-19/-585-billion-the-price-tag-for-global-trade-war-uncertainty).

to make really short-term decisions almost week by week by week, because that's how quickly it's changing."[31]

1.4.2 Relocation of Production Base

When elephants fight, it is the grass that suffers. With the presence of global supply chains, the impact of imposing tariffs on China's products will have a spillover effect on the others, causing collateral damage to other economies. The impact of the China–US trade war is not just an affair between two countries. Specifically, China has been the principal assembly line of mobile phones in the world, illustrated by the strong statistical relationship between the share price of Apple Inc. and Chinese exports (Figure 1.11). The main production line of Apple is in China. Japan, South Korea, and the US supply critical components along the supply chain. If the US continues to point fingers at China,

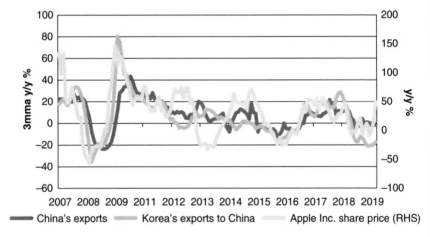

Figure 1.11 North Asia Exports and the Share Price of Apple Inc.
Sources: PRC Customs, Korea MTIE, ANZ Research

[31]Reuters. Drowning in uncertainty: Trade questions slow investment, squeeze profits across U.S. (December 10, 2019). (https://www.reuters.com/article/us-usa-trade-uncertainty/drowning-in-uncertainty-trade-questions-slow-investment-squeeze-profits-across-u-s-idUSKBN1YE185).

the manufacturers will need to find an alternative in response to the persistent uncertainty.

However, even if the US can limit imports from China, businesses will relocate their production base to other economies. Some electronic giants have considered Vietnam as an alternative to China.[32] There was an example of this substitution effect. In 2009, president Obama approved "safeguard" tariffs of 25–35% on motor tires from China for three years. As a result, the total imports of new radial tires for cars declined 28% in 2010. However, other economies like South Korea, Thailand, and Indonesia filled the void; the shipments from these countries to the US doubled. This suggests that the substitution effects amongst different offshore production centers can offset the effect of tariffs.

Data in the first few months of 2019 illustrated the substitution effects of this trade war (see Table 1.4). The US imports from China decreased by 13.1% in the first four months of 2019 compared with the same period a year ago (US exports to China also dropped 20.8%).

Table 1.4 US trade data January–April 2019.

US total trade Jan–Apr 2019, % year-on-year	Export	Import
World	0.5	0.4
Mainland China and HKSAR	-20.8	-13.1
Advanced Asia	3.7	10.2
Canada & Mexico	-1.1	2.1
EU	8.7	6.3
Tech trade		
World	1.9	1.4
Mainland China and HKSAR	9.5	-24.8
Advanced Asia	-8.9	21.8
Canada & Mexico	2.1	5.2
EU	3.5	18.4

Source: US BEA

---

[32]The *Korea Herald*. Samsung heir heads to Hanoi with prospects of new investment (October 30, 2018). (http://www.koreaherald.com/view.php?ud=20181030000698).

But the US imports from other advanced Asian economies rose 10%. On tech import, the US imported less from China (-24.8%). But its imports from advanced Asia increased 21.8%. This suggests that, for some products, suppliers can realign their production base in response to a country-specific import tariff. The production line in China is seen to be extremely efficient and massive relocation will be unlikely.

1.4.3 Negative Impact on US Business and Consumers

The US has plenty at stake in the Sino–US economic relationship. Import tariffs can also penalize American entities. Again, Apple's iPhone has been frequently used to illustrate this point. Kraemer et al. (2011) concluded that 58.5% of the distribution value of the iPhone went to Apple's profits while the labor cost of China accounted for merely 1.8% of total costs. Some tech experts suggested a less aggressive figure of 45%.[33] Furthermore, since an import tariff applies to the gross value of imports, the cost will also be passed to content suppliers in the US, such as R&D and marketing.

Trump claimed that China footed the bill for the tariffs. According to the US Customs and Border Protection, the government collected USD 15.6 billion through tariffs imposed between February 2018 and March 2019. Tariff revenue in the first half of the fiscal year, which began on October 1, 2018, surged 89% from a year ago to USD 34.7 billion. "We have billions of dollars coming into our Treasury, billions, from China. We never had 10 cents coming into our Treasury; now we have billions coming in," he said on January 24, 2019.

However, the tariff was imposed on US importers, not the Chinese sellers. The US merchants could pay the tariff or pass the cost to consumers in order to stay financially neutral. In practice, the import tariff involved burden sharing between American business, consumers, and Chinese exporters.[34] Cavallo et al. (2019) found that retailers in the US bore significant share of the costs. The impact on consumer welfare

---

[33]Digital Trends. July 26, 2013. (http://www.digitaltrends.com/mobile/iphone-cost-what-apple-is-paying/).

[34]*Washington Post.* Trump's China tariffs have not caused Americans to pay $1,000 more a year. Here's why. (January 17, 2020).

depended on how much the US importing businesses were willing to absorb the costs.

In theory, an import tariff artificially raises the cost of goods. Sellers will tend to pass the costs to consumers, especially if the products are price inelastic, i.e. buyers are not price sensitive. Redding et al. (2019) found that in some sectors, such as steel, import tariffs caused foreign exporters to reduce their prices substantially, enabling them to export relatively more than in sectors where tariff pass-through was complete. Hale et al. (2019) estimated if the US were to impose 25% of import tariff on all Chinese goods, consumer prices and investment prices could increase by 0.3 percentage point and 1.0 percentage point, respectively. John Williams, president of the New York Federal Reserve, believed an import tariff on Chinese goods would result in higher inflation and slower growth in the US.[35]

1.5 Trade War and Deglobalization

Trump's administration seems to have turned the overall US policy towards China much more hawkish than before. Regardless of the outcome of the next presidential election, the US will likely continue to be tough on China. Former Vice President Joe Biden, who may represent the Democratic Party in the 2020 election, argued that the US needs to curb China's "abusive" economic behavior. Even though he did not agree with Trump's import tariff plan, he still called for a more aggressive stance to China through forming a "united front" with economic partners against China.[36] The attitudes of the Republican and Democratic parties towards China will likely be indifferent.

Meanwhile, China has adopted a hardline stance against the US. Prior to Osaka's G20 where Xi and Trump held a bilateral meeting, China's State Council issued a White Paper titled China's Position on

---

[35]Reuters. Fed's Williams says tariffs boost U.S. inflation, weigh on growth. (May 14, 2019).

[36]CNBC. Biden slams Trump's trade war even as he calls to "get tough" on China. (July 11, 2019).

the China–US Economic and Trade Consultations,[37] reiterating that "China does not want a trade war, but it is not afraid of one and it will fight one if necessary." The Chinese government condemned the US' non-satiation: "But the more the US government is offered, the more it wants. Resorting to intimidation and coercion, it persisted with exorbitant demands, maintained the additional tariffs imposed since the friction began, and insisted on including mandatory requirements concerning China's sovereign affairs in the deal, which only served to delay the resolution of remaining differences."

The Chinese government believes that the country can sustain the impact of the trade tension. Since exports to the US represent only one-fifth of China's total exports, the US trade appears to be something "nice to have" but not essential to China's survival. In May 2019, Xi Jinping called for the nation to embark on a new "Long March" and "start all over again."[38] As external demand deteriorated, the government launched several measures to stabilize growth, including tax cut and monetary policy accommodation in 2019. The government prepared for a persistent trade tension with the US. "When necessary we will fight back, but we have been working actively to try not to have a trade war," said Xi publicly in November 2019.[39]

Indeed, China has become less export oriented (see Figure 1.12). In 2018, net exports contributed negatively to GDP growth with a figure of -0.6 percentage point. It was running out of its population advantage as the country had passed the Lewis Turning Point.[40] The value added from exports could not catch up with the value of imports. Its manufacturing base could no longer focus on providing simple assembling services for other countries. To upgrade its economy, China rapidly expanded its global presence through acquiring overseas assets and

---

[37]The State Council Information Office of the PRC (2019). China's Position on the China–US Economic and Trade Consultations (June).

[38]*South China Morning Post*. Xi Jinping calls for "new Long March" in dramatic sign that China is preparing for protracted trade war (May 21, 2019).

[39]*South China Morning Post*. China wants a US trade deal – but will fight back if necessary, says president Xi Jinping. (November 22, 2019).

[40]Das, M., N'Diaye, P. (2013). Chronicle of a Decline Foretold: Has China Reached the Lewis Turning Point? IMF Working Paper. WP/13/1326 (January).

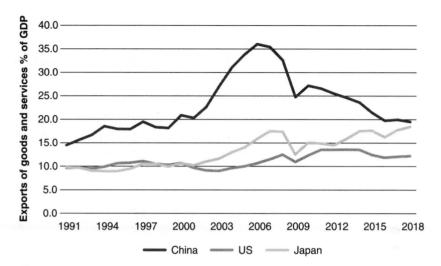

Figure 1.12   Total trade as a % of GDP.
Sources: World Bank

technology companies. In addition, the US' sanction on Huawei and ZTE reinforced the belief that China should be self-sufficient, especially in technology.

In the near term, China can only count on domestic consumption to drive growth. Of the GDP growth of 6.6% in 2018, final consumption contributed 5.0 ppt or 75% of total growth. To do so, the government will need to encourage household spending. To this end, the policy direction is to increase wage growth at a faster pace. This requires an improvement of total factor productivity. Technology becomes the critical piece in the puzzle. How China and the US proceed with the Phase Two negotiation and resolve the issue of forced technology transfer will have a significant implication for China's long-term economic prospects.

If the US decides to withdraw from multilateralism, globalization will be replaced by regionalization. Kevin Rudd, former prime minister of Australia and a veteran China expert, warns that China and the US are about to enter "a new Cold War, a new doctrine of containment as well as this notion of economic decoupling."[41] He said, "The world will

---

[41]Rudd, K. (2013). The Trade War, Economic Decoupling and Future Chinese Strategy Towards America. Speech at Lowy Institute (June 13).

likely see two radically different digital worlds—one anchored in America, the other behind one form or other of the Chinese firewall. And third countries, particularly Belt and Road countries, may find themselves in an increasingly uncertain no-man's-land in between."

Indeed, the greater openness of the Chinese economy could be an attractive proposition. Bown (2019) examined the import tariff schedule of China since the trade war commenced. He found that the average tariff level of China charged to other countries declined from 8.0% to 6.7% by March 2019 but the levy on US imports rose from 8.0% to 20.7%. In view of China's large consumer market, some countries will prefer China's friendly policy. The relationship between China and its long-term rival Japan warmed in 2018. When Prime Minister Shinzo Abe visited China in October 2018, the two countries agreed on USD 2.6 billion in business deals. Abe said, "I believe active trade will deepen ties between Japanese and Chinese people further." The trade war seems to have pushed China closer to Japan.

The trade war will reinforce China's belief in strengthening the economic tie with Eurasia. In March 2019, Italy became the first G7 country to sign up the BRI, even though many European countries like France and Germany insist China must improve access and fair competition for foreign firms. Germany's Economic Minister Peter Altmaier said, "In the big EU states we have agreed that we don't want to sign any bilateral memorandums but together make necessary arrangements between the greater European Economic Area and the economic area of Greater China." An EEA–China trade bloc, if it happens, may define a new regime within the era of globalization.

However, the Belt and Road may not end up being the vehicle of the new regionalization. First, by design, it is a foreign policy agenda of Xi Jinping. It is not a specific proposal to establish a free trade zone. In fact, there are still many commercial and governance issues facing different projects (Russel and Berger 2019). Secondly, many Western observers deem the Belt and Road a Chinese version of neocolonialism. This thought will be shared not only by the US allies but also other countries.[42] Finally and more importantly, given the rise of unilateralism,

---

[42]Kleven, A. (2019). Belt and Road: Colonialism with Chinese Characteristics. Lowy Institute (May 6).

it is doubtful whether countries are still committing to trade agreements involving more than two countries. Since 2002, China, Japan, and South Korea have mulled a tri-party free trade agreement. But the bilateral relationships of the three countries have been hindered by their political history. Forming a new trade bloc will require a great effort of harmonization. This will be difficult against the backdrop of neo-nationalism.

In conclusion, the US–China trade war is an interesting subject in contemporary economics. It is a head-to-head dispute between the two largest economies in the world. One is the captain of the advanced world and one represents the emerging market. It is a conflict between two countries that hold very different political ideologies. Trade negotiation will not provide a permanent fix to the trade imbalance. After reviewing the development over a two-year period, we can safely conclude that the global economic order in the twenty-first century will not be the same. After this trade war, China and the US will unlikely restore a normal economic relationship similar to the one prior to the trade war. If the past success of their bilateral economic tie was a symbol of globalization, the trade war signaled that the world would enter a period of deglobalization, resulting in a painful and costly process of economic transition.

Do we have a second chance? Can we prevent this from happening? Yes, and this book attempts to propose a solution. But we need to do that step by step.

In Chapter 2, we explain that the US trade imbalance with China is merely a symptom of a bigger economic problem. It is an inevitable outcome of the fiat money regime. This dollar-centric regime will be knocked as globalization is rolling back, as suggested in Chapter 3. In Chapter 4, we argue that China can fix this problem via financial decoupling and, indeed, it is doing so. As the world economy enters the digital era, outlined in Chapter 5, the recent development of cryptocurrency will present a prominent alternative to the dollar regime. Chapter 6 will provide a layman's explanation of a blockchain-based monetary system. As the largest holder of foreign currency reserve, China has the market power to initiate a digital-monetary regime as proposed in Chapter 7. Only if the power of money creation goes to the right hand (as in Marvel *Avengers': Endgame*), can we finish the endless trade disputes of the US.

Annex A: China's Belt and Road Initiative

In 2013, Xi Jinping unveiled the Belt and Road Initiative during his visits to Kazakhstan and Indonesia. His vision can be inferred from his interpretation of the "New Era," which "offers a new option for other countries and nations . . . to speed up their development while preserving their independence," and it offers "Chinese wisdom and a Chinese approach to solving the problems facing mankind." He is keen on elevating China's soft power to that of the US, which has successfully reaped the benefits from its intangible assets such as brand value and culture via Hollywood movies, Silicon Valley technology, Big Macs, and the Yankees.

Contrary to the general impression, Belt and Road has not really expanded into a trade bloc. Instead, it serves as a general platform for China to develop a "friendly relationship" instead of a free trade agreement. The activities are not limited to goods and services trade but also cultural exchange. In fact, many countries alongside the Silk Road Economic Belt and the 21st Century Maritime Silk Road do not seem to offer much commercial value. The initiative appears to be a white paper outlining Xi Jinping's thought on foreign affairs. This initiative was ultimately added to the constitution of the China Communist Party in 2017.

According to the Chinese government, 131 countries and 30 international organizations have joined the initiative, through which China has made investments of more than USD 90 billion (see Table A1).[43]

Table A1 Country profile of Belt and Road Initiative.

(Based on the official Belt and Road website maintained by China government)	
GDP per capita	Country
>USD 20,000	Luxembourg, Qatar, Singapore, Austria, New Zealand, Israel, UAE, Italy, South Korea, Brunei, Cyprus, Malta, Kuwait, Bahrain, Slovenia, Portugal, Saudi Arabia, Cook Islands

[43]China Government Belt and Road website (https://eng.yidaiyilu.gov.cn/qwyw/rdxw/89501.htm).

Table A1   (Continued)

USD 10,000–19,999	Estonia, Czech, Greece, Oman, Barbados, Slovakia, Uruguay, Lithuania, Antigua and Barbuda, Seychelles, Trinidad and Tobago, Latvia, Panama, Chile, Hungary, Poland, Croatia, Maldives, Costa Rica, Lebanon, Romania, Equatorial Guinea, Turkey, Grenada, Niue, Russia
USD 5,000–9,999	Malaysia, China, Kazakhstan, Cuba, Bulgaria, Dominica, Montenegro, Dominican Republic, Gabon, Venezuela, Prue, Turkmenistan, Thailand, Ecuador, South Africa, Serbia, Suriname, Jordan, Namibia, Belarus, Fiji, North Macedonia, Jamaica, Iran, Bosnia and Herzegovina, Iraq
USD 2,000–4,999	Libya, Albania, Guyana, Tonga, Angola, Samoa, Azerbaijan, Georgia, Algeria, Sri Lanka, El Salvador, Armenia, Indonesia, Egypt, Mongolia, Tunisia, Bolivia, Cape Verde, Micronesia, Morocco, Vanuatu, Philippines, Bhutan, Palestine, Papua New Guinea, Syria, Ukraine, Laos, Vietnam, Moldova, Timor-Leste, Congo
<USD 2,000	Nigeria, Djibouti, Kenya, Ghana, Cote d'Ivoire, Pakistan, Bangladesh, Uzbekistan, Zambia, Cameroon, Cambodia, Myanmar, Mauritania, Zimbabwe, Kyrgyzstan, Sudan, Senegal, Tanzania, Tajikistan, Chad, Guinea, Rwanda, Liberia, Uganda, Gambia, Togo, Afghanistan, Yamen, Somalia, Sierra Leone, Madagascar, Mozambique, Burundi, South Sudan

Source: Data from Hong Kong Trade Development Council website (December 2019)

Annex B: Official Statements from the US and China

USTR 2018 Report to Congress on China's WTO Compliance
https://ustr.gov/sites/default/files/2018-USTR-Report-to-Congress-on-China%27s-WTO-Compliance.pdf

Section 301 Investigation process on China
https://ustr.gov/issue-areas/enforcement/section-301-investigations/section-301-china/investigation

Section 301 Report into China's Acts, Policies, and Practices Related to Technology Transfer, Intellectual Property, and Innovation

https://ustr.gov/sites/default/files/Section%20301%20
FINAL.PDF

China Section 301-Tariff Actions and Exclusion Process

https://ustr.gov/issue-areas/enforcement/section-301-investi-
gations/tariff-actions

Joint Statement of the United States and China Regarding Trade
Consultations

https://www.whitehouse.gov/briefings-statements/joint-state-
ment-united-states-china-regarding-trade-consultations/

Bureau of Industry and Security - Entity List

https://www.bis.doc.gov/index.php/policy-guidance/lists-of-
parties-of-concern/entity-list

Economic and Trade Agreement between the Government of
the United States of America and the Government of the
People's Republic of China

https://ustr.gov/countries-regions/china-mongolia-taiwan/
peoples-republic-china/phase-one-trade-agreement

国务院关税税则委员会对原产于美国的部分进口商品中
止关税减让义务的通知

http://www.mofcom.gov.cn/article/b/g/201805/
20180502744874.shtml

商务部公告2018年第34号 关于对原产于美国的部分进
口商品加征关税的公告

http://www.mofcom.gov.cn/article/b/e/201804/
20180402728516.shtml

中美就经贸磋商发表联合声明

http://www.gov.cn/xinwen/2018-05/20/content_
5292160.htm

国务院关税税则委员会决定对原产于美国的659项约500亿
美元进口商品加征25%的关税

http://www.mofcom.gov.cn/article/b/g/201807/
20180702769198.shtml

国务院关税税则委员会关于对原产于美国约160亿美元进口商品加征关税的公告

税委会公告〔2018〕7号

http://www.gov.cn/xinwen/2018-08/08/content_5312624.htm

中华人民共和国商务部公告2018年第63号对原产于美国的5207个税目约600亿美元商品，加征25%-5%不等的关税

http://www.mofcom.gov.cn/article/b/g/201809/20180902786225.shtml

国务院关税税则委员会关于对原产于美国的部分进口商品提高加征关税税率的公告 税委会公告〔2019〕3号

http://www.gov.cn/guowuyuan/2019-05/13/content_5391208.htm

《关于中美经贸磋商的中方立场》白皮书

http://www.scio.gov.cn/zfbps/32832/Document/1655898/1655898.htm

国务院关税税则委员会关于对原产于美国的汽车及零部件恢复加征关税的公告

http://www.gov.cn/xinwen/2019-08/24/content_5424154.htm

国务院关税税则委员会关于对原产于美国的部分进口商品(第三批)加征关税的公告

http://www.gov.cn/xinwen/2019-08/24/content_5424152.htm

中国相关企业暂停新的美国农产品采购

http://www.mofcom.gov.cn/article/ae/ag/201908/20190802887951.shtml

中国商务部关于发布中美第一阶段经贸协议的公告

http://www.mofcom.gov.cn/article/ae/ai/202001/20200102930845.shtml

China files WTO complaint over the United States' tariff measures on Chinese goods https://www.wto.org/english/news_e/news18_e/ds543rfc_05apr18_e.htm

China initiates dispute complaints against US solar cell duties, renewable energy measures

https://www.wto.org/english/news_e/news18_e/ds562_563rfc_16aug18_e.htm

China initiates WTO dispute complaint against US tariffs on Chinese imports

https://www.wto.org/english/news_e/news18_e/ds565rfc_27aug18_e.htm

https://www.wto.org/english/news_e/news19_e/ds587rfc_04sep19_e.htm

United States files WTO complaint on China's protection of intellectual property rights

https://www.wto.org/english/news_e/news18_e/ds542rfc_26mar18_e.htm

Treasury's decision on China's status as a Currency Manipulator

https://home.treasury.gov/news/press-releases/sm751

https://home.treasury.gov/system/files/136/20200113-Jan-2020-FX-Report-FINAL.pdf

Annex C: Major Timeline of the Trade War

Pre-war period: April 2017 – March 2018

In this period, the United States prepared the attack and began to impose non-China specific tariffs on solar, steel, and washing machines.

- April 6–7, 2017: Chinese president Xi Jinping visited the US president Donald Trump's Mar-a-Lago estate in Florida. The two leaders agreed to set up a 100-Day Action Plan to resolve trade differences.
- August 18, 2017: The USTR started to investigate China's practices in technology transfer, intellectual property and innovation.

- February 7, 2018: The US implemented "global safeguard tariffs" of 30% on all solar panels except for those from Canada, and 20% tariff on washing machines.
- March 22, 2018: USTR issued the Findings of the Investigation into China's Acts, Policies, and Practices Related to Technology Transfer, Intellectual Property, and Innovation under Section 301 of the Trade Act of 1974
- March 23, 2018: US imposed a 25% tariff on all steel imports (except from Argentina, Australia, Brazil, and South Korea) and 10% tariff on all aluminum imports (except from Argentina and Australia).

First round of the fight: April 2018 – November 2018

In the first round, the US initiated an import tariff after the publishing of the Section 301 report. China retaliated by applying a tariff to the same amount of US goods.

- April 2, 2018: China imposed tariffs of 15–25% on 128 US products (worth USD 3 billion) including fruit, wine, seamless steel pipes, pork, and recycled aluminum in retaliation to the US steel and aluminum tariffs.
- April 16, 2018: US Department of Commerce concluded that ZTE violated US sanctions, prohibiting US companies from engaging business with it.
- April 17, 2018: China announced antidumping duties of 178.6% on imports of sorghum from the US.
- May 18, 2018: China and the US released a Joint Declaration of ceasefire.
- June 7, 2018: US agreed to relax the restrictions towards ZTE.
- July 6–10, 2018: The 25% tariff on List 1 (USD 34 billion) was officially imposed; China retaliated with 25% tariff on an equal value of US goods.
- August 23, 2018: US and China implemented a second round of tariffs.
- September 18, 2018: China announced it would impose a tariff on USD 60 billion worth of US goods (List 3) on September 24.

The first trade truce: December 2018 – April 2019

G20 is always the turning point. The two presidents agreed on a truce after the Argentina summit. Administrators talked again before the tension escalated.

- December 1–2, 2018: Xi and Trump had dinner at the G20 Summit in Buenos Aires and agreed on a trade truce for 90 days.
- March 31, 2019: China extended the suspension of additional tariffs on US autos and auto parts, a day before implementation.
- April 30, 2019: Robert Lighthizer and Steven Mnuchin held a trade talk with Liu He. The two sides were expected to conclude with a formal agreement. However, there was no formal release after the meeting.

Second round of the fight: May 2019 – October 2019

Tariff rates were lifted in this phase as the US decided to increase the collateral. Yet Osaka G20 appeared to have enriched the understanding of both leaders, paving the way for another truce in the year end.

- May 10–13, 2019: The US increased tariffs on USD 200 billion worth of Chinese goods (List 3) from 10% to 25%; China announced it would tax USD 60 billion worth of US goods from June 1, 2019.
- May 16–31, 2019: The US included Huawei on its Entity List; China announced it would establish an Unreliable Entities List in retaliation.
- June 2, 2019: China issued a White Paper on US–China Economic Relations.
- June 21, 2019: US added five more Chinese companies to its Entity List.
- June 29, 2019: Xi and Trump agreed a truce after a meeting in Osaka G20 Summit.
- August 6, 2019: US declared China a currency manipulator; Chinese companies suspended new US agricultural product purchases.
- August 13, 2019: The US delays tariffs on certain products and removes items from the list. The USTR announced it would be delaying the imposition of additional tariffs on certain Chinese imports to December 15. A 10% tariff on a host of Chinese products is still to come into effect on September 1.

- August 23, 2019: China announces USD 75 billion in tariffs on US goods; Trump threatens tariff increases on Chinese goods.
- September 1, 2019: US imposed 15% tariff (originally 10%) on List 4a while delaying the tariff on List 4b to December 15.

The second truce: October 2019 – at the time of writing

The Phase One agreement is widely regarded as a truce. The 96-page document outlined many requests from the US. However, the deal only reduced the tariff rate imposed on List 4a by half while the tariff on previous goods remained unchanged. Phase Two negotiation will touch on many enforcement issues.

- October 11, 2019: Trump leaked that the US had reached the Phase One deal with China after a trade talk with Liu He in Washington, DC.
- November 1, 2019: China wins WTO case, able to sanction USD 3.6 billion worth US imports.
- January 13, 2020: US removed China from the currency manipulator list.
- January 15, 2020: Trump and Liu He signed the Phase One deal in Washington, DC, reducing the September's tariff from 15% to 7.5% in exchange for many pledges by China.

Chapter 2

Trade Imbalances and the Greenback

2.1 The Missing Link between Trade and Currency

Officially established in 1995, the World Trade Organization (WTO) was previously called the General Agreement on Tariffs and Trade (GATT) and was supposed to be the global platform for member states to reduce trade and investment barriers. GATT was formed in 1947 shortly after the establishment of the IMF and the International Bank for Reconstruction and Development (of the World Bank Group) in 1944. Immediately after the war, the Allies mostly agreed to rebuild the global economy through closer economic cooperation. They could quickly reach a consensus to develop the financial order of the world. But for trade, the proposal to set up an International Trade Organization was not approved by the US Congress (Fergusson 2007).

The outcome of the Bretton Woods Conference had already implanted a disconnection between trade and monetary policy. This disconnection continued to persist. In the US–China trade negotiation, Chinese Vice Premier Liu He and the US Trade Representative Lighthizer were bargaining their terms of trade ranging from the amount of goods China promised to buy, the level of import tariff, the extent of market access China granted to US companies, and perhaps even the companies included in the Entity List. Their trade talks also touched on China's exchange rate practice, a subject the first course of International Finance could cover.

The US Treasury designated China as a currency manipulator when the trade war heated up in August 2019. But they removed the designation in January 2020 when the Chinese side pledged not to adopt competitive devaluation. The policymakers recognized the role of currency in determining terms of trade. However, the US administration still believed that exchange rate adjustment could reduce the trade imbalance. They believed that an appreciation of the Chinese yuan could restore trade competitiveness of the US. They did not appreciate the historical development following the Plaza Accord; that is, currency revaluation did not reduce the US current account deficits with Japan and West Germany. Somehow, they did not really understand the underlying economics between monetary policy and trade.

Apparently, someone was missing in the trade negotiation process. Did Donald Trump invite the Fed Governor Jeremy Powell to attend the trade talk when PBOC's Yi Gang joined the Chinese delegation? Did Liu He and Lighthizer chat about the Federal Open Market Committee's (FOMC) monthly decision in the past two years? Did China explain to the US Treasury that it was the Fed hiking the interest rate too fast in 2019, causing the yuan to break the psychological handle of 7.0? Was there any coordination between monetary policy and trade policy at all? At the international level, have we seen any joint statement issued by the IMF and WTO? Somehow, there is a disconnection between monetary policy and trade policy.

In fact, the Fed is the most important stakeholder in global trade. The US dollar is the most widely held global reserve currency. The PBOC has a significant economic interest in this currency. It invests heavily in US dollar assets, cycling the foreign currency earnings accumulated from China's trade surplus. Other countries like Japan,

Korea, and Saudi Arabia do the same. The US dollar enjoys a premium. The special status of the dollar prevents the currency from adjusting to a proper equilibrium level that could regulate trade balance. Dollar recycling of exporting countries support the US current account deficits. No matter how many times the US presses its trading partners to strengthen their currencies, the safe haven demand continues to support the value of the US dollar.

This chapter argues that the special status of the US dollar in the global reserve system is the root cause of US trade imbalance. As the US was empowered to print money "infinitely" after the Nixon shock in 1971, they can always fund the balance-of-payment (BOP) deficits externally. China is also responsible for fueling this negative feedback loop because it continues to invest in US dollar assets. Trade agreement with a clause against competitive devaluation cannot solve the structural issue of a global saving glut. To address the issue of US trade imbalance, policymakers need to reform the international monetary system. The world should look for an alternative to replace the dollar-centric, fiat money regime.

2.2 Stubbornly Persistent US Trade Deficits

2.2.1 Stylized Facts of the US Trade Balance

Current account balance is an important bellwether in assessing a country's economic health. It is measured as the net earnings of a country, received from the rest of the world. It indicates whether a country is globally competitive. When a country's goods and services balance is positive, its products are received favorably by other countries. There is a normative aspect or a "good or bad" interpretation for this number. Therefore, trade balance not only carries an economic meaning but also a political implication. As the IMF rightly highlights, "the current account is the point at which international economics collides with political reality. When countries run large deficits, businesses, trade unions, and parliamentarians are often quick to point accusing fingers at trading partners and make charges about unfair practices" (Ghosh and Ramakrishnan 2017).

The US current account balance has been under the spotlight of policy debate for many years because of two reasons.

First, the deficit balance has been stubbornly persistent. Since 1982, except for a brief period in H1 1991, the balance has never returned to surplus on an annual basis. After several years of severe deficits from 1982 to 1987, the stock market crash hit the US in October 1987. The economy entered a period of recession and the current account deficit gradually reduced. However, the improvement did not last long. The economy experienced a long period of robust expansion after Bill Clinton took over at the White House. The deficit rose again. It reached its historical peak at 5.8% of the GDP in 2006, followed by the Global Financial Crisis (GFC). After the crisis, the deficit gradually returned to 2.7% in 2009 (see Figure 2.1).

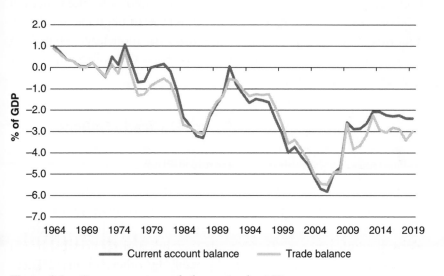

Figure 2.1   Current account balance in the US.

Source: Federal Reserve Bank of St. Louis Economic Data (FRED)

Secondly, the US appears to be the only country that picks up the bill. That is, its deficit absorbs most surpluses from the rest of the world. In 2018, the US deficit reached USD 491 billion whereas the EU, Japan, Korea, and China registered a surplus of USD 334 billion, USD 174 billion, USD 72 billion, and USD 49 billion, respectively. The BOP situation was very one-sided. Mathematically, if there are N-1 surplus countries, the remaining one has to be negative. The US was not the only economy experiencing a long period of current account deficit. The EU also had current account deficits for more than a decade prior to 2012. But it returned to surplus after the European Sovereign Debt crisis.

Interestingly, China's current account surplus was not the largest in the world, lagging behind the EU, Japan, and Korea. For the US, however, China has been the major driver of its deficit. The US balance began to deteriorate after the Nixon shock. By the 1980s, the US was in trade deficits with almost all countries (Figure 2.2). But the deficit with China began to explode in the 2000s. In 2002, the first full year after China's accession to the WTO, the US trade deficit in goods with China was USD 103 billion. In 2018, this figure was fourfold, reaching USD 419 billion, or 2% of the US GDP (Figure 2.2). In 2018, the US registered total trade deficit in goods of USD 891 billion or 4% of GDP. The expansion of this bilateral imbalance was very visible. If Trump's China policy can eliminate this bilateral trade deficit, the US can reduce its overall deficit by half.

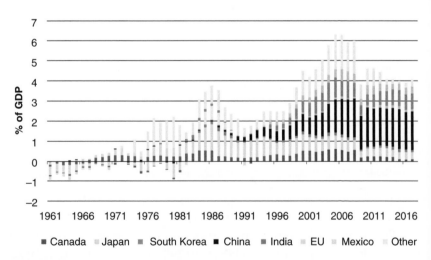

Figure 2.2   The US trade deficits with other countries.

Note: Negative figure = trade surplus

Sources: IMF, FRED

2.2.2 The Economics of Trade Balance

Apparently, classical trade theory cannot explain the persistency of the US trade deficits. If comparative advantage is the basis of international trade, the US should be able to export some products equally valuable to make its trade viable. However, David Ricardo's theory applies to the barter economy (i.e. goods for goods) in a static manner. His theory was developed in the context of the nineteenth-century world, focusing primarily on merchandise trades (he used wine and cloth as an example). With the presence of service trade and international capital mobility, the BOP issue is beyond what the classical theory can reach.

Supply shock used to be a transient factor behind the US trade deficit. The US actually began the trade deficit regime in 1974, a few years after the Nixon shock. In October 1973, the world was hit by the oil shock. Crude price doubled from USD 3.4 per barrel in 1972 to USD 6.9 in 1974 (see Figure 2.3). The US was the major buyer and imported 6 million barrels a day. High crude price dragged the US external balance. When its current account deficit hit 5.8% in 2006, the US imported more than 12 million barrels a day. In an extensive review, the IMF (2016) concluded that many previous current account

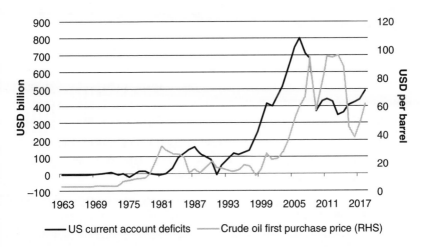

Figure 2.3   Crude oil price and US current account deficit.

Sources: US Energy Information Administration, FRED

imbalances were exacerbated by higher energy prices. In particular, the increase in oil prices since 2003 was responsible for the US deficit by over 1% of GDP.[1] However, the US net imports of oil have declined substantially since the GFC. Although it also became a net exporter of all oil products in 2019, its overall trade deficit barely improved.

The business cycle is a factor driving the current account balance. Clausen and Kandil (2005) studied the current account behavior of nine advanced economies, excluding the US. They found that both economic growth and higher energy prices raised imports of goods and services, resulting in a deterioration of current account balance. Stronger growth should be positively correlated with higher oil price. Even after controlling for this endogenous factor, this study suggested that current account deficit was pro-cyclical. Indeed, as mentioned previously, the deficit in the US experienced some improvement after the crises in 1987 and 2008. A cyclical upturn should be responsible for larger imports.

However, it remained difficult to explain the negative balance of the US over the past four decades during which the US had gone through both a cyclical upturn and downturn. Haltmaier (2014) separated the structural portion from the cyclical impact on current account balances of 35 countries. While the study showed that the changes in current account balances varied across countries in response to the changes in output gap, a considerable number of global imbalances remained unexplained.

Another reason for the structural deficit of the US trade balance is that the supply chain arrangement is irreversible. The way global business organized trade and investment today cannot be entirely captured by country-based economic theory. Globalization involves foreign direct investments beyond the geographical boundary of nations. Realistically, after the manufacturing sector moved out from the US, it was costly for it to retrench from China. The trade surplus of China includes the retained earnings of US entities. By the end of 2018, offshore assets held by the US amounted to USD 25.2 trillion, 22% higher than the level in 2007 (see Figure 2.4). The US has experienced net inflows of income since 2008, following an extended period of deficits in the period 1992–2007 and partially offsetting of its trade deficits in goods and services. In 2018, the net income reached USD 139 billion. Indeed, there had been

---

[1]IMF World Economic Outlook, April 2016.

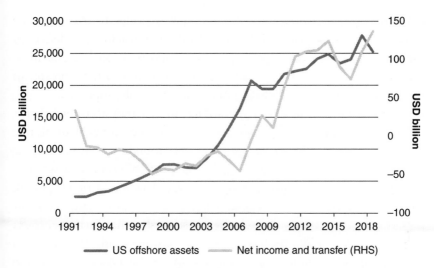

Figure 2.4 Offshore assets of the US and net foreign income.
Source: FRED

a lot of policy debate when Trump's administration launched the Tax Cuts and Jobs Act, which lured repatriated profits of USD 465 billion in the first two quarters of 2018.[2]

Notwithstanding the impressive contribution of foreign income, the trade deficit remains a structural issue facing the US economy. No country can overspend forever without paying the price. Prior to the GFC, some economists warned that the US current account was unsustainable and would ultimately reach the tipping point for massive economic disorder (for example, Edwards 2005), even though some others held a more complacent stance and called for "living with" the imbalance because the country was an attractive place for foreign capital inflows (Cooper 2005).

For emerging markets, overspending is not sustainable because their ability to accumulate foreign liability is constrained by the amount of foreign currency reserve. They also have difficulty retaining long-term investment. The Asia Financial Crisis was a potent example in the

---

[2]MarketWatch. Repatriated profits total $465 billion after Trump tax cuts – leaving $2.5 trillion overseas. (September 19, 2018). (https://www.marketwatch.com/story/repatriated-profits-total-nearly-500-billion-after-trump-tax-cuts-2018-09-19).

emerging market setting. The substantial and prolonged current account deficits of Thailand prior to the crisis had already sown the seeds of the financial meltdown. The level of foreign reserve could not sustain an acute redemption of foreign debts. When foreign investors pulled out, the Thai bhat tumbled. This type of emerging market crisis is a standard recipe for macro hedge funds in considering speculative attacks.

An educational website run by the Federal Reserve Bank of San Francisco quotes, "The U.S. economy has been doing very well for many years now, making it an attractive place for foreigners to invest in. As a result, they have been willing to finance growing U.S. trade deficit in the 1990s. While the deficit has reached unprecedented levels, the dollar has shown no consistent signs of weakening over this decade. Thus, trade deficit can be sustainable for a very long time, making the short run relationship between trade deficit and the dollar very tenuous." The text was written in 1999. Apparently, the author did not notice the looming threat of a financial blowup in 2008.

Indeed, the GFC was the best lesson for us to understand the very nature of structural imbalance. Many economists now hold the view that the external imbalance of the US is due to its domestic saving-investment imbalance. This idea can be expressed by the simple identity in macroeconomics (Ghosh and Ramakrishnan 2006), the gap between investment and saving net of fiscal deficit equals net export:

Imports − Exports = Investment − Saving = Net increase in foreign liability

Current account balance, defined simply as the difference between the value of exports and the value of imports, can be expressed as the difference between national (both public and private) savings and investment. If a country buys more than it sells to another country, there are two ways to fund the gap. The country can settle the net amount by drawing from its previous savings or foreign reserve. If there is no foreign reserve, as in the case of the US, the deficit or overspending means a new liability.

Borio and Disyatat (2015) believed that policymakers had overlooked the financial operation of this saving-investment imbalance. They suggested that this simple identity for explaining current account imbalance failed to capture the financial side in the real world. Global imbalances were almost synonymous with current account imbalances.

In reality, financial imbalances were the source of macroeconomic dislocations. Excessive attention to current account imbalances could not fully capture financial risks involved in cross-border investment. The authors thought that the excess saving of trade surplus countries was not the reason for the GFC. The uncontrolled credit creation was the real problem before the previous crises.

The saving-investment framework can fill an important intellectual gap in understanding the outcome of persistent trade imbalance. Although the mechanics of the saving-investment gap has long been understood, the identity carries little predictive power for financial sustainability. The GFC highlighted the fragility of modern financial systems and actually confirmed that the ugly outcome was a prolonged period of current account deficits.

Obstfeld and Rogoff (2009) pointed out that the rapid evolution of financial markets can pose untested hazards that trigger economic disorders. However, they expressed the potential crisis in a sharp adjustment of the US dollar exchange rate instead of a financial crisis. In an earlier paper, Obstfeld and Rogoff (2005) predicted that for the US trade balance (in 2004) to return to zero, the real effective exchange rate of the dollar should depreciate by 33%. The beauty of their economic model was that it combined the dynamics of current account imbalances with the changes in the international investment position. The model included a mechanism that captured interest rate differentials between the US dollar and other currencies. However, this simulation model took exchange rate adjustment as an outcome, responding to some exogenous change (e.g. sudden increase in the US saving rate). An intentional dollar devaluation could close the trade imbalances. But the model did not have a mechanism to prevent another overvaluation in the future.

The right question we need to ask is why the US dollar is overvalued. What makes the US dollar so strong? What is the role of the international monetary system? Why are dollar-denominated assets a default or preferred option for investment? What prevents the exchange rate from adjusting the external imbalance? Will the China–US trade war result in another Plaza Accord or a one-off revaluation? In a world with almost perfect international financial flows (especially with the Chinese yuan increasingly convertible), these questions concern not only the political economy but also investment implications.

2.3 Is the Exchange Rate to Blame?

2.3.1 Currency Revaluation

Currency revaluation is an unavoidable topic in all trade disputes. Our discussion has established the framework that external and domestic imbalances are two sides of the same coin. The US trade deficit with the rest of the world is an outcome of its own dissaving. If the world is completely dollarized, we just need to search for an equilibrium price between US import and export that can help the current account break even. In this dollarized setting, there is only one interest rate. If this interest rate is exogenously determined by a central bank, the saving-investment profile will be given. The equilibrium price of import–export should be adjusted to be consistent with this profile.

In a multicurrency world, the policy consideration will be more complicated. Ideally, the nominal exchange rate between the US dollar and other currencies should need to fulfill the long-running relationship of purchasing power parity (PPP). In equilibrium, the same Big Mac should be sold at the same price in US dollar terms. At the same time, the exchange rate should also satisfy uncovered interest rate parity. The nominal interest rate on a US Government bond must equal the interest rate of a comparable foreign bond plus the expected change in the nominal exchange rate over the period of maturity. Using these parity conditions to evaluate the fair value of currency could be an academic interest. In the actual policy setting, it is almost impossible to coordinate the monetary policy of different countries that are subject to varying degrees of domestic price rigidity.

Given domestic price rigidity, a floating exchange rate regime should have facilitated the adjustment of current account balance via the change of exchange rate. What was ironic was that the US had a positive current account in almost the entire Bretton Woods regime. Its current account deficit became the norm after the country switched to the fiat money regime. The financial market might have attained no arbitrage condition under interest rate parity via the capital/portfolio account. From the angle of PPP, the US Treasury still believed other countries undervalued their currencies. In this regime, the norm has been the administration pressing other countries to strengthen their currency value in order to fix its own trade deficits.

The real effective exchange rates (REER) compiled by the IMF can be used to depict the trend of purchasing power of different currencies (Figure 2.5). If we use 1995 as the base year (Bayoumi et al. 2005), the REER of the US was the strongest amongst these countries. Japan and Germany were the two nations willing to strengthen the currencies in Plaza Accord 1985. But their currency continued to depreciate in the mid-1990s. On the contrary, China was alleged by the US as a currency manipulator. But its REER strengthened substantially in the last decade. All these currencies registered a persistent trade surplus with the US. But their currency value followed different paths, suggesting the exchange rate was playing a small role in the US trade issue.

Indeed, pressing other countries to strengthen their currency offered little help. Frankel (2015) provided a good historical background of the Plaza Accord: "The 26% appreciation of the dollar between 1980 and 1984 was not difficult to explain based on textbook macroeconomic

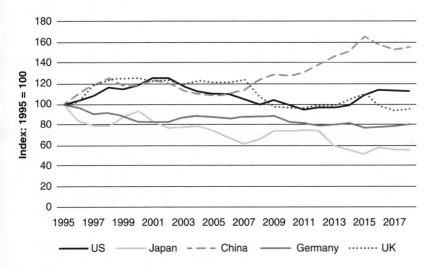

Figure 2.5 Real effective exchange rate.

Source: IMF

fundamentals. . . . Whatever the cause, the trade deficit reached USD 112 billion in 1984 and continued to widen. Some who had hitherto supported a freely floating exchange rate for the dollar began to change their minds." The G5 ministers agreed on a 10–12% depreciation of the dollar. The market subsequently pushed the dollar to the weaker side by buying Japanese yen, eventually pushing the exchange rate of the dollar against the yen to fall by 51% from 1985 to 1987.

Simple economics predicted a revival of US export competitiveness after the Plaza Accord. However, history did not evolve as the theory predicted. Even though the Accord successfully weakened the US dollar, the trade imbalance issue did not abate. The US trade deficit in goods and services peaked in the third quarter of 1987 at USD 38 billion. By 1991, it continued to come down. Frankel believed the dollar devaluation had the desired effect. But he also noted that the US recession was also an important reason for reduced imports in the period 1990–1991. The impact, however, was short-lived. The trade deficits continued to expand throughout the 1990s.

As an opposite argument, the US trade balance may not necessarily worsen under a fixed exchange rate regime. Hong Kong is an interesting example (see Figure 2.6). The Chinese port, which has dollarized

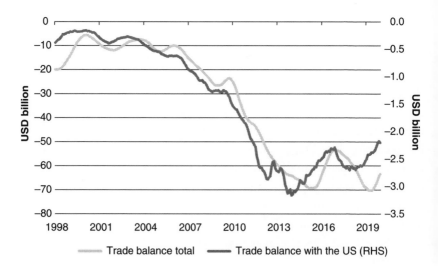

Figure 2.6 Hong Kong – Trade balance of a dollarized economy.
Source: Hong Kong C&SD

since 1983, is one of the few economies the US enjoys persistent trade surplus with. The US trade with Hong Kong can be considered a trade with China in a fixed exchange rate regime. The Hong Kong dollar is pegged at 7.75–7.85. The FOMC makes interest rate decisions for the city, as the Hong Kong Monetary Authority follows the exact decision of the former in the morning. Adjusted for local liquidity conditions in the banking sector, the interest rate level of HKD largely follows that of the USD. The city relies on domestic price movement for economic adjustment. There has not been revaluation during the past 37 years.

2.3.2 Exchange Rate in Trade Talks

Most economists favored a floating exchange rate regime in the aftermath of the Nixon shock. It was believed to be an efficient method to curb trade imbalances. McKinnon (1990) noted that this view primarily assumed a separation of monetary policy and exchange rate policy as countries were insulated and, hence, financial arbitrage (or interest rate differentials) played a small role in exchange rate determination. If currency weakening indicated an expectation of monetary policy easing, the trade deficits would be even larger. Exchange rate revaluation was not an effective tool in regulating the trade balance. When he wrote in 1990, he predicted that the dollar weakness post-Plaza Accord could not improve the US current account. Instead, this could push the inflationary pressure of the American economy.

Today, more than 30 years after the Plaza Accord, the US government continues to adopt a similar mindset in dealing with its trading partners. The Department of the Treasury publishes a semiannual review of international economic and exchange rate policies: "If any of the U.S. trade partners meets the standards of the '1988 Act,'[3] the Treasury Department must conduct an enhanced analysis." By the Trade Facilitation and Trade Enforcement Act of 2015,[4] there are

---

[3]The US Treasury. Omnibus Trade and Competitiveness Act of 1988 (H.R. 3) (https://www.treasury.gov/resource-center/international/exchange-rate-policies/Documents/authorizing-statute.pdf).

three criteria in assessing whether a country is a "currency manipulator" (see Table 2.1). When a country meets all of them, the US government will label it as a currency manipulator and the US will try to solve this via bilateral negotiations:

1. A significant bilateral trade surplus with the US is one that is at least USD 20 billion;
2. A material current account surplus is one that is at least 3% of GDP; and
3. Persistent, one-sided intervention occurs when net purchases of foreign currency are conducted repeatedly and total at least 2% of an economy's GDP over a 12-month period.

Table 2.1 Treasury thresholds under the 2015 Act.

Criteria	Benchmark	Previous Threshold	New Threshold
Major trading partner coverage	Total bilateral goods trade (net imports)	12 largest trading partners	USD 40 billion
Significant bilateral trade surplus with the US	Goods surplus with the US	USD 20 billion	USD 20 billion
Material current account surplus	Current account balance	3% of GDP	2% of GDP
Persistent one-sided intervention in FX markets	Net FX purchases	2% of GDP	2% of GDP
	Persistent of net FX purchases	8 of 12 months	6 of 12 months

Source: The US Treasury (https://home.treasury.gov/system/files/206/2019-05-28-May-2019-FX-Report.pdf)

---

[4]The US Congress. Trade Facilitation and Trade Enforcement Act of 2015 (https://www.congress.gov/114/plaws/publ125/PLAW-114publ125.pdf).

On August 5, 2019, the US Treasury eventually designated China as a currency manipulator after many years of consideration. The US claimed to engage with the IMF to eliminate the unfair competitive advantage created by China, according to the government statement.[5] The Treasury decision was based on the following rationale:

> China has a long history of facilitating an undervalued currency through protracted, large-scale intervention in the foreign exchange market. In recent days, China has taken concrete steps to devalue its currency, while maintaining substantial foreign exchange reserves despite active use of such tools in the past. The context of these actions and the implausibility of China's market stability rationale confirm that the purpose of China's currency devaluation is to gain an unfair competitive advantage in international trade.

The decision to designate China as a currency manipulator sparked a concern about a currency war. A day following the US' decision, the PBOC seemed to have become hands-off in managing the value of yuan. Without imposing a so-called counter-cyclical adjustment factor on the daily fixing, the value of renminbi against the USD broke the psychological level of 7.0 (see Figure 2.7). Within a month, the spot rate surged to 7.18 on September 3 compared with 6.88 on July 31. Prior to the Treasury's decision, Trump publicly complained about the strength of the dollar on a number of occasions, claiming that it could hurt American competitiveness. The market was worried that the US would intentionally weaken the value of the dollar, even though it was unclear how the US government would conduct direct intervention in the financial market.

This currency manipulation report legitimizes the US trade measures towards other countries. Many exporting countries are used to this type of unilateral accusation by the US government. The US can also modify the criteria to suit its own interest. Proponents supporting this practice believe other central banks intervene in the

---

[5]The US Treasury. Treasury designates China as a currency manipulator. Press release (August 5, 2019) (https://home.treasury.gov/news/press-releases/sm751).

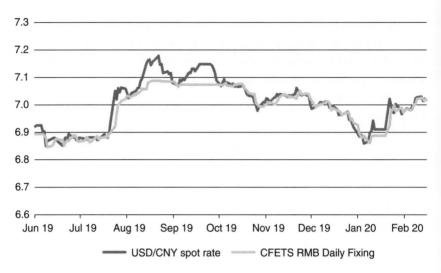

Figure 2.7   Daily renminbi exchange rate, USD/CNY.
Source: CFETS

foreign exchange market in order to boost their export competitiveness. The problem is that many countries actually want to stabilize rather than weaken their currencies. Their motivation is financial stability instead of trade.

Clearly, there is a disconnection between the US trade policy and monetary policy. In countries like China and Japan, the central banks can buy and sell in the foreign exchange market because they have a sizeable amount of foreign currency reserve. Exchange rate can be an implicit policy target in considering import inflation and export competitiveness. In contrast, the US Treasury and the Federal Reserve System have different mandates. The Fed is responsible for attaining the macroeconomic targets (i.e. inflation) via interest rate policy. However, it is also a provider of the global reserve currency. The exchange rate of the dollar is beyond the mandate of the Fed even though its interest rate policy does influence the value of the dollar. Instead, the Treasury has been very vocal in exchange rate discussion because of the trade policy.

In theory, decline in export competitiveness should be translated into dimming growth prospect. That should be a driver for the Fed to cut the interest rate and hence weaken the currency. If interest rate parity holds, the widening of interest rate differential should witness some flows from US dollar to higher yield currency. The reality is that the dollar safe haven status dictates capital flows in the opposite direction. Despite slower growth, cutting the interest rate can propel a bull run in US government bonds. The "risk-off" environment in the financial market sees a portfolio reallocation by global fund managers towards the US Treasury, resulting in a flight from the emerging market and commodity currencies. We see more capital inflows into US dollar assets. The reserve currency status becomes the biggest obstacle to the exchange rate channel in regulating US balance.

This US–China trade war follows the same script. Authers (2019) raised an interesting point that "at least two other organizations have more power over markets than the White House. They are the US Federal Reserve and the Chinese Communist Party." By flagging this trade war against China, Trump put pressure on China to stimulate the economy. By firing up global tensions, he also pressed the Fed to cut the interest rate abruptly in 2019, despite a set of good employment statistics. The inverted yield curve in early 2019 proved to be an unreliable signal of a US recession. Nonetheless, the yield of 10-year US government securities fell to below 2.0% in late 2019 (see Figure 2.8). Trump wanted a weaker dollar. However, his tariff plan actually induced more foreign flows into the dollar fixed-income market. The US dollar strengthened.

2.4 Exorbitant Privilege of the Dollar

2.4.1 Triffin Dilemma

In 1960, Professor Robert Triffin (1960) at Yale University expressed his concern about the gold-exchange standard, commonly known as Triffin's dilemma. In late 1950s, the Bretton Woods system was the main architecture in international finance. The US dollar was backed by a

Figure 2.8 The US 10-year government bond yield and USD exchange rate.
Source: FRED

simple promise of gold convertibility, and other currencies were backed by the greenback. In essence, the dollar only served as an intermediary. Triffin predicted that if the US corrected its persistent BOP deficits, the growth of world reserves could not be fed adequately by gold production at USD 35 an ounce. But if the US experienced deficits persistently, its foreign liabilities would be unsustainable. The gold convertibility could not sustain. Indeed, when other countries lost confidence and demanded for gold, Richard Nixon had to abandon the gold standard in 1971, fulfilling the prophecy of Triffin.

Bordo and McCauley (2017) provided a critical literature review on the Triffin dilemma. They pointed out that Triffin's theory referred to the sustainability of gold–dollar convertibility with little coverage on current account or trade imbalances. The BOP deficit Triffin referred to was the US liability position to the rest of the world, as the country needed to fulfill its global duty to supply foreign reserve. It was a variant version of Triffin's dilemma of what they called a "current account Triffin" that related trade balance with the role of the US dollar in other central banks' reserves. Nonetheless, this extended implication of the "exorbitant privilege" enjoyed by the dollar could still explain the underlying reason for the persistent US trade deficit.

According to Eichengreen (2011), the term "exorbitant privilege" was coined in the 1960s by Valéry Giscard d'Estaing, the then French Minister of Finance, but was misattributed to Charles de Gaulle. With this exorbitant privilege, the US virtually had unlimited power to issue money and fund international spending (including both capital account and current account items). As Eichengreen put it beautifully, "It costs only a few cents for the Bureau of Engraving and Printing to produce a USD 100 bill, but other countries had to pony up USD 100 of actual goods in order to obtain one." The international duty performed by the US (i.e. the Fed) of supplying international reserve currency was rewarding, as the US could enjoy a natural advantage (or an "original sin") as a debtor country internationally.

The exorbitant privilege was first granted to the dollar under the Bretton Woods Agreement in 1944, which was a fixed exchange rate regime. Revaluation was allowable only with the IMF's agreement if they saw it could fix a "fundamental disequilibrium" of balance of payments (IMF website).[6] In the aftermath of the Nixon shock in 1971, there had been several attempts to adjust the value of US dollar against gold with a hope to restore the fixed exchange rate regime (e.g. Smithsonian Agreement). In 1973, the developed countries admitted the failure of Bretton Woods. The major currencies began to float. However, the US dollar remained the global reserve currency given its first mover advantage.

The US enjoyed the exorbitant privilege in two periods:

1. In the Bretton Woods regime (1944–1973), the US dollar was an intermediary currency backed by gold at USD 35 per ounce. Global exchange rates were fixed;

---

[6]IMF website. Cooperation and reconstruction (1944–71) https://www.imf.org/external/about/histcoop.htm.

2. Post-Bretton Woods (1973–current) or a fiat money regime, the dollar was not backed by any physical collateral. The world became a floating exchange rate regime.

Under the Bretton Woods regime, other countries endorsed the US to be the supplier of global reserve. Their willingness to hold the US dollar was based on their confidence in gold convertibility. In the period 1944–1973, the US dollar leveraged on its gold holding to create money. Technically speaking, gold was still the definitive reserve in the monetary system.

It was the fiat money regime that took the special status of the US dollar to the next level. Money supply by the Fed was not constrained by the amount of gold available anymore. Now, the US monetary policy is decided by the FOMC, which consists of twelve members. These twelve members are empowered by the government of the US (not the IMF, not China) to decide on the supply of the global reserve currency. After the GFC, the FOMC decided to expand the balance sheet of the Federal Reserve from less than USD 1 trillion in 2008 to USD 4.5 trillion within a few years by purchasing the liability of the US government, US mortgage agencies, and some American financial institutions

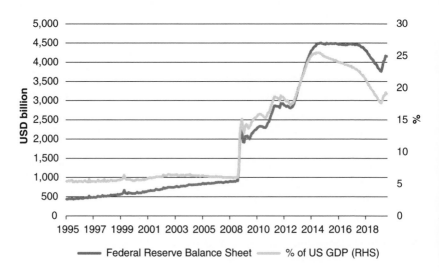

Figure 2.9 Balance sheet of the US Federal Reserve.
Source: FRED

(Figure 2.9). None of these decisions relates to their global responsibility. The amount of money supply does not anchor the level of gold holding, but rather the votes inside the boardroom.

2.4.2 Quantitative Easing

In the first few years following the GFC, the US Fed had adopted an unconventional monetary policy. By pressing the interest rate to almost zero and implementing a series of quantitative easing, the Fed did help achieve financial stability. One could also argue that the policy stimulus helped improve the external balance of the US because the current account deficit decreased from the historical peak of 5.8% of the GDP in 2006 to 2% in 2014, the year prior to the tapering and policy normalization from 2015 onwards (see Table 2.2). However, as mentioned

Table 2.2 Current account and trade balance of the US.

Year	Fed Policy	M2 Growth	Current Account as % of GDP	Trade Account as % of GDP
2006		5.9	–5.8	–5.5
2007		5.7	–5.0	–4.9
2008	QE1 Nov 2008–Oct	9.7	–4.7	–4.9
2009	2010: Bought MBS,	3.7	–2.6	–2.7
2010	bank debts, Treasury securities with a total amount of about USD 1.3 trillion	3.6	–2.9	–3.3
2011	QE2 Nov 2010:	9.8	–2.9	–3.5
2012	Launched QE2 and bought Treasury securities of USD 600 billion	8.2	–2.6	–3.3
2013	QE3 Sep 2012–Oct 2014:	5.4	–2.1	–2.7
2014	Open-ended bond purchase.	5.9	–2.1	–2.8

(Continued)

Table 2.2 (Continued)

Year	Fed Policy	M2 Growth	Current Account as % of GDP	Trade Account as % of GDP
2015		5.9	–2.2	–2.7
2016		7.1	–2.3	–2.7
2017		4.9	–2.3	–2.9
2018		3.7	–2.4	–3.1

Source: FRED

earlier, the sharp fall in oil price, decline in domestic demand, and the rise in foreign income also contributed to the improvement in the current account. The cyclical factor was responsible for the sharp decline in trade deficit, which shrank to 2.6% in 2009 from 4.7% in 2008. With the subsequent quantitative easing, the trade deficit actually enlarged again to 3.5% in 2011. When the Fed started to print money, the trade deficit rose again.

There was a strand of empirical studies covering the impact of the Fed's unconventional monetary policy on current account imbalance. Through a structural VAR econometric model, Adler and Buitron (2017) found that monetary tightening (quantified as 1% point decrease in 10-year US government bond yield) could lead to a significant improvement in trade balance (0.7% of GDP) in the US. Vice versa, monetary easing allowed the US to import more and sustained its trade deficit. When he discussed the Fed's policy in the context of trade in 2015, Bernanke (2015) expressed that the negative effects of a weaker dollar (due to monetary easing) on the exports of US trading partners were substantially offset by the positive effects of higher US incomes. In other words, the consequence was an adversity of the US trade balance.

Let's take a step back. The Fed could react to the GFC without a piece of physical gold. The twelve members led by Chairman Ben Bernanke had clearly utilized the power given to them in addressing the domestic crisis. However, their actions also exhibited a governance issue of the fiat money regime. Bernanke admitted that the Fed policy affected the availability of dollar credit in emerging markets which were subject to a liquidity premium in their cost of borrowing. The Fed inherits a natural advantage compared with other central banks. With the exorbitant privilege, the US could "finance its trade deficit in large part through the risk premium it earns from issuing safe liabilities and investing in risky assets" (Bernanke 2015).

Even in the very critical review of "Triffinesque," Bordo and McCauley (2017) did not reject the idea of "current account Triffin." The authors cited a number of empirical studies and identified some flaws of the studies supporting the theory of exorbitant privilege. They concluded that "the finding that the US current account deficit is larger than one would expect from underlying variables like income level, demographics, and so on, leaves open the question of why this is so." Their conclusion was that the US did not necessarily register current account deficits despite being the registered supplier of global reserve currency. However, the idea that the currency status facilitated a pro-longed current account deficit remained plausible. Statistically, we do see

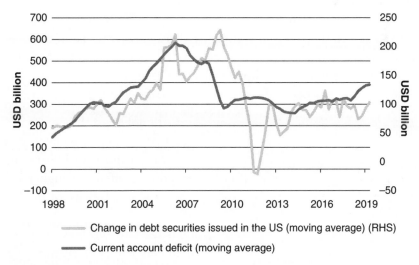

Figure 2.10   US debt securities and current account deficit.
Source: FRED

a parallel development of current account balance and the US securities issued (Figure 2.10).

The exorbitant privilege in the fiat money regime created a negative spiral that dragged the US economy into a "twin deficits" country, i.e. current account deficit and fiscal deficit. The Fed can issue paper by buying US government securities at no cost. To fulfill the reserve currency status, the Treasury performs its duties to supply debt instruments that are seen to be risk-free. US households can save less than other countries. Corporate America can increase their leverage more easily. Public and private spending can be easily debt-funded. They can buy more from other countries than selling to them indefinitely.

2.5 Dollar Recycling and the Global Saving Glut

2.5.1 Petrodollar Recycling

Ben Bernanke (2005) coined the concept of a global saving glut, i.e. the imbalances arising from excess supply of saving over investment. He proposed that the significant increase in the global supply of saving caused the increase in the US current account deficit and, thus, the relatively low level of long-term real interest rates in the world. In essence, Bernanke equated the saving-investment imbalance to external imbalances, as we highlighted in the previous section. But he was skeptical about the idea of twin deficits as he thought that the empirically, the relationship between fiscal balance and current account balance was weak in the US in the period 1996–2000. In his view, the main reason was the very substantial shift in the current accounts of developing and emerging market nations that transformed these countries from net borrowers to large net lenders. The global imbalance was due to the fact that these countries saved too much.

The global saving gluts were facilitated by a process of dollar recycling. The basic idea was that trade surplus countries converted their earnings into US dollar assets. Dollar recycling of different countries took different forms and was based on different motivations. Oil exporters invested their proceeds from the pump into dollar assets. China and other Asian economies also turned their export earnings into dollar assets. Because the dollar was a default currency in international trade, these countries had to invoice or settle their trade. They also regarded the dollar, an investment currency because it was a risk-free, reserve currency (will the US government default?). The trade surplus countries lent money to fund the US deficits.

Nsouli (2006) suggests two channels through which recycling takes place. The absorption channel has the oil proceeds in the US dollar used for consumption. Technically speaking, this is not entirely a recycling act because the funds or trade surpluses are not flowing back to the US. Wealthy Saudi Arabia may spend the money on a Ferrari. The process involves exchanging the US dollar proceeds into euro via a commercial bank before going into the pocket of the Italian car maker. The global banking system pools the dollar earnings and ends up in the Eurodollar market. If the funds did not return to the US, it can hardly be called recycling.

Another channel is the capital account. This is the channel through which the petrodollar contributes to global imbalances. The oil proceeds are not spent, but saved and invested. Central banks or sovereign wealth funds of oil-exporting countries invest in the US. In fact, the New York Fed provides the custodian services for some 250 foreign central banks and foreign governments, keeping USD 3.3 trillion of their sovereign wealth (Spicer 2017). The investment often takes the form of US government securities or agency debts. From a BOP perspective, it is a liability position of the US. Persistent trade deficits due to oil imports in the US are booked as the country's liability.

Petrodollar is a potent example of the dollar recycling process. Following the collapse of the Nixon shock in 1971, the US government attempted to stabilize the US dollar. However, they failed to restore the fixed exchange rate regime until 1973. The turning point was when OPEC nations agreed to accept the US dollar exclusively for their oil exports, because petroleum was a major import for most countries in the world. These countries needed to buy the dollar for their oil procurement. Naturally, they also maintained substantial foreign reserves in US dollar assets to match their oil imports. This strategy created a natural currency hedge. Currency matching is a major consideration for corporate treasurers engaged in global business today.

Saudi Arabia played a central role in petrodollar recycling. In 1974, the US and Saudi Arabia established a Joint Commission on Economic Cooperation.[7] The aims of the Commission were:

1. Fostering closer political ties between the two countries through economic cooperation;
2. Assisting Saudi industrialization and development while recycling petrodollars;
3. Facilitating the flow to Saudi Arabia of American goods, services, and technology.

This agreement raised several interesting points. First, it established a formal mechanism to tie the oil proceeds to the interests of American corporations that were involved in the bilateral trades. Secondly, the technical assistance was funded almost entirely from the Saudi Arabian Trust Account in the US Treasury. This account was interest bearing. Saudi Arabia needed to deposit an amount equal to the estimated annual costs of infrastructure projects the US provided.

With this agreement, the oil proceeds were recycled to the US. In August 1974, the Assistant Secretary of State for Near Eastern and South Asian Affairs noted that "In helping the Saudis to find a way to invest their large and growing financial reserves, we will give them added incentive to continue to produce oil in the quantities needed to meet world demands at stable, and hopefully, lower-price levels." Saudi Arabia's foreign reserve became the liability of the US Treasury.

The dollar quickly regained its global status because the dollar-oil agreement stabilized its value. The traditional gold standard of USD 35 per ounce was transformed into a regime of "black gold." The physical reserve of gold and oil were both limited. The durable nature of the two commodities also made them an ideal candidate for backing currencies. The difference between oil standard and gold standard was the exchange rate regime. The value of USD is not fixed to oil at USD

---

[7]The U.S.–Saudi Arabian Joint Commission on Economic Cooperation ID-79-7: Published: March 22, 1979. Publicly Released: March 29, 1979. (https://www.gao.gov/products/ID-79-7).

35 per barrel. The price of petroleum itself is floating in accordance with supply and demand. Furthermore, the world is now largely a floating exchange rate regime. The values of other currencies against the USD are not fixed.

This "oil standard" is a loosely defined concept rather than an institutional arrangement. The "oil standard" is manifested at the country level. Member countries of Gulf Cooperation Council did peg their currencies with the US dollar. Between October 1978 and November 1980, Bahrain, Qatar, and the United Arab Emirates (UAE) pegged their national currencies to the US dollar at a rate of 0.38, 3.64, and 3.67, respectively. The Omani rial and Saudi riyal were pegged to the dollar at 3.8 and 3.75 in 1986. To maintain the peg, these countries often need to intervene in the market. Pinto calculated that in the period 2015–2017, when global oil prices fluctuated massively, the GCC accumulated an estimated USD 353 billion in fiscal deficits, USD 76 billion in current account deficits, and USD 270 billion in foreign-exchange reserve losses (Pinto 2018). By April 2019, countries like Saudi Arabia, UAE, and Kuwait (USD 176.6 billion, USD 55.7 billion, and USD 40.2 billion, respectively) still held a large amount of US government securities, so that they could defend their currencies if needed.

Needless to say, some observers extended to view the oil standard from a geopolitical point of view. Rowley at al. (1989) wrote that the reason for Saudi Arabia to enter the 1974 agreement with the US was to exchange oil for military protection. This could be called the "Armadollar-Petrodollar Coalition." Rowley postulated that the interaction during the 1970s of rising military exports to the gulf and growing oil exports from the region provided a basis for the cooperation between major armament and energy corporations. Under this thesis, Saudi Arabia was willing to embrace the dollar exclusively in oil trade and be engaged in petrodollar recycling.

2.5.2 China's Factory-Dollar Recycling

Another major dollar recycling since 1990s has been the rise of emerging Asia, notably China. If the petrodollar is built on the exports of oil reserves, the vast amount of manpower reserve in Asia has offered another channel of dollar recycling. With scarce natural resources, these countries have relied on their labor supply to support their exports of manufacturing products. Their factories have been the engine of economic growth. Similar to oil exporters, these countries have accumulated a large amount of trade surplus in the past few decades. Their sovereign wealth invests heavily in the US dollar assets. They are also a major investor in dollar assets.

In the past two decades, China accumulated foreign earnings through exports continuously. When China gained its access to the WTO in 2001, its foreign reserve was only USD 212 billion. By the middle of 2014, the level of sovereign wealth reached the peak at USD 3.99 trillion before a period of rapid depletion in the aftermath of the infamous exchange rate reform on August 11, 2015. China not only derived much of its sovereign wealth through net exports but also attracted a huge amount of foreign direct investment. According to the latest data by the State Administration of Foreign Exchanges (SAFE), China allocated 58% of its foreign reserves in US dollar assets in 2014. Assuming that this proportion has not changed, the amount of US dollars asset held by the Chinese government could be USD 1.8 trillion in December 2019.

Today, the SAFE Investment Company and China Investment Corporation (CIC) are amongst the largest sovereign wealth funds (SWF) in the world. The Chinese SWFs together with their peers, like Korea Investment Corporation, Government Investment Corporation (GIC) and Temasek from Singapore, are the operating vehicles in the factory dollar recycling process. Even though these funds do not always disclose their currency portfolio, they should have a significant share allocated to the dollar assets, both inside and outside the US.

China's factory dollar recycling showcases Bernanke's global saving glut. To develop the manufacturing sector, China has invested heavily in its productive assets, funded primarily by domestic saving. National saving rates are typically high. For instance, China's national saving rate was 38% of GDP in 2000. Since its accession to the WTO, the saving rate had risen tremendously. At one point, China's national saving rate reached 52% of GDP in 2008. Given the government's effort to transform the economy from an investment-led, export-oriented economy into a consumption-driven one, the saving rate has declined gradually in the past few years. In absolute terms, however, the rate of 45% was still translated into USD 6.1 trillion. This number is 2.5 times the value of USD 2.4 trillion in 2008.

Bernanke attributed the decline in long-term real interest rates to the increase in external surpluses and high saving rate in China, as the imbalances propelled strong inflows into US dollar assets. Like West Germany and Japan in the 1970s and 1980s, China accumulated a huge amount of trade surplus over the years. It also quickly became a major holder of US government securities and contributed to dollar recycling. In nominal USD, China is estimated to have contributed one-quarter of the world's gross national savings in 2018 (see Figure 2.11), compared with 9% in 2005 when Bernanke first spoke of the global savings gluts. China's foreign reserve holding amounted to USD 3.1 trillion, a lot higher than Japan's (the world's second) USD 1.29 trillion. China held USD 1.1 trillion of the US Government securities and is the top foreign creditor of the US government (see Figure 2.12).

The operation of factory dollar recycling differs slightly from the petrodollar story. Oil exporters derive much of their dollar earnings directly from exporting natural resources whereas China plays an intermediary role in the global supply chains. Even though China runs a huge amount of trade surplus with the US, its trade balances with many

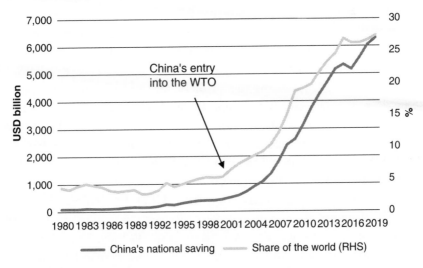

Figure 2.11   Gross national savings in nominal USD.

Source: IMF

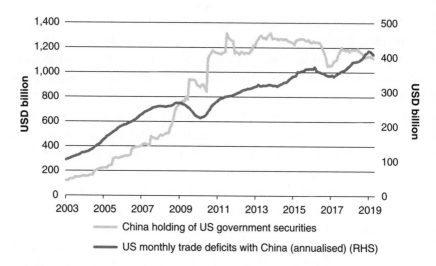

Figure 2.12   China's holding of US Government Securities.
Sources: US TIC, FRED

economies in the upstream are negative, such as Korea and Australia. China acts as an assembler and puts together many parts and components from Japan, Korea, and even the US into final products. Typically, manufacturers in China receive US dollars from their export receipts and they use the money to fund their imports. In petrodollar recycling, oil exporters have the choice not to follow the dollar standard. In the case of China, the factory dollar recycling process is due to the network advantage of the dollar in trade transactions.

The US dollar remains the primary foreign currency in China's cross-border flows. In 2018, Chinese commercial banks bought USD 1.89 trillion and sold USD 1.95 trillion of foreign exchange. The banks received and paid foreign currency of total USD 5.5 trillion. Of the total, 88% was US dollars. On a net basis, China experienced a net dollar receipt of USD 223 billion in 2018. Besides the amount these banks squared with the central bank, there were USD 731 billion of foreign deposits sitting in the banking system. Chinese banks processed a total amount of cross-border net payment of USD 86 billion in 2018, supporting foreign trade and investment flows. The demand for foreign currency by local residents is high.

China's factory-dollar recycling plays an important role in global saving glut. It is the best explanation for the persistent trade deficits in the US. As long as the world maintains the fiat currency standard, the US trade imbalances will remain sticky. Given the exorbitant privilege, there is an implicit moral hazard for the US to fund its twin deficits by printing money. The trade war is an outcome of the disconnection between monetary policy and trade policy. Against this backdrop, trade measures such as the import tariff will be unable to reduce the US trade deficit. Neither multilateral negotiation over the WTO platform nor the bilateral trade talks can fix the global saving glut, not to mention the Phase One agreement the US concluded with China in the first month of 2020.

Chapter 3

Deglobalization Prompts De-Dollarization

3.1 Anti-Multilateralism and Anti-Sovereign Movement

Just two decades ago, globalization was a buzz word. Emerging markets—notably Brazil, Russia, India, and China (BRIC)—were deemed the next "Big Thing" and offered a greenfield for Corporate America. With a combined population of 2.5 billion in 2000, the BRIC countries were believed to be a huge opportunity for consumer business. China's manufacturing sector and India's outsourcing services provided a low-cost option for multinational corporations (MNCs). In those days, global business was the preferred stream of almost all MBA students.

During the past few years, however, the narrative of globalization has turned sharply. Public opinion has shifted. International trade is faced with an increasingly hostile environment, as it is perceived to be the culprit behind rising inequality within and between countries. Global supply chains are accused of being a major threat to jobs. Massive manufacturing and construction are blamed for being environmentally unfriendly. Within the policy circle, multilateralism is hardly functioning. The World Trade Organization (WTO) has made little progress in the Doha Round of negotiations after the breakdown in 2008. Instead, the Global Financial Crisis (GFC) has prompted policymakers to question the earlier promise of international finance. Politicians who take a hawkish stance towards trading partners have risen to prominence. Populism shapes the direction of global trade and economic affairs.

Free trade has been the fundamental belief in economics. By David Ricardo's comparative advantage, all nations should have their own competitive edges. Economic integration is said to unlock latent economic value. After China's accession to the WTO, the world has experienced a hugely positive supply shock. Although the expansion of a cheap labor pool has absolutely increased consumer welfare by lowering the cost of production, this "China shock" has also resulted in rapid declines in US manufacturing employment due to import substitution (Autor et al. 2016). The adjustment process was painful. Globalization does not guarantee Pareto's improvement. The rise of populism is a wake-up call. Voters are demanding for equality instead of efficiency. A critical task for policymakers is to identify the winners and losers so that the government can redistribute the gains of the former to the latter.

As the trade war intensified in 2018, China was celebrating the 40th anniversary of its market reform. From the 1950s to the middle of 1970s, the Communist nation stayed behind the iron curtain when the Western world was going through a period of postwar globalization. When the late Deng Xiaoping took power, he opened up the country for trade and investment. Since then, a massive influx of foreign capital and know-how into the coastal region, combined with the huge pool of hard-working labor, has propelled China's so-called miracle. The country quickly became an integral part of the world economy and also took globalization to another level. China's GDP per capita quadrupled. Chinese workers, businesses, and the government were the winners in global trade and investment.

Who were the gainers in the US? Besides the underappreciated consumer welfare, MNCs having presence in China were clearly a beneficiary. Given the access to cheap dollar funding, the US financial sector is also a winner. In 1997, WTO members agreed to soften restrictions on banking services, securities trading, and insurance services. The commitment entered into force in March 1999. The scale of financial liberalization covered approximately 95% of worldwide financial services.[1] The Bank for International Settlements (BIS 2017) suggested that trade and financial openness were intertwined. Financial integration grew substantially as emerging markets liberalized their financial markets and adopted a policy of capital account liberalization. As the primary dealer of risk-free capital, US banks captured the opportunities and expanded their global presence because of the dollar's dominant position in trade settlement.

The US dollar was almost a symbol of globalization. Its position was also questioned when the promise of financial integration was at risk. When the GFC broke out a decade ago, China began to question whether the dollar standard remained legitimate and started to promote the yuan as an alternative currency in trade and investment. As the biggest country by size of merchandise trade, China's action brought a significant implication on the future position of the US dollar. With the rise of protectionism, other countries will also question the authority of the US in globalization. If China advocates direct currency conversion with other countries and bypasses the dollar in trade, de-dollarization seems to be a natural outcome on the back of deglobalization.

The globalization–dollarization cycle stresses on the circular role played by the currency regime as the US dollar is both a product and a cause of global trade. The rise of global imbalances frustrates the US within the country. Protectionism emerges and, in turn, triggers deglobalization and hence de-dollarization. As discussed in the previous chapter, the fiat money regime has supported the US trade deficits persistently. Once the dollar loses its superpower, its value can be adjusted to where it should be. There is a possibility for the world to restore its balance.

This chapter begins with a historical review of globalization. We reaffirm a very obvious observation: The popularity of a currency ultimately ties to a country's political and economic power at the global stage. This golden rule is a simple extension of Mercury and Mars hypotheses recently referred by Eichengreen et al. (2017). As financial institutions

---

[1] WTO. Statement by WTO Director-General Renato Ruggiero on the agreement on financial services. Press release (December 12, 1997).

play a pivotal role in populating the dollar globally, I also discuss the process of financial integration that the world has gone through. This will shed light on the outlook of the US dollar if the US begins to drive the deglobalization. In fact, financial integration is also a suspect propelling inequality between and within countries and, in turn, promoting populism. With this in mind, de-dollarization will likely be a natural consequence of deglobalization.

3.2 The Globalization Cycle

3.2.1 Globalization 1820–1914

Globalization is a vague economic concept without a precise definition. Loosely, it refers to a process of economic integration with massive mobility of goods, capital, people, and technology. Nowadays, we should also include information flows. Countries have been trading with each other for a few thousand years. But the scope of economic integration in the past was very narrow. Economic ties amongst neighboring countries could only be labeled regional trade. To be called globalization, a wide geographical coverage around the time zone of 24 hours is a must. Only a highly developed transportation network can support globalization. To a certain extent, the trades between the East and the West along the Silk Road could also be considered a primitive version of globalization.

In the contemporary context, however, a truly globalized world should be defined by the level of interdependence. Countries are not only trading finished products but also factors of production. Economic relations go beyond trade. Foreign investments symbolize the level of economic integration. Multinational corporations (from the Dutch East India Company to IBM) have played a central role in the globalization process. Capitalists follow trade and investment flows. Resources in different countries are organized as some forms of supply chains. The management board of MNCs may have a larger influence on local economies than government officials. The concept of national boundaries is increasingly blurred.

The world has experienced two waves of globalization according to Baldwin and Martin (1999). The first one was led by the UK in 1820–1914 whereas the second one began in 1960, led by the UK and the

Allies. By the end of the eighteenth century, Great Britain had become the world's superpower, with many colonies across the world. The UK economic might was boosted by technological development as a result of the First Industrial Revolution. In those days, a weaving machine was a hot and necessary property, just like the mobile phone today (see Figure 3.1).

Transportation played a pivotal role in the first wave of globalization in the nineteenth century. Steamships and trains carried goods across continents. Clark (2005) wrote, "The area of the British Isles is only about 0.16% of the world land mass. Yet Britain then produced two-thirds of world output of coal and one half of world production of cotton textiles and iron. Output per worker was higher in Britain than in any other country." Besides the Industrial Revolution, Clark also attributed the British success to the Demographic Revolution, Agricultural Revolution, and Transportation Revolution. These revolutions happened in the period 1760–1860 and laid a solid foundation for the global expansion of the Anglo-Saxon world.

Figure 3.1   Picture of the Industrial Revolution.

Original source: https://commons.wikimedia.org/wiki/File:Hartmann_Maschinenhalle_1868_(01).jpg

Expansion of international trade was a visible outcome in the first wave of globalization. In the middle of the nineteenth century, UK's trade to GNP ratio surged tremendously (Figure 3.2). Bairoch and Burke (1989) indicated that between 1815 and 1914, the total volume of exports in Europe probably expanded nearly 40-fold, compared with only double or treble a hundred years earlier. That was the time the British Empire extended its reach from London all the way to Asia. In the first wave of globalization, the US economy had lower economic openness than the Brits.

Rapid expansion of international trade in the first wave integrated different economies across the seven seas. The combination of technology and transportation established the first generation of the global supply chain, exploiting natural resources endowed in different parts of the world. An example cited by the World Economic Forum was the invention of the refrigerated cargo ship in the 1870s. The "reefer ship" enabled Argentina and Uruguay to experience their golden age. The South American countries started to export meat from cattle reared on their vast lands. Perishable goods were previously impossible in the long-haul trade. But technological breakthrough helped overcome the geographical boundary and expanded access to factors of production.

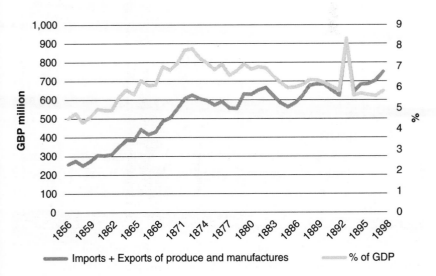

Figure 3.2   UK's trade in the nineteenth century.

Sources: FRED, author analysis

In those days, people were proud of how fascinating the global logistics were, similar to what we do today. There is a quote of John Maynard Keynes (1919) frequently cited in the literature of globalization:

> The inhabitant of London could order by telephone, sipping his morning tea in bed, the various products of the whole Earth, in such quantity as he might see fit, and reasonably expect their early delivery upon his doorstep; he could at the same moment and by the same means adventure his wealth in the natural resources and the new enterprises of any quarter of the world, and share, without exertion or trouble, in their prospective fruits and advantages, or he could decide to couple the security of his fortunes with the good faith of the townspeople of any substantial municipality in any continent that fancy or information might recommend. . . Most important of all, he regarded this state of affairs as normal, certain and permanent except in the direction of further improvement, and any deviation from it as aberrant, scandalous and avoidable.

Economic historians distinguished four subperiods within the first wave of globalization: The rise of British liberalism (1815–1846), the spread of European free trade (1846–1860), the liberal period (1860–1879), and the Continent's return to protection while Britain remained open (1879–1914) (see Baldwin and Martin 1999). In the final stage of the first wave, protectionism emerged in Continental Europe. Although farmers benefited from trade measure, the decline in wheat prices offset the gain from protectionism. For industrial goods, by contrast, the new tariffs were imposed to prevent the competition from imports, especially from Great Britain (see Figure 3.3).

According to Bairoch (1993), the reduction in agricultural growth dragged the European economy for two decades. Per capita GDP growth, which had averaged approximately 1% to 1.3% between 1830 and 1870, slipped to 0.1% in the 1870s and 1880s. Meanwhile, nationalism (the modern German, Belgian, and Italian states were formed around this time) began to rise in Continental Europe. Protectionism emerged rapidly. The notion of free trade was rejected, led by Bismarck who

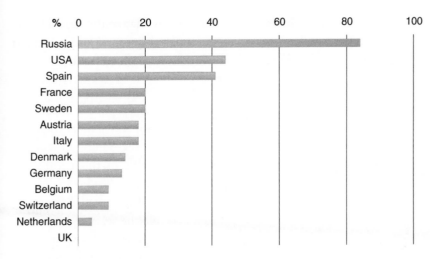

Figure 3.3 Average tariff rates on manufactured products, 1913.
Source: Data from Baldwin and Martin (1999)

insisted that Germany's industry was being handicapped by the influx of foreign goods (Mathias and Pollar 1989):

> The only exception is England, and that will not last long. France and America have both completely forsaken that direction. Austria, instead of reducing its protective duties, has increased them. Russia has done the same, not only through the gold coinage, but in other ways. Therefore, no-one can expect Germany to remain permanently thee dupe of an honest conviction. Hitherto the wide-opened gates of our imports have made us the dumping-place of all the over-production of foreign countries. . . . It is the surfeiting of Germany with the over-production of other lands which most depresses our prices and checks the development of our industry and the restoration of our economic condition. (Bairoch and Burke 1989)

At the country level, globalization was believed to be a culprit behind global inequalities. The rise of Western powers saw a rapid deterioration of the ancient states that failed to catch up with the technological development. Some countries like India, China, and many African states did not adapt to the global trend of industrial adjustment. In addition, farmers and blue-collar workers in the industrialized countries did not benefit from globalization, as their work was replaced with domestic industrial machineries or foreign imports. There were winners and losers in the first wave of global economic integration, sowing the seed of subsequent protectionism and nationalism.

The first wave of globalization ended with the outbreak of World War I in 1914. The global economy did not truly recover until the 1950s, even with the presence of the US as an "emerging market" in the interwar period. Historians also related the Great Depression to the end of the boom in South America (Drinot and Knight 2014). By the end of World War II, trade as a percentage of world GDP had fallen to 5%.

In summary, the first wave of globalization went through several phases: (1) Industrial Revolution; (2) expansion of international trade; (3) rising inequalities and protectionism; and (4) military conflicts and deglobalization. Various political ideologies emerged in the course of globalization. It may have been the fate of capitalism. When rising inequalities spell the end to free trade. The start of globalization was promising. The endgame is costly. As Rodrik (2017) concluded, "economic history and economic theory both provide ample grounds for anticipating that advanced stages of economic globalization would produce a political backlash."

3.2.2 Postwar Globalization

Globalization is a cycle. Before World War II, the end of the first wave marked the beginning of a new one. After dropping atomic bombs on Hiroshima and Nagasaki, the US became a new global hegemonic power. Similar to the Britons, the US was riding the tide of the Second Industrial Revolution, symbolized by automobile and aircrafts. The global transportation network boosted the goods flows and passenger flows at a much faster pace. Trade picked up rapidly after the war.

The World Economic Forum (2019) separated the Second Globalization into two stages. Before the fall of the Berlin Wall in 1989, the Cold War divided the world into two spheres. Globalization remained partial. After the Iron Curtain fell in 1989, German unification turned Europe into a super growth engine and helped turn the EU amongst the world's largest economic bloc. In the Far East, Deng Xiaoping reassured

China's open-door policy after his visit to Shenzhen in 1992. The massive pool of Chinese workers combined with the influx of foreign capital created another economic dynamo. The world started to capture the full potential of true globalization in the early 1990s.

Unlike the first wave of globalization in the nineteenth century, the postwar one has made good use of multilateral organizations. Reglobalization began at the end of the second world war with the Bretton Woods agreement of 1944 and the General Agreement on Tariffs and Trade (GATT) in 1947 (Daunton 2005). A decade later, Belgium, France, Italy, Luxembourg, the Netherlands, and West Germany signed the Treaty of Rome, laying the ground for the creation of the European Economic Community (EEC) and a customs union. Even within the Soviet Union, there was an internal market amongst the affiliated states. The world economy became truly globalized in the second stage of the postwar globalization. In 1995, the GATT was formalized into a standing organization called the WTO, a symbol of multilateralism. In 2001, China was formally admitted as a member state. The world factory had begun to fire the engine, full speed ahead.

The multilateral world has pushed the notion of globalization to a new high. Globally, total trade as a percentage of GDP was just 24% in 1960 (see Figure 3.4). After a stagnant 1980s, the figure started surging

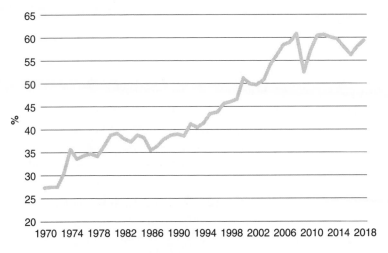

Figure 3.4   World's trade as % of GDP.

Source: World Bank

after China's liberalization and German unification. Just before the out-break of GFC in 2008, the ratio surpassed 60%. In this second wave of globalization, the UK saw its trade-to-GDP ratio at 61% in 2018, even higher than its level in the nineteenth century. Although the ratio of the US was relatively low at 27% in 2017, the figure still doubled that of the nineteenth century.

As discussed earlier, the first wave of globalization in the nineteenth century ended with a rising political movement towards nationalism. The US had also experienced the surge of a "Jacksonian" in the nineteenth century, holding a critical view on economic openness and overreliance on the global economy. If history is to be of any guidance, we are prob-ably staying in the third phase of the globalization cycle (see Table 3.1).

Table 3.1   Globalization cycle—political–economic perspective.

	British Empire 1820–1914	The US and the Allies 1960–now
Technology breakthrough	Industrial Revolution Demographic Revolution Agricultural Revolution Transportation Revolution	Financial services Home appliances Automobile and airplane Telecommunications
Global trade expansion	Rising trade relative to GDP Trade liberalism Dutch East India and the like	Rising trade relative to GDP GATT in 1947 MNCs
Populism and protectionism return	Bismarck's tariff hike on agricultural and manufacturing products France's Meline tariff 1892	Trump's tariff on Chinese goods Brexit Japan–Korea trade conflict
Deglobalization	World War I 1914 Great Depression 1929 Smoot-Hawley Tariff 1930 World War II 1937–1945	Is it coming?

Source: Author, based on insight from Rodrik (2017), Baldwin and Martin (1999)

This assessment is not conclusive because the century-long globalization in the period 1820–1914 was the only prominent reference of the globalization cycle that involved the whole world. But the emerging populism after the GFC appears to follow the script precisely.

3.3 Currency Globalization

3.3.1 Financial Integration and the Hubs

Money follows trade. There were two corresponding waves of financial integration when the world globalized in the nineteenth and twentieth centuries. The rising economic and political power of Great Britain in the nineteenth century and the US in the postwar globalization coincided with the degree of global acceptance for the pound sterling and the dollar. Their timing seemed to be consistent with the aforementioned globalization cycle. And there were similarities and differences in the internationalization of the two currencies.

The two globalizations also saw their respective financial cycles with the following features: (1) Trade-induced financial flows; (2) A network of financial hubs; (3) Expansion of portfolio flows; and (4) Financial crises and subsequent stabilization measures.

The perception was that financial flows in the nineteenth century were induced by trade. However, capital mobility actually resulted from saving–investment imbalance. In the years 1871–1913, British investors invested significant amounts of money overseas, representing 4% to 8% of its GNP. The level was higher than that for other developed nations at the time (Goetzmann and Ukhov 2005). With the "global" adoption of the Gold Standard in the 1870s, exchange rates were stable, similar to the beginning of the Bretton Woods era. Financial institutions in London facilitated enormous flows of capital, searching for the investment opportunities. The capital flows fostered foreign direct investment in the "settler" economies in the colonies occupied by Europeans. Mining booms were everywhere. The FDI flows at that time were very similar to the emerging market flows (e.g. BRIC) we witnessed in the past few decades.

Taylor (1996) presented an expanded set of historical data on the evolution of current account for twelve countries dated back to the

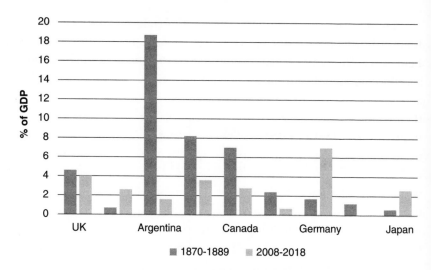

Figure 3.5 Capital flows (proxy by absolute value of current account) 1870s vs. 2008s.

Sources: Taylor (1996) cited by Baldwin and Martin (1999), author updated 2008–2018 using IMF data

nineteenth century. In Figure 3.5, I append his data from 1990 to 2018. In terms of absolute value, the average current account balances in many countries (as a % of GDP) in the nineteenth century were actually comparable to the postwar period. In Britain, the average was 4.6% of GDP during the period when many countries were joining the Gold Standard from 1850 to 1914. This figure still stands higher than all subsequent periods.

The capital flows of Britain and the US dropped significantly during the interwar period. Before the First World War, the average size of capital flows was quite high for certain resource intensive countries, such as Argentina and Australia, in the 1880s. During the deglobalization period, capital flows dropped in most countries including the UK. Prior to the second round of globalization, capital flows remained low in the 1950s. Only after the reglobalization stage, the flows picked up again from the 1970s. After the dollar became a fiat money, capital flows in the US surged significantly. From 1997 to 2007, the figure surpassed 4%. After the GFC, the level declined to 2.6%.

There was an academic interest in studying the intensity of financial integration during the two periods of globalization. The Feldstein–Horioka (1980) puzzle stated that high capital mobility should correspond with low correlation between domestic investment and savings. However, they could not reject this hypothesis. Nonetheless, their study sparked the interests in examining the degree of international capital mobility. Some studies concluded that financial integration in the postwar period was higher compared to the one in the end of the nineteenth century (Mauro et al. 2002, Volosovych 2011) while other studies were less conclusive (Zevin 1992). It appeared that more recent studies (after 1995) could get a hold of a larger data set, which could support their conclusion of higher capital mobility in the fiat money regime.

Financial hubs played a significant role in global financial integration. As the political and commercial capital of the British Empire, London was undoubtedly the leading financial center before 1870. Soon after, New York grew to become a major provider of financial services for the US. Berlin and Paris served alongside other cities in Continental Europe (e.g. Amsterdam, Brussels, Zurich, and Geneva). Countries are eager to develop an international financial center in their own soil, as financial activity is an important source of economic value added, reminding policymakers when they decide to withdraw from globalization. Since London has benefited from massive amounts of financial inflows since joining the EU in 1973, there has been a growing concern about its leading status in financial services going forward after Brexit on January 31, 2020.[2]

Given the prominent position of London in the nineteenth century, the pound sterling became a global reserve currency. It was widely circulated in the British Empire, which expanded geographically via the colonial presence. Many Commonwealth territories pegged their own currency even after issuing their own currency, like Australia. A group of countries continued to deposit their exchange reserves at

---

[2] *The Guardian*. New York surges ahead of London as financial centre, survey finds. January 27, 2020. (https://www.theguardian.com/business/2020/jan/27/new-york-london-financial-centre-brexit).

the Bank of England in order to gain access to London's financial market. After Britain left the gold standard in September 1931, some non-Commonwealth countries unexpectedly linked their currencies to sterling, forming the sterling area.[3] This suggested that the location of international financial hubs secured the currency status.

Pound sterling was a symbol of globalization, and financial integration during the first wave of globalization which ended in 1914. Eichengreen et al. (2017) cited the data presented by Lindert (1967, 1969) that showed the change in composition of global foreign exchange reserves in 1899 and 1913 (see Figure 3.6). In 1899, sterling accounted for 65% of the total. French francs and German marks accounted for some shares of the total (15% and 17%, respectively). Sterling's dominance declined over the subsequent decade, with gains mainly accruing to the French franc, which was held by Russia and a number of other countries. The share of sterling in global currency reserve fell from the peak of 65% in 1899 to 48% in 1913, which was the year before World War I.

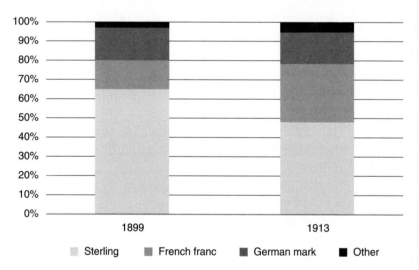

Figure 3.6   Currency composition of foreign exchange reserves 1899 vs. 1913.

Source: Eichengreen et al. (2017)

---

[3]The National Archives. The sterling area and stabilization. (https://www.national-archives.gov.uk/cabinetpapers/themes/sterling-area-stabilisation.htm).

During the period of World War I, the British relied on a pegging arrangement with the US dollar at USD 4.765. However, the UK borrowed heavily from the US to fund the war. By 1920, British foreign assets had fallen to one-quarter of their 1914 level. The exports of capital goods during the war transformed the US from a debtor to a creditor nation (Federal Reserve 1989). Winston Churchill wanted to resume the value of sterling through reintroducing the gold standard in 1925. But this was unsustainable. In 1931, the UK abandoned the gold standard again. In the interwar period, the dollar was gaining its influence, paving the way for the gold-exchange standard after World War II.

3.3.2 Currency Standard and Trade Bloc

There have been many policy debates on the role of currency in economic integration. Typically, the issue is whether an economic union should use a common currency so as to maximize the benefit of free trade. In principle, this policy question should only require a few seconds to answer: A trade bloc could be theoretically considered as a single country within which all economic transactions are not subject to any trade barriers. There is no reason for a single country to have different currencies amongst different provinces and states (except for China, which allows Hong Kong to run "one country, two systems"). To maximize the power of free market, one would remove any artificial barrier that involves price distortion or transaction costs. New Yorkers and Californians use the US dollar. People in Shanghai and Beijing transact using the Chinese yuan. For a trade bloc, countries naturally prefer a single currency regime or a fixed exchange rate system.

Gold had played a special role in promoting the currency integration, manifested in pound sterling and the US dollar, respectively. In 1792, the US adopted bimetallism and passed the Coinage Act, defining the US dollar as equivalent to 24.75 grains of fine gold and 371.25 grains of fine silver. In 1816, the UK kicked off the gold specie standard by pegging the pound to a specific quantity of gold under the UK's Coinage Act. These landmark events established a principle of implicit convertibility in money creation. In the second half of the nineteenth century, many British colonies and some Nordic countries tied their currencies to pound sterling. The US basically shifted from bimetallism to a "true gold standard" in the period 1879–1933 (Elwell 2011).The concept of a "promise to convert" was embedded in paper money, silver coins, or other certificates. Effectively, a large part of the world began to adopt the gold exchange standard. Only some Spanish-speaking nations and China remained on bimetallic or silver standards, respectively.

In 1996, Bordo and Rockoff (1996) suggested the gold standard as a "good housekeeping seal of approval." Historically, government bond yields in the period 1870–1914 showed the countries with good track records of adhering the gold standard could issue at lower coupon rates. In essence, the gold standard (or a gold exchange standard) provided a mechanism to discipline fiscal and monetary policies. The gold standard was virtually a fixed exchange rate regime as the value of different currencies fixed with gold. By Mundell's impossible trinity, balance of payments (BOP) adjustments could only be adjusted through capital flows because exchange rates were inflexible. During the period of the gold standard in the late 1800s, international capital mobility was high, facilitating many foreign investments and growth.

In the fiat money regime, the idea of creating a currency bloc was hotly debated in Europe. The euro was the biggest man-made experiment in modern economic history. The idea was originated from the Economic and Monetary Union (EMU) backed in 1992 with the Treaty of Maastricht. On January 1, 1999, the eurozone began in 11 European countries. The euro circulated alongside the Deutsche mark, French franc, Spanish peseta, Italian lira, Dutch guilder, Portuguese escudo, Belgian franc, Luxembourgish franc, Finnish markka, Austrian schilling, and Irish pound. Since the first additional inclusion with Greece in 2001, many more EU members have switched their sovereign currency to the common one.

In the beginning, the eurozone seemed to be an attractive option for EU members. Many countries wanted to join the monetary union and believed in the merit of scale economics. The EU had to establish a qualification scheme for member states to adopt the common currency. It was called the euro convergence criteria, which the member states were required to strive in order to enter the third stage of the Economic and Monetary Union (EMU). Under the current scheme, there are five criteria involving fiscal, debt, and deficit qualifications, based on Article 140 of the Treaty on the Functioning of the European Union in 2007. As of 2019, the eurozone covered 19 nations (see Figure 3.7).

The formation of the monetary federation can be explained by the gravity model. Geographical proximity is a natural reason for countries to share a common currency. Obvious examples are Monetary Union of Gulf Cooperation Council (GCC); West African Economic and

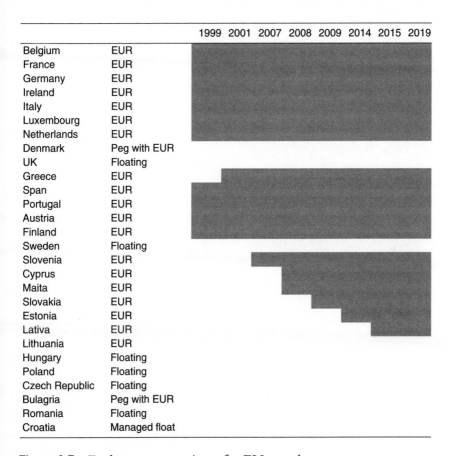

		1999	2001	2007	2008	2009	2014	2015	2019
Belgium	EUR								
France	EUR								
Germany	EUR								
Ireland	EUR								
Italy	EUR								
Luxembourg	EUR								
Netherlands	EUR								
Denmark	Peg with EUR								
UK	Floating								
Greece	EUR								
Span	EUR								
Portugal	EUR								
Austria	EUR								
Finland	EUR								
Sweden	Floating								
Slovenia	EUR								
Cyprus	EUR								
Maita	EUR								
Slovakia	EUR								
Estonia	EUR								
Lativa	EUR								
Lithuania	EUR								
Hungary	Floating								
Poland	Floating								
Czech Republic	Floating								
Bulagria	Peg with EUR								
Romania	Floating								
Croatia	Managed float								

Figure 3.7 Exchange rate regimes for EU members.

Source: EC Convergence Report 2018

Monetary Union (UEMOA); Southern Africa's Common Monetary Area (CMA); and Asian Monetary Unit proposed by Japan's Research Institute of Economy, Trade and Industry (RIETI). Many currency unions were inherited from the colonial era given the strong economic and cultural links with Europe.

When globalization was still the dominant thought, academic discussions were focused on questions like the pros and cons of joining a currency bloc or the qualifications required for member admission. Nobel Laureate Robert Mundell (Mundell 1961) pioneered the discussion with his seminal paper for the theory of Optimum Currency Area (OCA). In the 1960s, many countries were still maintaining fixed exchange rates. Mundell's concern was primarily the potential merits of flexible exchange rates. In terms of the economic consideration of single currency areas, Mundell's idea was:

> If the world can be divided into regions within each of which there is factor mobility and between which there is factor immobility, then each of these regions should have a separate currency which fluctuates relative to all other currencies. This carries the argument for flexible exchange rates to its logical conclusion. But a region is an economic unit while a currency domain is partly an expression of national sovereignty. Except in areas where national sovereignty is being given up it is not feasible to suggest that currencies should be reorganized; the validity of the argument for flexible exchange rates therefore hinges on the closeness with which nations correspond to regions. The argument works best if each nation (and currency) has internal factor mobility and external factor immobility. But if labour and capital are insufficiently mobile within a country then flexibility of the external price of the national currency cannot be expected to perform the stabilization function attributed to it, and one could expect varying rates of unemployment or inflation in the different regions. Similarly, if factors are mobile across national boundaries then a flexible exchange system becomes unnecessary, and may even be positively harmful, as I have suggested elsewhere.

Beyond economics, joining a currency bloc is also a political symbol. In doing so, member countries effectively give up their monetary autonomy. They surrender the capacity to rule the monetary policy. This applies not only to a formal currency union but also the decision of pegging with another country. For instance, as part of China, the Hong Kong dollar has been repeatedly questioned about its peg with the US dollar. The economic argument was sound as the yuan was not fully convertible. However, politicians could make story from the sovereignty perspective. In another extreme, the US, Mexico, and Canada do not have a currency union despite decades of NAFTA. Relative to the euro, discussion about forming a monetary union in North America has been scant. Maybe the sovereignty consideration was too obvious to deserve further consideration.

The academic literature has also been focused on modeling the formation of the currency bloc (Alesina et al. 2002, Yehoue 2004). Countries are modeled to evaluate the benefit on trade dynamically. If trade has expanded to a level that exceeds their threshold, the country will be willing to join the currency union. The process lasts until it reaches the steady state. There is also another series of studies assessing the actual benefit of the euro. After two decades of history, researchers can now conduct empirical studies on the economic impact of single currency. For instance, Glick and Rose (2016) found that the currency union significantly boosted EMU trade by 50%.

Although the idea of currency union was appealing in early years, the European debt crisis in 2012 started to challenge the one-sided view about the benefit. For instance, Ryan and Loughlin (2018) reviewed the experience of historical monetary union, namely, the Latin Monetary Union (LMU), the Scandinavian Monetary Union (SMU), and the Austro-Hungarian Monetary Union (AHMU). They argued that robust supranational institutions, such as a common central bank and a unified fiscal policy, are necessary for the union to be sustainable. Some type of fiscal federalism was needed. For instance, EU Economic governance "Six-Pack"[4] and the European Fiscal Compact (European Commission 2011) asked the member nations to tighten existing fiscal rules such as upper deficit and debt limits written into countries' constitutions and secondary legislation. The euro experience suggested that having a single

---

[4]EU Economic governance "Six-Pack" enters into force. Press memo. December 12, 2011. (https://ec.europa.eu/commission/presscorner/detail/en/MEMO_11_898).

central bank dealing with many local governments without proper coordination might not be sustainable. Trade, monetary, and fiscal policies should be considered holistically.

3.4 Financial Deglobalization

3.4.1 Capital Mobility and Financial Crises

Historically, the nature of financial globalization at the end of the nineteenth century differed from the contemporary one (Bairoch and Kozul-Wright 1996). Capital mobility a century ago was primarily FDI-related and hence is stickier. In contrast, capital flows in the twentieth century tended to be liquid, related to the growing portfolio investment. In the contemporary globalization, the size of portfolio investments in equities, fixed income, and foreign exchange markets are gigantic. The development of information communications has enabled speedy and significant flows. The level is disproportional to the scale of cross-border trade and investment. Countries receiving capital inflows need to withstand massive traffic. Financial integration concerns financial stability or crisis management.

In considering financial globalization, Broner and Ventura (2016) developed a model to analyze the different treatments on domestic and foreign capital. In an imperfect world where governments cannot discriminate foreign and domestic capital inflows, the outcomes of financial liberalization can be very different. In summary, cross-border capital flows expose the weakness of domestic institutions and debt enforcement mechanisms. Influx of foreign capital can be beneficial but also introduce adverse effects because of poor institutional arrangement domestically. The probability of a financial crisis depends on a country's characteristics, including the level of productivity, domestic savings, and the quality of institutions.

The policy view on financial integration and currency union changed over time. Shortly after World War II, the consensus was that capital controls could help avoid the exchange rate volatility. The fixed exchange rate regime under the Bretton Woods agreement was just a measure to ensure financial stability so that the countries could rebuild their economies. However, when the gold-exchange standard broke down in the early 1970s, the thought shifted to the merits of flexible exchange rate. By Mundell's impossible trinity, capital mobility became a logical policy mandate. Meanwhile, the theme of globalization emerged in the 1990s. Multilateral organizations like the IMF, OECD, and the EU all advocated capital account liberalization. This view was reconsidered after the GFC in 2008 as the policy agenda turned to financial stability. The view supporting financial integration was downgraded. Macroprudential measures became a buzzword in the policymaking circle.

The literature has also become critical to financial globalization since the GFC. The narrative is that policymakers need to evaluate the risk and benefit from opening up their capital account. Capital inflows can induce higher investment and growth. But the governments are reminded to consider how vulnerable the domestic financial sector is. Kose et al. (2009) pointed out that there might be certain threshold levels of financial depth and institutional quality different countries needed to attain before opening. Once these thresholds are overcome, financial liberalization could benefit the domestic economy tremendously.

Financial crises happened in the two waves of globalization. Events like the Asia Financial Crisis in 1997 and the GFC in 2008 remain fresh in our minds. But financial contagion also dates back to 1792 when the newly formed US government began its first central bank treasury operation (The Economist 2014). The Panic of 1857 also caused the banking crisis across the Atlantic Ocean (Calomiris 2007) (see Figure 3.8). Aliber and Kindleberger (2015) documented more than 22 financial panics between 1870 and 1914. Almost all financial crises involved contagion effects across countries and continents. A common theme of those crises was the banks' exposure to bond stresses triggered by falling commodity prices. The downside of financial integration is that contagion can span across Europe, North America, Asia, and Latin America quickly.

The rising criticism of financial globalization in the last decade was clearly triggered by the GFC when the policymaking circle became more aware about the role of global saving glut in US subprime crises, financial overengineering, and incentive schemes for investment bankers. In

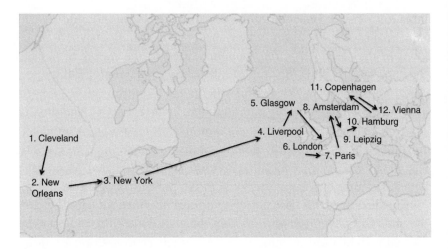

Figure 3.8   The Panic 1857—Contagion across the Atlantic.

Source: Author drawing based on the sequence described by *The Economist* (2014)

the literature, financial globalization was found to be empirically related to financial crises. Reinhart and Rogoff (2009) produced a chart repeatedly cited in other papers. It nicely shows that the periods of financial globalization and the incidence of banking crises coincide almost perfectly. Banking crises and financial globalization rise and fall together.

The US subprime crisis exhibited the downside risk of financial engineering. The financial community (and investors) took the blame of excessive risk-taking, over-leveraging and lack of consumer protection. This event surprised the world as it challenged the perception that financial crises were mostly emerging market-related. In contrast, the US subprime problems and the European sovereign crises in 2012 happened in advanced economies. They were supposed to have proper supervisory oversight. However, financial contagion could still occur rapidly. European banks, such as UK's Northern Rock, suffered from US subprime credits. This is very much akin to the intercontinental panics in 1825, 1857, and 1890 (see Table 3.2). Globalization, financial integration, and financial crises have formed a fellowship.

Table 3.2   Three cross-border financial crises in each of the two globalizations.

The First Wave 1820–1914	The Second Wave World War II
1825 Latin America Bond Crisis	**1973 Oil crisis**
By the 1820s London had overtaken Amsterdam as Europe's main financial hub. Between 1822 and 1825 many Latin American states including Colombia, Chile, Peru, Mexico, and Guatemala issued bonds worth £21m in London. But the bonds were sold off subsequently. UK banks were exposed to the debt and to mining firms. The panic caused many bank runs in 1825.	OPEC countries abruptly halted oil exports to the Western countries, causing a severe spike in crude prices. The oil crisis triggered high inflation and economic stagnation, giving birth to the term "stagflation" (stagnation plus inflation). The US turned into a current account deficit country. It also loosely pegs the USD with Saudi Arabian oil, i.e. petrodollar.
1857 Railway shock	**1997 Asia Financial Crisis**
The railroad concept was hot property in the gold rush. But railroad stocks started to fall in 1857. Ohio Life, which was highly leveraged and overexposed to railway, tumbled in August and resulted in a contagion rippling through the banking system. Short of liquidity, banks refused to convert deposits into currency. The impact spilled over across the Atlantic. Glasgow and Liverpool, and then London felt the impact, before spreading to Paris, Hamburg, Copenhagen, and Vienna.	Thai baht was sold off in July 1997 and quickly spread to the rest of East Asia. Foreign investors pulled out their investments. Indonesia bond market tumbled. Foreign reserves in many countries were drawn out. Some countries, notably South Korea, require the bailout packages from the IMF. Malaysia decided to impose capital control. Property market dropped by half in Hong Kong and Singapore. China insisted not to weaken the currency and help stabilize the market sentiment.

(Continued)

Table 3.2   (Continued)

The First Wave 1820–1914	The Second Wave World War II
1890 Barings Bank Crisis	**2008 Global Financial Crisis**
The crisis was similar to 1825's Latin America Bond crisis. Barings led UK banks in financing many projects in Latin America, channeling an impressive £13.6 million into Argentina alone between 1888 and 1890. But the bank was about to bankrupt in November 1890 due mainly to excessive risk taking. As Barings was too big to fail, the Bank of England arranged a bailout package to guarantee Barings' liability. The risk spilled over to Brazil and Uruguay. Concerns about the Latin American economy caused a reduction in capital inflows from Europe.	Triggered by the collapse of the housing bubble in the US, the GFC sparked the Great Recession, the most-severe financial crisis since 1929's Great Depression. The overuse of financial engineering resulted in the collapse of Lehman Brothers (one of the biggest investment banks in the world). The trouble spilled to other financial institutions across the US and Europe. Governments stepped up to bail-out the too-big-to-fail. The US Fed initiated unconventional monetary policy to stabilize the market. Many governments tightened financial regulations to tame risk-taking behavior in the market.
1907–1913 Trust crisis and the Fed	**2020 Coronavirus and dollar shortage**
Trust companies were large and powerful in the US in early 1900s. They invested in spicier assets but lightly regulated. Augustus Heinze and Charles Morse, two businessmen who made their fortune from copper mining, suffered from falling copper price. When they drew funds from banks and other smaller lenders, the panic spilled to Knickerbocker Trust in 1907. After they declined some depositor demand for	In December 2019, the deadly virus outbreak began in Wuhan, China. The government implemented a lockdown just before the Lunar New Year. Economic activity was virtually completely shut down for two months in China. In March, the virus affected the rest of the world, with cases in all continents soaring. Worry about some Western countries acting too late and too weak spook a

Table 3.2 (Continued)

withdrawal, confidence in trust companies eroded. Efforts by John Pierpont Morgan failed to calm the market. For the economy to function, the private sector issued their own money, totaled USD 500m. The US passed the Federal Reserve Act 1913 as the lender of last resort.	global recession concern. Travels were almost fully banned. Global equities were sold off. Cash was king. Saudi Arabia and Russia feud over oil prices in early March 2020 triggered further sell-off across almost all asset classes from sovereign debts to gold. All central banks cut interest rates and pledged cash.

Sources: The Economist (2014), Mitchener and Weidenmier (2007), *Encyclopedia Britannica*[5]

3.4.2 Financial Crises and Populism

In the aftermath of financial crises, the public started to question globalization and financial integration. The European Sovereign Debt Crisis in 2012 was a stress test of the sustainability of euro area. Although there have been many different explanations for the crisis, the consensus is that individual sovereign countries need to discipline their own fiscal position and implement structural economic reforms. Financial globalization could risk national economic collapses given the example of Greece, Spain, Portugal, and Ireland, fueling the rise of neo-nationalism amongst EU members (and possibly Brexit). For the US subprime crisis that resulted in massive foreclosures, Wall Street took the blame. Occupy Wall Street in 2011 mirrored the growth of populism and echoed the anti-globalization campaign in Seattle in 1999. Globalization, financial integration, and financial crisis are fellow sufferers.

In fact, this is where the political economics contributes to the cycle of globalization. Financial integration facilitates the substitution of foreign capital for domestic labor and is believed to have driven inequalities (Jaumotte et al. 2013). Furceri et al. (2018) found that financial globalization increased output in countries with high financial depth

---

[5]Britannica. Five of the world's most devastating financial crises.

and those that avoided financial crises. The distributional effects were more noticeable in countries with low financial depth and inclusion and whose liberalization was followed by a financial crisis. Financial crises play a large part in the rising populism as foreign investment amplifies the distributional issue in the domestic economy.

Parallel to rising protectionism in the US, the public started to dislike foreign involvement in the local economy even if foreign investment could create jobs. Free trade is labeled as "Chinese workers stealing our jobs." Social tension heightens in countries experiencing an influx of immigrants and foreign workers. Building a wall along the Mexico border seems by many to be a "sensible choice." Politicians call for capital account restriction rather than liberalization as young couples cannot cope with the rise of property prices. Wealthy Asians are perceived to be responsible. Whether the ethnic groups are local citizens and have the right to buy does not matter.[6]

When prejudice and nationalism dominate, the line of psycho-economic research developed by Daniel Kahneman and Amos Tversky can also explain today's opinion towards globalization. As Sabet (2016) noted,

> When it comes to foreign trade, the "foreign" aspect of the issue presents the most prevalent mental shortcut. International trade involves dealing with "others". Research on globalization opinion suggests that the average individual's opinion on trade comes not from rational (and mentally demanding) assessments of costs and benefits, but gut-level decisions guided by attitudes toward out-groups and foreignness.

Regardless of whatever the academic explanations, the reality is that globalization is hitting the inflection point.

---

[6]New Zealand Stuff. Labour's "half-baked" property data turns Chinese buyers into "scapegoats". (July 11, 2015).

3.5 End of Cycle: De-Dollarization

3.5.1 The Transition Regime

Protectionism, populism, and neo-nationalism are growing. We see the trade war and unilateralism. We see that the US government is indebted to the Chinese government, as the latter holds US government securities. We see a setback of financial globalization with global financial institutions realigning their business due to global regulatory tightening. We see the competition of financial hub status. Hong Kong, Singapore, Shanghai, Dubai, and Frankfurt all want to share IPO, loans, or FX activity in New York and London (while Tokyo remains a source of carry trades for Japanese residents). The recent developments all suggest that we are entering the latest stage of the second wave of globalization, pointing to another major regime shift.

With multilateralism breaking down, de-dollarization appears to be an inevitable consequence. As the US begins to withdraw itself from globalization, other countries will also respond with diversification. Governments also want to reduce their dependence on the US dollar and claim their monetary policy autonomy. Using domestic currencies to settle foreign trade can facilitate the access to trade credit provided by local banks and reduce settlement risk.[7] In fact, Catão and Terrones (2016) observed a noticeable trend for emerging economies to de-dollarize from early 2000s, but the process stalled or even reversed after the GFC. Several rounds of quantitative easing by the US Fed was too powerful to flood the already dollar-centric market.

What did history tell us? As the first wave of globalization ended after the outbreak of World War I, the sterling-centric regime also broke down. The UK needed to fund the war. The gold specie standard was replaced with a gold exchange standard, as the amount of physical gold reserve could not support the expansion of credit (Bordo and Schwartz 1997). In the interwar period, countries that previously pegged their currencies with the sterling tended to deviate from the original

---

[7]ASEAN. Ways to promote foreign trade settlements denominated in local currencies in East Asia (https://www.asean.org/wp-ontent/uploads/images/archive/documents/ASEAN+3RG/0910/Sum/16.pdf).

standard, providing some flexibility of monetary policies in considering domestic fiscal deficits.

Eichengreen and Flandreau (2008) provided a historical account for the global currency regime in the interwar period. They found that the US dollar had already overtaken the pound and became the leading reserve currency in the 1920s. Although Churchill's attempt seemed to help the pound to catch up in the 1930s, the dollar had taken off. Two major currencies coexisted. The growing influence of the greenback paved the way for its formal status as the reserve currency in the Bretton Woods system. The rise of New York as the new international financial center also shared the business from London and Paris. The dollar became "the designated one." The emergence of New York appeared to be an event evolved from the political economic condition in the interwar period.

Today, countries wishing to market their own financial hubs and currencies through a carefully crafted plan may not achieve the same outcome. Japan has been eager to develop Tokyo as a global financial center for many decades (Shirai 2017). In 1984, the government began to internationalize the Japanese yen. Subsequently, Japan deregulated its financial system and liberalized its capital markets. The campaign developed the euro-yen market and the Tokyo offshore market for non-residents in 1986 (Japan Ministry of Finance 1999). However, even though the Japanese yen is amongst the league of G10 currencies and is the 3rd heavily traded currency in the financial market (2019: USD 1.1 trillion vs. EUR's USD 2.1 trillion), still less than half of Japanese exports are invoiced in yen today. The share in Japan–US trade was 12.5% in 2018, which was deemed unsatisfactory (Ito et al. 2019).

Nonetheless, the process of de-dollarization will likely be lengthy. Data suggests the status of the US dollar and other G10 currencies are still light-years away. The BIS Triennial Survey showed that the US dollar represented 44% (88 out of 200) of total FX turnover in April 2019 and the share had actually rose since the formation of euro in 1999 (see Table 3.3). The second heavily traded currency was euro with a share of only 16%. This result suggested that the impact of regional trade and currency bloc could not beat the economics of network externalities (perhaps due to more EUR/USD transactions). It will take a long time to give birth to another global dominant currency, or it may not happen at all.

Table 3.3 BIS Survey on OTC foreign exchange turnover April 2019.

Daily Averages, in USD Millions	Total	Spot Transactions	Outright Forwards	FX Swaps	Currency Swaps	FX Options
Total, "net-net" basis	**6,595,471**	**1,987,441**	**999,318**	**3,202,667**	**108,486**	**297,522**
by currency						
USD	5,824,036	1,687,179	883,119	2,905,785	101,895	246,058
EUR	2,129,114	615,509	255,673	1,141,653	26,012	90,267
JPY	1,108,495	360,221	145,256	515,729	24,054	63,234
GBP	843,698	239,765	108,735	444,190	19,071	31,937
AUD	446,511	170,020	52,827	186,332	12,077	25,254
CAD	332,053	121,791	42,963	145,739	7,168	14,392
CHF	327,022	85,683	36,237	194,094	1,961	9,047
CNY	285,030	96,896	35,600	136,851	1,564	14,120
Other currencies	1,894,984	597,818	438,227	734,959	23,170	100,736
Total, "net-gross" basis	**8,300,586**	**2,378,712**	**1,182,332**	**4,234,248**	**143,751**	**361,493**

(Continued)

Table 3.3 (Continued)

Daily Averages, in USD Millions	Total	Spot Transactions	Outright Forwards	FX Swaps	Currency Swaps	FX Options
United Kingdom	3,576,409	1,143,755	541,629	1,645,696	78,001	167,328
United States	1,370,119	475,773	246,079	579,155	6,550	62,562
Singapore	639,869	153,862	98,318	335,724	7,063	44,890
Hong Kong SAR	632,108	111,701	58,619	417,161	21,686	22,934
Japan	375,505	97,614	61,133	195,279	6,049	15,421
Switzerland	275,719	64,203	29,941	161,148	36	20,389
France	167,123	22,866	19,752	117,885	2,513	4,083
Mainland China	136,017	43,302	5,466	84,347	344	2,557
Germany	124,448	18,916	6,982	95,725	1,157	1,668
Other countries	1,003,271	246,719	114,412	602,128	20,351	19,661

Source: BIS Triennial Central Bank Survey of Foreign Exchange and Over-the-counter (OTC) Derivatives Markets in 2019

3.5.2 De-Dollarization and the Trade War

China's de-dollarization effort is believed to be a natural development as the size of its economy continues to expand. The policy to internationalize the renminbi was also motivated by a domestic reason, i.e. monetary policy independence. In his seminal speech in 2009, PBOC Governor Zhou Xiaochuan called for reforming the international monetary system because the outbreak of the current crisis in the US had spilled over to the emerging world.[8] China also cared about its massive holding of the foreign currency reserve, which was largely allocated to US dollar assets. The unconventional monetary policy of the Fed had significant impact on China's currency value and local money supply. Even though many observers related China's effort to internationalize the renminbi to Belt and Road Initiative (Meng 2019), the reality was that internationalization of the yuan began in 2009, much earlier than Xi Jinping's chairmanship.

However, the efforts by the Chinese government in the past ten years have not seen significant breakthrough. In 2019, daily average turnover of CNY in the FX market was USD 285 billion compared with USD 5.8 trillion of the dollar (Table 3.3). There are several reasons for this. First, network externalities continue to favor the incumbent currency. The hurdle for a rival to beat the leader is high. Secondly, if the trade war represents a breakdown of globalization, the negative impact also hits China. During the trade war, the RMB exchange rate has weakened significantly. Global investors continue to be concerned about the vulnerability of the Chinese economy against the trade shock. China can settle some commodity contracts in local currencies. But the US dollar will continue to retain its leading position.

Eichengreen and Flandreau (2008) pointed out, "When a country has serious economic and financial problems, like France in the 1930s, Japan in the 1990s and, not inconceivably, China in the future, acquiring reserve-currency status is even more difficult than holding onto it." For the yuan to be a safe haven currency, China needs to prove that its economy is bulletproof and resistant to external shocks. In recent years,

---

[8]Zhou, Xiaochuan (2009). Reform the international monetary system. Essay presented to BIS. (March). https://www.bis.org/review/r090402c.pdf.

China has proactively pushed itself to be an innovative economy with a dedicated policy package of Made in China 2025. The government embraces the concept of Industry 4.0, attempting to integrate the new concepts like Internet of Things and 5G transmission into the entire supply chains. If the industrial policy can transform the country into a competitive one, the old story of US–UK interchange could repeat itself. Ironically, this policy activism in technology development was exactly the reason for the US to call for the trade war.

As discussed in the previous chapter, the "exorbitant privilege" of the dollar was the main culprit behind the trade conflict. De-dollarization could actually be a solution to restoring US trade balance and end the trade disputes. Since the trade war does not favor China's technological development and hinders its economic transformation, it is still difficult for the yuan to replace the position of the US dollar in the near term. Given this negative feedback loop, the interwar experience of dollar-displacing-sterling is not strictly applicable to the current situation.

Chapter 4

China–US Financial Decoupling

4.1 Trade War and the Yuan

Exchange rates have been a subject of debate in many trade disputes, and the China–US one is no exception. When the tension escalated in August 2019, the US Treasury labeled China as a currency manipulator. According to the official release, the US planned to engage with the International Monetary Fund (IMF) to eliminate the unfair competitive advantage created by China's latest actions.[1] In January 2020, the US revoked the decision a few days before the Phase One deal.[2]

---

[1] The US Treasury. Press release. August 5, 2019 (https://home.treasury.gov/news/press-releases/sm751).

[2] The US Treasury. Press release. January 13, 2020 (https://home.treasury.gov/news/press-releases/sm873).

This back-and-forth decision on China's status by the Treasury was not new. China was designated a currency manipulator in 1992–1994. For many years, China has been frequently alleged to have kept the yuan undervalued.

Whether the yuan is overvalued or undervalued has long been subject to many debates in the financial market. The IMF assessment in recent years concluded that the yuan exchange rate was in line with fundamentals. After the exchange rate reform in 2015, the Chinese government has clearly allowed the spot rate to be more market-determined. However, economic slowdown and the trade war itself pressed the yuan weaker and the People's Bank of China (PBOC) was busy to prevent the yuan from depreciating. This policy intention should favor Trump's trade policy. Interestingly, the US administration did not seem to understand (or intentionally ignore) the reality.

Due to the trade war, the foreign exchange (FX) market sentiment flip-flopped between risk-on and risk-off modes. On average, investors mostly preferred safe haven currencies at the time of uncertainty. When the trade war intensified, the market was pricing in the negative impact on China's exports. A weaker yuan could offset the impact of import tariff on Chinese goods and restore price competitiveness in US dollar terms. Its safe haven status discounted the effort of trade hawks. If the Chinese authorities were to shift the exchange rate regime from managed float to free float, the yuan could have been even weaker. Market force could have fully neutralized the effectiveness of import tariff.

Indeed, often misinterpreted as competitive devaluation, the exchange rate reform on August 11, 2015, meant to allow the yuan to float more flexibly, as I stressed in a media interview.[3] This "811 reform" announced a one-off alignment of the daily official exchange rate (i.e. daily fixing at 9:15am Beijing time) with the prevailing market level. The aim was to improve the transparency of the infamous fixing scheme. This was an effort to prepare the yuan for inclusion in the IMF's Special Drawing Rights (SDR). China decided to allow a greater degree of cross-border

---

[3] Reuters, March 5, 2019. https://uk.reuters.com/article/uk-china-economy-yuan/china-state-planners-yuan-flexibility-pledge-sparks-speculation-idUKKCN1QM121.

capital flows. The intention was to reduce the pressure on foreign currency reserve as market liberalization required a larger volume of foreign exchange transactions. China wanted to adopt a more flexible exchange rate regime.

The exchange rate is an essential part of China's overall monetary policy reform. By Mundell's theorem of impossible trinity, a non-dollarized open economy needs to give up its interest rate autonomy if the exchange rate remains fixed. As the second-largest economy, China wants to increase its ownership of the monetary system to be similar to other advanced economies one day. The authorities prefer to use interest rate policy to deal with its output gap and maintain price stability. In the past few years, China launched many policy instruments to enhance its monetary policy transmission mechanism in order to promote the central bank's influence on market interest rates. Meanwhile, the country has liberalized its capital accounts. To be a global reserve currency, China will need to allow the renminbi to be "freely usable."

China also wants to preserve its holding of FX reserve of USD 3.1 trillion. For emerging economies, the foreign reserve defines the purchasing power of the country, both domestically and overseas. During the market turbulence in the period 2015–2016, China experienced significant capital outflows. The PBOC intervened to stabilize the currency market. The foreign reserve depleted rapidly, falling from the 2014 peak of USD 4 trillion to slightly less than USD 3 trillion. It shocked market confidence and fueled the expectation of currency depreciation. To avoid this scenario again, the central bank has gradually increased exchange rate flexibility. The government actively promotes the use of local currency in trade and investment. To this end, China needs to increase the attractiveness of the yuan so that it will eventually become a safe haven currency similar to the US dollar and the Japanese yen.

For most global investors in the US and Europe, the yuan is simply an attractive alternative in their emerging market portfolio. They are willing to increase the exposure to China if the opportunity is risk-rewarding. Many fixed-income investors would include dollar bonds issued by Chinese entities. But the actual exposure to renminbi denominated assets remains limited. Unlike the US dollar, which has maintained its status as a risk-free currency, the Chinese yuan still needs to offer a premium in order to increase its acceptance. The economics of network externalities remains in favor of the US dollar. Even the euro and the yen have difficulty challenging the greenback. Unless the global economy were to experience a major paradigm shift, the yuan could at most be something nice to have.

However, this trade war is unconventional; the world economy is on the edge of a paradigm shift. The sociopolitical trend indicates that we may be at the outset of deglobalization. The global economy is experiencing a structural shock that warrants a reform of the global monetary policy system. This type of change may not be organized multilaterally like the Genoa Conference 1922 or the Bretton Woods Conference 1944. In a unilateralist world, regime shift will likely be pushed by an unexpected event, another Nixon shock. The new regime will likely be consistent with the actual economic and social conditions in the twenty-first century.

To prepare for the paradigm shift, China has expressed their view on their reserve management. The goal will be to preserve the real value of savings. Because the amount is sizable, any change in China's asset allocation of their foreign reserve will have a significant impact on the market because of the herd behavior of other central banks and global investors. If China decides to back the renminbi by a specific metal or a currency basket, the target could potentially become a new global benchmark. If China de-dollarizes its portfolio, the "exorbitant privilege" of the US dollar will be shaken. The good news is that this Chinese action can provide a solution to resolve the trade conflicts between China and the US.

This chapter starts with a brief review of the exchange rate regime of China. My conclusion is that China has determined to float the yuan, as it is important to claim its monetary policy autonomy. I will then provide an update on how the policymakers promote international acceptance of the renminbi (RMB). It appears that the PBOC has followed a prescriptive approach to internationalizing its own currency by replicating the features of the US dollar. To conclude this chapter, I will discuss how China manages its sovereign wealth. Contrary to the topic of RMB internationalization, China's reserve management has not received much coverage in the literature. But this topic is very instructive in forming a forward-looking view of how the reform of the global monetary regime would be.

4.2 The Yuan in the Monetary Policy Context

4.2.1 Reforms in the Transitional Period 1979–2004

Stability has been the overall management philosophy of the Chinese leaders. In 1953–1978, China was isolated. Since the country began to open up in 1979, the government was taking a baby step in exchange rate reform. The basic assumption was that China was a poor country. It ranked amongst the lowest GDP per capita in the world and had no capacity to cope with external shocks. One policy mistake might affect 1 billion people. In Deng Xiaopeng's era, the policy philosophy was to "wade across the stream by feeling the way." Market reforms were executed through learning by doing. Every policy commenced with a pilot scheme and every regulation was labeled as a provisional measure to start with. This philosophy generated the impression for Western observers that China's reform was slow.

In 1979, China began to allow exporters (including local governments participating in the export process) to retain a share of foreign exchange earnings based on a quota. It was called foreign exchange retention system (外汇留成制度). In 1981, the State Council decided to develop a dual exchange rate system because a significant portion of the domestic economy still used an inherited price system from the planned economy. Many prices were not set by the market and often deviated significantly from the international level. Between 1981 and 1984, the government divided the economy into a tradable sector and a non-tradable sector. For current account transactions related to tradable goods, the government applied an internal settlement rate at CNY 2.8 per USD. For non-trade-related transactions, the official rate of CNY 1.5 per USD continued to apply.

From 1985 to 1993, this dual exchange rate regime continued to evolve. Besides the internal FX settlement system, there existed many semi-official currency swap markets (外汇调剂市场) around the country for firms to convert foreign currencies (mainly the US dollar, Hong Kong dollar, and Japanese yen). The exchange rate was supposed to reflect the supply–demand condition. On the other hand, the government started to undergo a stepwise devaluation of the official rate successively from CNY 1.5 per USD in 1981 to CNY 5.8 per USD in

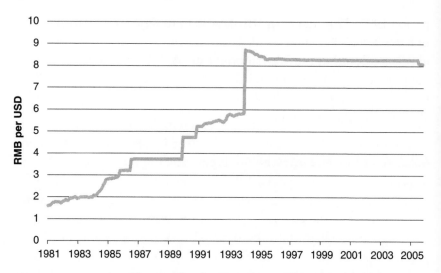

Figure 4.1 RMB exchange rate against the US dollar.

Source: Bloomberg

1993 (Figure 4.1). In the same period, China also went through a painful transitional period of domestic price reform (a dual track system). The hyperinflation in the late 1980s triggered social unrests, leading to a political event in 1989. China was sanctioned by the western countries until the early 1990s.

After several years of political consolidation, Deng Xiaopeng reiterated that he would adopt market economic reform after visiting the Shenzhen Special Economic Zone in 1992. China's relationship with the West also warmed. In 1994, China decided to unify the official rate with the market rates traded in the swap centers. However, the action also included a one-off devaluation of 33% overnight to CNY 8.7 per USD. Another important development was the establishment of the China Foreign Exchange Trade System (CFETS) in April 1994. Two years later, China allowed the yuan to be fully convertible under the current account. Between 1994 and 1997, China strengthened the currency to CNY 8.28 per USD.

In the period 1997–2005, China had almost pegged its currency to the US dollar. When many Asian currencies weakened significantly, China held the exchange rate for the sake of regional stability. In the period 1997–2000, the yuan was allowed to trade at a very narrow range of 8.2760–8.2800 against the dollar. When other Asian currencies weakened significantly in the aftermath of the Asia Currency Crisis, China committed to a fixed rate and did not devaluate. In December 2001, China was admitted into the WTO. The government pledged to gradually adjust its currency regime.

4.2.2 A Tightly Managed Floating Regime 2005–2015

As China's current account surplus continued to surge after its accession to the WTO, its policy of dollar pegging was criticized severely. The government was under pressure to respond and reform its exchange rate regime. On July 21, 2005, China announced that it would publish the official exchange rate based on market supply and demand with reference to a basket of currencies. Based on this basket, the PBOC started to publish the daily fixing rate against the US dollar before the start of the trading session. This basket had been a black box and attracted significant interests of many market analysts who developed their proprietary model to forecast the fixing every day. This fixing rate became the midpoint and defined the allowable range for intraday movement.

The preference was to maintain "stability" in the "flexible" exchange rate regime. When the daily fixing scheme was established, USD/CNY (Quote convention: how much CNY per one USD) was only allowed to fluctuate within a tight band of -0.3% around the central parity (in May 2007, the band was widened to -0.5% in May 2007; -1% in April 2012; and -2% in March 2014). For other currencies that were convertible in CFETS, namely, EUR, JPY, and HKD, the band was wider at -1.5%. In 2005, there was already an understanding that the PBOC would increase the band over time. The reform also came with a one-off strengthening of the exchange rate by 2.1%, pushing USD/CNY from 8.28 to 8.11. This adjustment was consistent with the long-held view that the renminbi was undervalued.

The reform in July 2005 was eventful not only because it was truly a shift to the floating regime but also a huge surprise in the market. Two months before the reform was launched, Prime Minister Wen Jiabao was still hawkish in the public arena, saying, "Reform of RMB exchange rate system is matter of China's sovereignty and any pressure and speculative exploitation of the issue or any attempt to turn the economic issue into a political one will not be conducive to resolving it."[4] In hindsight, his statement was understandable. If the central bank revealed its plan prior to its implementation, the market participants could have profited from arbitrage. Exchange rate reforms had to happen like lightning. In addition, the exchange rate reform turned out to alleviate some political pressure of the US. At that time, the US government still believed in mutual consultation when they dealt with China.[5]

The Chinese authorities pegged the currency with the US dollar during the global financial crisis (GFC) before allowing it to float again in June 2010. From 2010 to 2015, there had been little change in the exchange rate mechanism. The market continued to guess the daily rate set by the PBOC, as the central bank never disclosed the model behind. Another frequently asked question in the market was when the PBOC widened the trading band. Bank analysts often published speculative reports. During this period, the US had launched a series of quantitative easing policies. Hot money was flowing into China. Given the impressive economic performance shortly after the GFC, China attracted a lot of capital inflows, resulting in property and financial bubbles. This situation was similar to the situation in Thailand before the outbreak of the Asian Financial Crisis. The PBOC had to reform its exchange rate policy in order to avoid repeating history.

4.2.3 Managed Floating Post "811"

From 2005 to 2014, China was busy dealing with the problem of capital inflows. The authorities needed to sterilize the influx of hot money that fueled the asset bubbles. The best way to characterize the capital flows

---

[4] Embassy of the PRC. China never yields to outside pressure on yuan (May 17, 2005). (http://www.china-embassy.org/eng/zt/1/t195998.htm).

[5] *New York Times.* Bush's Choice: Anger China or Congress Over Currency. (May 17, 2005). (https://www.nytimes.com/2005/05/17/business/worldbusiness/bushs-choice-anger-china-or-congress-over-currency.html).

was the strong accumulation of foreign exchange reserves, which was increasing from USD 733 billion in July 2005 to a peak of USD 3.99 trillion in June 2014. The current account was also a contributor to the build-up. Over-invoicing in trade was also commonly used to mask the inflows of capital that took advantage of high onshore yield.[6]

Prior to 2012, the Chinese yuan was under a strong pressure of appreciation, rising 26% against the USD (in effective terms, i.e. trade weighted currency basket, the appreciation was 44% nominal, 58% real). This "managed" appreciation reflected the view of the government that the economic fundamental of China remained healthy. However, this predictable trend combined with higher interest rate differential (due to the Fed's unconventional monetary policy) had attracted many carry trades. Financial risks were accumulating. In the summer of 2015, the IMF External Sector Report assessment report declared that the yuan was no longer undervalued.

On August 11, 2015, the PBOC made another bold step of exchange rate reform, aiming to make the daily fixing scheme more "market friendly." This "811 reform" turned out to be a market rout. The PBOC surprised the market with a very brief statement explaining the change in the daily fixing mechanism. Under the new mechanism, banks were asked to submit quotes with reference to the closing rate of the previous day, in conjunction with the value of the yuan against a basket of currencies. Since there had been a gap between the spot rate in the previous trading day and the fixing, the reform required a one-off, immediate downward adjustment of the RMB exchange rate by 1.9% (Figure 4.2).

Prior to the "811 reform," the PBOC daily fixing scheme had been criticized for lack of transparency. The intent was to reform the fixing mechanism and aim at shifting towards a more "market friendly" regime. With the benefit of hindsight, the State Council flagged such a move in July 2015, when it stated, with the usual tone, that they considered to improve the exchange rate mechanism and expand the allowable trading

---

[6] Kessler, M. and Borst, N. (2013). Did China really lose $3.75 trillion in illicit financial flows? [Blog post]. PIIE Blog (https://www.piie.com/blogs/china-economic-watch/did-china-really-lose-375-trillion-illicit-financial-flows).

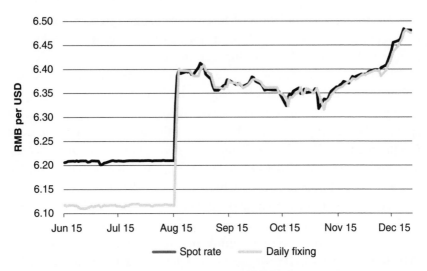

Figure 4.2   USD/CNY spot rate and daily fixing.
Sources: PBOC, Bloomberg

range. But the statement was taken lightly. The reform might have been an action taken by the PBOC in response to the IMF Report on SDR considerations on August 3, 2015, although there was no evidence that the IMF specifically recommended to change the fixing methodology.

The "811 reform" the market by surprise. The explanation by the PBOC failed to calm the market. Instead, weaker fixings in the two trading sessions following August 11 were interpreted by the market as an intentional devaluation as opposed to merely conforming to the new fixing mechanism. This forced the central bank to intervene directly and aggressively to curb dollar buying. The depreciation expectations led to a pickup in capital outflows that required more than just FX intervention to quell. Capital account flows were tightened and margin requirements on forward transactions were imposed in an effort to rein in outflow pressures.

The "811 reform" was taxing. The outflows doubled from an average of around USD 100 billion in Q3 and Q4 of 2014 to a quarterly average of USD 200 billion in H2 of 2015. In sum, China's foreign currency reserve fell sharply from the peak of USD 3.99 trillion before

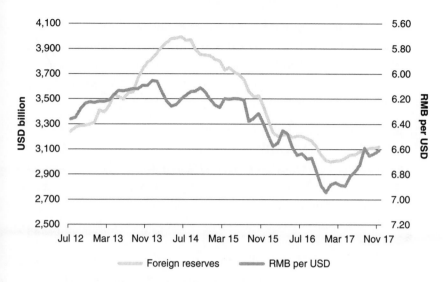

Figure 4.3 China's FX reserves.
Sources: SAFE, PBOC, Bloomberg

stabilizing at USD 3.0 trillion in 2017 (see Figure 4.3). Market anecdotes suggested two reasons for the massive outflows:

1. Short-covering the carry trade position: Prior to the event, the FX market had built up a large short-term position through onshore–offshore financial products such as "Nei Bao Wai Dai" (offshore borrowing guaranteed by onshore deposits) and structured products such as Targeted Redemption Forward (TRF). Market participants were short on US dollar. After the shocked change in expectation of the forward exchange rate, there were massive (estimated to be USD 500 billion) capital outflows from the mainland to unwind the market position.

2. Increased demand for FX hedging: With the expectation of RMB depreciation firming up, onshore residents began to hedge the exchange rate risks via acquisition of offshore assets. These were done via official channels, such as outward direct investment or outbound tourism, or unofficial channels, such as over-invoicing of current accounts or even money laundering.

The reform was intended to increase the flexibility of the yuan exchange rate regime (Das 2019 discussed the policy implication comprehensively). But it eventually turned out to be an event that motivated the authorities to "invent" more measures to manage market expectation and tighten cross-border control.

1. Alternative policy benchmark: In December 2015, CFETS published the CFETS RMB index, aiming at shifting the market focus from a single currency pair of USD/CNY to a basket of currencies. Benchmarking the value and volatility of RMB with the basket of currencies should allow for greater two-way variability in USD/CNY. Currency volatility in terms of the basket should be less than that of a single currency pair. Today, the US dollar remains the major currency pair traded in the onshore market and constitutes more than 95% of total turnover, most market participants believe that the PBOC's policy is to maintain the stability of the CFETS RMB Index, not the US dollar.

2. Windows guidance: In early 2016, the authorities announced they would refine the methodology of daily fixing after taking "the recommendation by the panel banks." They stated that they would be adjusting the previous closing rate for the impact of the changes in cross-rates among basket currencies during the previous trading day and overnight. On May 26, 2017, the government said the panel banks could adjust their quotes by imposing a "counter-cyclical adjustment factor" (CCF). The aim was to reduce the impact of excessive movement due to herd behavior. It was said that individual banks had their own model to calculate the factor. But many market participants viewed the CCF as a tool for the authorities to impose its policy preference. The CCF was suspended in January 2018 when the renminbi regained strength, and resumed in August amidst the depreciation pressure triggered by the trade war.

3. Macroprudential measures: On October 15, 2015, the PBOC imposed a reserve requirement on banks' forward position. Banks needed to set aside 20% of their clients' FX forwards positions in US dollar reserves to be held for a year at no interest. The base for calculating reserves was the nominal value of new contracts clients signed with the banks to purchase dollars or banks' dollar sales to clients. This policy introduced

a frictional cost to banks' forward business. Since the reserve was in the US dollar, this policy reduced the dollar liquidity banks could commit to their open positions in their forward book.

Since "811" in 2015, the authorities have allowed the yuan to trade with the dollar more flexibly over a period of time. Amidst the trade war, USD/CNY touched the strongest level of 6.3 in Q1 2018 to the weakest level of 7.1 as at August 2019 (weakened by more than 10%). Although the official policy tone is to maintain the renminbi exchange rate "basically stable," the central bank has a greater tolerance level compared with the pre-"811" era. The general expectation held by market participants is two-way volatility rather than one-way appreciation. The forward market is generally traded with a reasonable range and the market pricing does not imply long-term depreciation of the yuan. In the past two years, the central bank seldom used the foreign reserve to intervene the spot market directly (although window guidance, CCF, and forward market intervention are still used according to market anecdotes).

Since China has implemented many measures to curb speculative transactions in the FX market and tighten capital outflows, the current regime is more capable of withstanding the deprecation pressure exerted by the trade war. The chaos in the aftermath of "811" will unlikely repeat. In fact, the pressure on the yuan's exchange rate and other emerging market currencies began in June 2018 when Trump's policy turned hawkish and China's growth momentum began to slow. The USD/CNY rate weakened quickly while the CFETS RMB Index dropped 6.5% between April and mid-August in 2018. However, the PBOC showed no sign of active market intervention because the market did not believe in long-term depreciation as signaled by the pricing in the forward market. The foreign reserve level continued to stay above USD 3 trillion. There were no significant capital outflows.

Our historical review shows that China's exchange rate reform has gone through several stages:

1. 1979–1993: A transitional period from planned to market economy through introducing a dual-track scheme.
2. 1994–2004: Pegging with the US dollar and letting the domestic price adjust to the international level.

3. 2005–2015: Allowing the nominal exchange rate to adjust to an "equilibrium level" that is no longer undervalued.

4. 2015–present: Introducing two-way volatility cautiously with a bottom line to preserve the FX reserve position no less than USD 3 trillion.

The last stage of reform is in line with the development of China's monetary policy framework. In a flexible exchange rate regime, the supply and demand of currency in the FX market can help offset the impact of external shocks on domestic prices. In theory, if China were to truly abandon an exchange rate target, the PBOC can focus on interest rate reform. Executing financial liberalization is a dynamic process. The implementation should proceed based on a sequence that is consistent with the prevailing condition of an economy (Johnston and Sundararajan 1991). There is increasing evidence that the PBOC has successfully improved interest rate transmission mechanism (Kamber and Mohanty 2018), providing a necessary condition for China to speed up capital account liberalization, an important step for the internationalization of the yuan.

4.2.4 Currency Outlook and Reforms

The yuan has become a global currency. Its value is determined not only by domestic fundamentals in China but also some cyclical factors in the global markets. For instance, in early 2014, USD/CNY reached the strongest level at 6.04. This could be traced to the reversal of the interest rate cycles between the Fed and the PBOC. The yield advantage that China had over the US was at its highest in late 2013, before the Fed started to taper their quantitative easing program. The yield differential continued to narrow when the PBOC started their rate-cutting cycle in late 2014, with larger moves in 2015 on expectations of Fed rate hikes. Nonetheless, sometimes the USD/CNY moves may not perfectly follow the yield gap if the liquidity condition of the market is tight.

But there is also a structural reason for the weakening of the renminbi. Since China's accession to the WTO in 2001, it has experienced an influx of foreign direct investment, taking advantage of cheap labor

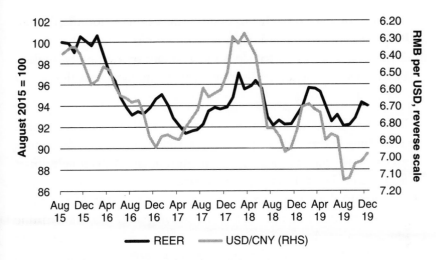

Figure 4.4 RMB real effective exchange rate.

Sources: BIS, FRED

and preferential government treatment towards manufacturing. However, the production costs in China are now getting expensive with nominal wage rates rising more than twofold since 2008. Compared with some other emerging economies, China is no longer as cost competitive. With productivity growth not keeping pace with wage growth, the real effective exchange rate (REER) needs to be adjusted. Especially after the RMB REER rose strongly between mid-2014 to early 2015, the currency became overvalued (Figure 4.4). The weakness of the renminbi offset a large part of this overvaluation.

The longer-term fate of the RMB rests with China's structural reforms. To assess the long-term prospect of the RMB, we need to see beyond what the inflation dynamic and monetary policy cycle imply. The consensus view is that China is poised to cross the Lewis turning point, from which China will move from a condition of labor abundance to labor shortage. Chinese policymakers, on the one hand, reiterate the need to lift productivity, but on the other hand, strive to promote the service sector, which now represents more than 50% of GDP and continues to grow at a pace faster than the manufacturing sector in the future.

In 2012, the World Bank published an influential report titled *China 2030: Building a Modern, Harmonious, and Creative Society*, shaping the thought of China's policymakers in subsequent years. To avoid falling into a middle-income trap, the report made six recommendations:

1. Implement structural reforms to strengthen the foundations for a market-based economy by redefining the role of government; reforming and restructuring state enterprises and banks; developing the private sector; promoting competition; and deepening reforms in the land, labor, and financial markets.
2. Accelerate the pace of innovation and create an open innovation system in which competitive pressures encourage Chinese firms to engage in product and process innovation, not only through their own R&D but also by participating in the global network.
3. Seize the opportunity to "go green" through a mix of market incentives, regulations, public investments, industrial policy, and institutional development.
4. Expand opportunities and promote social security for all by facilitating equal access to jobs, finance, quality social services, and portable social security.
5. Strengthen the fiscal system by mobilizing additional revenues and ensuring local governments have adequate financing to meet heavy and rising expenditure responsibilities.
6. Seek mutually beneficial relations with the world by becoming a proactive stakeholder in the global economy, actively using multilateral institutions and frameworks, and shaping the global governance agenda.

When China transforms itself from an investment-led to a consumption-driven economy, it needs to speed up the growth of total factor productivity. If China can successfully push forward with the structural reform and enrich the value added component in its industrial and service outputs, the value-added per worker will be lifted. Only with a sustainable growth of real wages will China's consumption continue to rise. These will eventually lead to a higher real exchange rate in the long run, as suggested by the Balassa-Samuelson theory.

In other words, if the structural reforms fail to boost China's productivity in the tradable sector, the renminbi will remain structurally weak. And there is a reason to worry. The growth of total factor productivity has slowed in China in recent years, according to estimates from the Penn World Table (Figure 4.5). On the positive side, there is still plenty of room to catch up compared with the advanced economies. The government has emphasized on technological development and innovation. Indeed, there is a noticeable expansion of some newly emerging industries. As China's export outlook is uncertain because of the trade tension with the US, it is reasonable to be cautious about the long-term prospect of productivity improvement, and hence the fundamental support of the exchange rate outlook of the yuan in the long term.

Ironically, China's technology push is exactly the concern of the US in this trade dispute while Trump's administration also claimed China's currency is undervalued. There is clearly a circular argument. Low-cost and low value-added products will no longer be competitive. China will likely focus on high-end exports. Even though this will mean head-to-head competition between the two countries, currency appreciation of

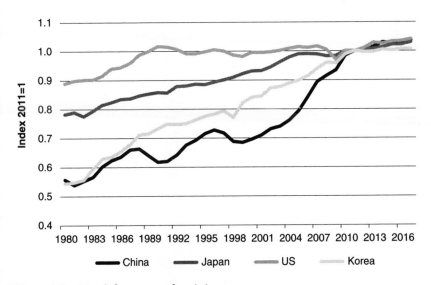

Figure 4.5 Total factor productivity.

Source: FRED

the yuan will at least facilitate the rivalry on a level playing field. If the US allows China to boost its tech and innovation development, chances are we would see a rapid appreciation of the yuan exchange rate. Allowing the yuan to become a prominent reserve currency will help resolve the trade imbalance.

Chinese corporates are increasingly eyeing offshore investment opportunities as yields in the domestic economy trend lower (Figure 4.6). On the back of relatively low funding costs, the RMB could soon become a major funding currency for offshore investment. As China eventually turns into a net exporter of capital, the yuan could potentially evolve, like the yen did, and become a carry trade currency, depending on the basis development in the offshore market.

If history repeats, the economic development of China may follow the footsteps of Japan. After an impressive domestic economic performance for decades, Chinese corporate will expand their investments abroad, making use of its sizeable foreign reserves. China may eventually reach a stage where the current account surplus continues to be sustained by foreign investment income. A common observation for North Asian economies including Japan and South Korea is that

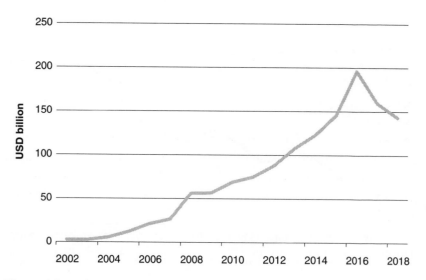

Figure 4.6   China's outward direct investment.

Source: Ministry of Commerce

even though domestic manufacturing seems to have declined with the rise of offshore production, these economies continue to attract capital inflows from either equity investment in the listed companies or profit repatriation. This prevents the currencies of these economies from depreciating.

Should the yuan become a "headquarters currency" of such, its exchange rate may start to behave like the Japanese yen or Korean won. Indeed, China is continuing to expedite its financial market development in Shanghai and also expand foreign participation in the onshore equity and bond markets. This development is very similar to Japan's financial liberalization in the 1980s. Despite a "hollowing out" of domestic manufacturing, the exchange rate of the Japanese yen experienced ups and downs within the range of 80–140 in the last three decades. However, the strength of the JPY nominal exchange rate has been one of the reasons behind the extended period of stagnation in Japan. Likewise, the renminbi exchange rate will likely fluctuate within a "reasonable" range rather than a one-way depreciation.

4.3 Globalizing the RMB in the Deglobalizing World

4.3.1 De-Dollarization

China's efforts to promote international use of the renminbi has been well documented in the academic literature (e.g. Frankel 2012, Park 2016), central banks' policy papers (e.g. Nabar and Tovar 2017, Windsor and Halperin 2018), and many analyst reports. Many papers on this topic were motivated by the question of whether the yuan will ultimately become a dominant currency in the global economy. In their analysis, the general assumption was that China's share in the global economy should take over the US one day and would continue to integrate into global trade and investment successfully, repeating the path the US had gone through.

However, the trade war signals another scenario. Protectionism and nationalism dominate the policy environment. Regionalization instead of globalization may be a more realistic or even the most optimistic assumption in the near term. The dollar centric regime may be replaced with a multicurrency regime. Countries are striving for monetary independence. De-dollarization is most likely driven by a greater use of local currency amongst neighborhood countries. The chance of seeing a rice trade between Thailand and Cambodia settled in euro, or the transfer fee of a soccer player between Barcelona and Liverpool quoted in Japanese yen, would be remote.

China is looking for monetary independence. It has a large and excessive US dollar exposure. USD/CNY represents 95% of all spot transactions in China's FX market. But the bilateral trade between China and the US, valued at USD 634 billion in 2018, only shared 14% of China's total trade. De-dollarization is justifiable. If China aligns its currency exposure in accordance with the portfolio of all external transactions, there should be a substantial reduction in the demand for the US dollar. China also holds a substantial amount of US dollars in its foreign reserves, estimated to be about USD 2 trillion. But China's FDI in the US was only USD 40 billion in 2018. The dollar exposure of China deviates substantially from the geographic profile of its trade and investment partners.

If China is only targeting the achievement of monetary policy independence, the scale and scope of RMB internationalization can be very narrow. If the goal is not to become a globally dominant currency like the US dollar, the authorities would not look for over-circulation of the yuan in the offshore market to allow investors to build up their speculative position. China would still encourage other central banks to hold the renminbi in their currency portfolio. But the amount required will just need to be sufficient for supporting their current account transactions. The yuan will still appear as a payment currency outside China's soil. The transaction will most probably be done by Chinese investors having residence in foreign markets, similar to the ecosystem of the Japanese yen.

In a deglobalized world, the goal of RMB internationalization will be less ambitious. China will most likely settle and invoice its cross-border transactions with Belt and Road countries in the yuan. China can pay for its imports or asset acquisitions offshore using local currency. A smaller amount of foreign reserve holdings will be adequate. Lesser demand for US dollar securities will alleviate the problem of the global saving glut, a culprit behind the trade imbalance with the US. In other words, internationalization of the yuan is a recipe to relieve the trade tension, contrasting the negative perception about this policy push based on the "China threat theory."

4.3.2 RMB Internationalization

A typical way to characterize the process of RMB internationalization is to depict all policy measures facilitating the growing volume of RMB-related transactions in the financial markets offshore. In the context of the globalization cycle we covered in Chapter 3, we will analyze the approach China adopted to promoting the currency. Incidentally, these strategies resemble the key features supporting the dominance of the dollar: (1) Nurturing RMB convertibility; (2) Establishing offshore RMB centers; and (3) Developing a yuan recycling process for trade partners.

Nurturing the Convertibility   At Bretton Woods, the US established an implicit contract with other nations on dollar-gold convertibility. The gold-exchange standard was virtually a brokerage arrangement and crowned the US the official intermediary status. The establishment of the supranational organizations based in Washington, DC enhanced the soft power and gradually drifted the center for global decision-making from London or Geneva to the US.

China follows a similar step in promoting the renminbi. The PBOC have entered bilateral local currency swap agreements with many other central banks. Since 2008, the PBOC has signed these swap agreements with 38 central banks (see Table 4.1). By the end of 2018, 30 of these agreements remained effective. The value of these agreements totaled CNY 3.48 trillion. Although these standing facilities seem to be symbolic because not many central banks actually utilize the lines, the nature of these agreements is an official recognition of convertibility between the yuan and other local currencies.

This convertibility is also made available for the private sector in the financial market. To facilitate the circulation of the Chinese yuan, the PBOC also appointed many RMB clearing banks in the offshore market (see Table 4.2). In the onshore market, CFETS set up many direct conversion schemes for other foreign currencies. Market making banks received some quotas for such conversions. This measure aims at facilitating market participants with genuine needs to buy or sell non-US dollar. For instance, a Korean manufacturer in China can convert Korean won into the renminbi to fund their investment in China. Trading volumes of other foreign currencies, such as SGD, AUD, EUR,

Table 4.1 Local currency swap agreements signed with the PBOC.

Counterparty	Entered/Renewed	CNY / FCY Billion
Bank of Lao PDR	January 2020	–
European Central Bank	October 2019	350 / EUR 40
Monetary Authority of Singapore	May 2019	300 / SGD 61
Central Bank Van Suriname	February 2019	1.0 / SRD 1.1
National Bank of Ukraine	December 2018	15 / UAH 62
Bank Indonesia	November 2018	200 / IDR 440 trillion
Bank of Japan	October 2018	200 / JPY 3,400
Bank of England	October 2018	350 / GBP 40
Bank Negara Malaysia	August 2018	180 / MYR 110
National Bank of Kazakhstan	May 2018	7 / KZT 350
Central Bank of Chile	May 2018	22 / CLP 2,200
State Bank of Pakistan	May 2018	20 / PKR 351
National Bank of the Republic of Belarus	May 2018	7 / BYR 2.22
Central Bank of Nigeria	April 2018	15 / NGN 720
South African Reserve Bank	April 2018	30 / ZAR 54
Central Bank of Albania	April 2018	2 / ALL 34.2
Reserve Bank of Australia	March 2018	200 / AUD 40
Bank of Thailand	December 2017	70 / THB 370
Central Bank of Russian Federation	November 2017	150 / RUB 1,325
Hong Kong Monetary Authority	November 2017	400 / HKD 470
Bank of Canada	November 2017	200 / CAD 30
Qatar Central Bank	November 2017	35 / QAR 20.8
Bank of Korea	October 2017	360 / KRW 64 trillion
Swiss National Bank	July 2017	150 / CHF 21
Central Bank of Argentina	July 2017	70 / ARS 175
Bank of Mongolia	July 2017	15 / MNT 5.4 trillion

Table 4.1   (Continued)

Reserve Bank of New Zealand	May 2017	25 / NZD 5
Central Bank of Iceland	December 2016	3.5 / ISK 66
Central Bank of Egypt	December 2016	18 / EGP 47
Central Bank of Hungary	September 2016	10 / HUF 416
Central Bank of the Republic of Serbia	June 2016	1.5 / RSD 27
Central Bank of Morocco	May 2016	10 / MAD 15
Central Bank of United Arab Emirates	December 2015	35 / AED 20
National Bank of Georgia	September 2015	–
Central Bank of the Republic of Turkey	September 2015	12 / TRY 5
Central Bank of Tajikistan	September 2015	3 / TJS 3
Central Bank of Armenia	March 2015	1 / AMD 77
Central Bank of Sri Lanka	September 2014	10 / LKR 225
Central Bank of Brazil	March 2013	190 / BRL 60
Central Bank of Republic of Uzbekistan	April 2011	700 / UZS 167

Source: PBOC

Table 4.2   Offshore RMB clearing banks.

Date of Appointment	Market	Bank
Dec 2003	Hong Kong	Bank of China (Hong Kong)
Sep 2004	Macau	Bank of China, Macau branch
Dec 2012	Taipei	Bank of China, Taipei branch
Feb 2013	Singapore	Industrial and Commercial Bank of China, Singapore branch
Jun 2014	Germany	Bank of China, Frankfurt branch

(Continued)

Table 4.2 (Continued)

Date of Appointment	Market	Bank
Jun 2014	UK	China Construction Bank, London branch
Jul 2014	South Korea	Bank of Communications, Seoul branch
Sep 2014	France	Bank of China, Paris branch
Sep 2014	Luxembourg	Industrial and Commercial Bank of China, Luxembourg branch
Nov 2014	Australia	Bank of China, Sydney branch
Nov 2014	Canada	Industrial and Commercial Bank of China (Canada)
Jan 2015	Malaysia	Bank of China (Malaysia)
Jan 2015	Thailand	Industrial and Commercial Bank of China (Thailand)
May 2015	Chile	China Construction Bank Chile Branch
Jun 2015	Hungary	Bank of China Hungary Branch
Jul 2015	South Africa	Bank of China Johannesburg Branch
Sep 2015	Argentina	Industrial and Commercial Bank of China (Argentina)
Sep 2015	Zambia	Bank of China Zambia
Nov 2015	Switzerland	China Construction Bank Zurich
Mar 2017	US	Bank of China New York
Mar 2017	Russia	Industrial and Commercial Bank of China Moscow
Mar 2017	UAE	Agricultural Bank of China Dubai Branch
Feb 2018	US	JP Morgan
Nov 2018	Japan	Bank of China Tokyo Branch

Source: PBOC

KRW, NZD, MYR, have risen substantially but the absolute amount remains small. Even after several years of operation, non-USD represents only 4–5% in the spot market. USD remains the major currency in China's FX market.

Another effort was to strive for inclusion in a global currency standard. In November 2015, the IMF agreed to change the SDR's basket currency composition, effective in October 2016 (see Table 4.3). The RMB joined the SDR basket in addition to the other G4 currencies. This inclusion was often interpreted as just a symbolic event, as the SDR was not a widely circulated "currency" in the financial market. Yet many central banks do have SDR sitting on their balance sheet, given their transactions with the IMF. The inclusion does represent an indirect demand for the renminbi.

In the early years of the RMB internationalization, some central banks were granted direct access to China's capital market. With the inclusion of the RMB into the SDR basket, more central banks added the yuan into their official currency reserve (Figure 4.7). Based on the COFER data of the IMF, total RMB reserves held by other central banks reached USD 202.8 billion, accounting for 1.89% of the total foreign exchange reserves by end of 2018, ranking 6th, and higher than the Australian dollar (1.62%) and the Canadian dollar (1.84%).

As the share of RMB in central banks' reserve portfolios increase, the chances for the yuan to become an anchor currency will also rise. Other central banks will formulate their monetary policies and link their currency value with reference to the yuan's exchange rate both implicitly and explicitly. In recent years, many countries have shifted from their US dollar target to other arrangements. The rise of RMB will certainly catch their attention when they reform their exchange rate arrangements. While it is still premature to expect major central banks in the advanced economies to peg their currencies with the

Table 4.3 IMF SDR basket.

%	2016	2010
USD	41.73	41.9
EUR	30.93	37.4
JPY	8.33	9.4
GBP	8.09	11.3
RMB	10.92	

Source: IMF

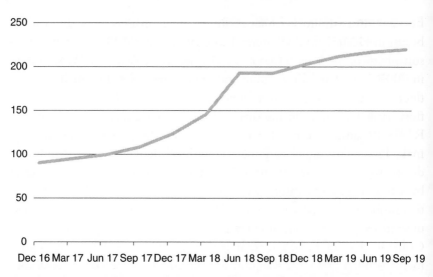

Figure 4.7   RMB reserves held by other central banks (in USD billion).
Source: IMF COFER data

RMB in the near term, RMB will certainly increase its influence on Asian exchange rates in the future (see Kawai and Pontines 2015 for the latest discussion on related empirical studies based on Frankel-Wei regression).

In 2013, China drove the establishment of the Asian Infrastructure Investment Bank (AIIB). The bank is widely seen as a rival to other supranational organizations established at the Bretton Woods conference. The AIIB is also believed to be an effort to lift the status of the renminbi. In addition, it is perceived that China has been frustrated with its underrepresentation at the IMF, World Bank, and Asian Development Bank, which it claims are heavily dominated by American, European, and Japanese interests.[7] As the headquarters of AIIB is located in Beijing, for the Western allies, the decision to join the organization is seen as a political expression following the line of thought under the "China threat theory."[8]

---

[7]Brant, P. (2014). Why Australia should join the Asian Infrastructure Investment Bank. Lowy Institute (September).

[8]Pitlo III, L. B. (2019). China May Be More Assertive, But Is It Really Ready to Lead? *The Diplomat.* (November 1).

Establishing Offshore RMB Centers. The offshore RMB business began in Hong Kong when the PBOC allowed the city to open a personal bank account in RMB in 2004.[9] But the offshore market took off in 2009 when the PBOC launched a pilot scheme for RMB trade settlement. Trade channels were the most traditional channels for RMB to flow in/out of offshore markets. With the development of cross-border RMB settlements since 2010, domestic Chinese importers started to make invoice payments in RMB, thus forming a pool of offshore RMB deposits (Figure 4.8). On the other hand, the receiving side of the yuan by Chinese exporters supported the returning flow of the currency to the onshore market. In 2018, the cross-border RMB settlement volume in the current account reached CNY 5.11 trillion. In early 2011, China also allowed domestic firms to conduct outward direct investments (ODI) in RMB. In 2018, the RMB ODI was CNY 805 billion.

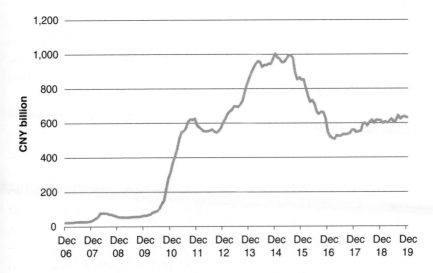

Figure 4.8 Hong Kong's RMB deposits, CNY billion.
Source: HKMA

---

[9]Hong Kong Monetary Authority. RMB Business in Hong Kong (https://www.hkma.gov.hk/media/eng/doc/key-functions/monetary-stability/rmb-business-in-hong-kong/hkma-rmb-booklet.pdf)

To provide USD/CNY or HKD/CNY conversion, banks in Hong Kong set up trading desks to convert offshore CNY, also called the CNH ("H" stands for Hong Kong). In 2003, Bank of China (Hong Kong) was appointed as the RMB clearing bank to square the position with the onshore market. The Hong Kong Monetary Authority (HKMA) signed a bilateral swap agreement with the PBOC. The Ministry of Finance regularly issued the first China Government Bond. All CNH-denominated bonds were called Dim Sum bond. The PBOC also issued the CNH bill in the money market in recent years.

The strategy is to spread the offshore RMB activities to other financial centers. More RMB clearing banks were appointed in subsequent years, including New York, London, Frankfurt, Singapore, Tokyo, and Paris. The RMB clearing facilities covered all global time zones. The offshore markets continued to build up the RMB liquidity pool, reflected by the size of CNH deposits. While Hong Kong's CNH deposits represented a substantial proportion of the total, other offshore markets (e.g. London, Taipei, Singapore, and Seoul) caught up quickly. This network has boosted the RMB payment flows. The global ranking in terms of SWIFT payments has climbed. However, the trade war has affected the Chinese trade flows negatively. In September 2019, the yuan was the fifth most active currency for global payments by value, sharing 1.95% of the total. The value decreased by 11.82% compared to August 2019 (Figure 4.9). In the same month, other payment currencies increased by 0.19%.

The CNH market resembles the Eurodollar market in London, which is a critical infrastructure for round-the-clock circulation of the US dollar. Outside Hong Kong, the City of London has also been keen to tap the RMB opportunity. According to SWIFT, London is the largest CNH market if we exclude Hong Kong (Figure 4.10). The *Financial Times* (February 8, 2019) wrote, "the city's charm offensive has paid off, with daily orders averaging USD 73 billion in October (2018). . .underscoring the UK's status as the world's biggest renminbi trading hub outside China." He and McCauley (2012) pointed out the Eurodollar market could help predict the evolution of the offshore RMB market by providing intermediary function between non-Chinese residents.

China also attempts to expedite capital account liberalization and deregulate cross-border transactions. The authorities launched

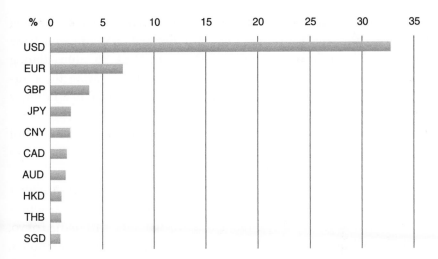

Figure 4.9 RMB share as a global payment currency, September 2019.
Source: SWIFT

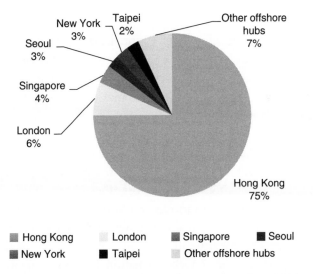

Figure 4.10 Top 15 offshore RMB markets, September 2019.
Source: SWIFT

some Free Trade Zones (FTZs). For years, foreign investors had trouble repatriating their funds sitting in mainland China. To support the cross-border flow, the regulators eventually allowed companies to move funds across the border in the form of inter-company loans based on a concept of cash pooling (although the scheme was halted after "811" due to massive capital outflows). In 2014, Shanghai began to liberalize and established Free Trade Units (FTU) in its banking system, facilitating an easier cross-border flow of funds. The FTZ initiative was also rolled out in other Chinese cities. However, growing speculative activities taking advantage of the regulatory loophole saw the backlash of the FTZ implementation initially. Currently, the pilots still proceed with great caution.

Of both the current and capital account transactions, the RMB represented only about one-third of total settlements even after 10 years of liberalization. In 2018, the amount of cross-border RMB settlements with Hong Kong accounted for 40% of total cross-border RMB settlements in terms of volume, followed by Singapore with a share of 9%, Germany of 4.2%, and South Korea of nearly 4%. In other words, excluding Hong Kong SAR of China, the RMB payment flows with other countries are a lot less (see Figure 4.11)

Developing a Yuan Recycling Process for Trade Partners. Petrodollar recycling was the key mechanism backing the global dominance of the greenback (see Chapter 2). The recycling process established an access to a deep and liquid capital market so that countries were willing to invest the net earnings from trade in dollar assets. The yuan may claim its status as a prominent currency by the impressive growth of trade-related payments in the RMB. But to call it a global reserve currency, China needs to establish a sizeable and liquid capital market for sovereign wealth funds and foreign institutional investors. This is an important step to close the loop. Exporting countries to China (e.g. Korea, Australia) can invest their RMB proceeds from trade into CNY-denominated investment grade financial instruments.

Many reports on the RMB internationalization compared the offshore RMB hubs with the size of their CNH deposits. In 2018, the gross value of RMB cross-border settlement amounted to CNY 15.85 trillion, increasing 46.3% (Figure 4.12). But the total receipts were CNY 8 trillion and total payments were CNY 7.85 trillion, resulting in a net inflow of CNY 154.4 billion back to China. That is, the "euro-yuan" market was not very much adding to its net long position in the RMB.

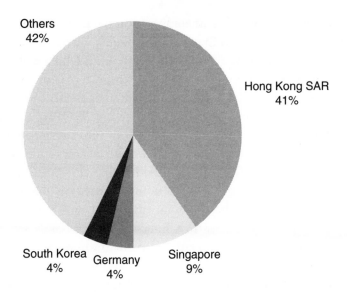

Figure 4.11 Cross-border RMB payments with maninland China by economies, 2018
Source: PBOC

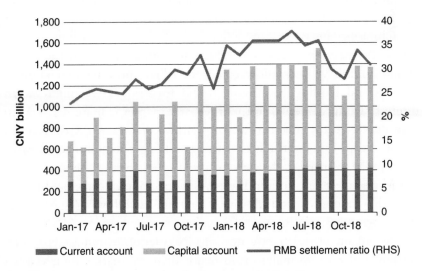

Figure 4.12 China's cross-border payment in RMB.
Source: PBOC

CNH liquidity was tight. The interest rate was high, hindering its role as a funding currency in the offshore loan market.

On the other hand, the net RMB inflows into China may actually be a positive sign of the yuan recycling process. In early years, China granted foreign countries a quota to invest their RMB funds via the RMB Qualified Foreign Institutional Investor (RQFII) scheme. In the past few years, the authorities opened up other channels including Bond Connect, Stock Connect, and direct access to China Interbank Bond Market (CIBM) by qualified financial institutions. These schemes have received great interest from financial investors. Particularly, Bond Connect has been an important channel for foreign financial institutions to invest in China's sovereign bonds and policy financial bonds. It is an important element to close the loop of the yuan recycling.

In fact, China's bond market is large enough to assist the yuan recycling. In 2018, the market size reached USD 12.9 trillion, larger than Japan (USD 12.5 trillion). China is now the second-largest bond market by market value in the world (Figure 4.13). China Government Bonds (CGB) and Policy Financial Bonds (PFB) issued by policy banks are heavily traded in the market and comprised 17.4% and 16.8% of outstanding bonds, respectively. Expressed as a ratio to GDP, however, China's bond market is considered to be less developed.

China has been very proactive in attracting foreign bond investors in the past few years. Since 2015, foreign central banks and sovereign funds have been allowed to trade all rate products (cash bonds, repos, bond lending/borrowing, bond forwards, IRS and forward interest rate agreements) in the interbank market (Figure 4.14). Foreign public-sector investors are also allowed to trade FX derivatives in the onshore market. China also has a large corporate bond market (credit). However, the lack of good credit rating scheme in the onshore market has limited the investment appetite of global investors who are used to considering the ratings by following Standard & Poor's, Moody's and Fitch.

To enhance the attractiveness of CNY-denominated assets, China actively seeks for an inclusion in major financial market benchmarks. On June 1, 2018, the Chinese A-share was formally included in MSCI Emerging Markets Index and Global Standard Index, which was

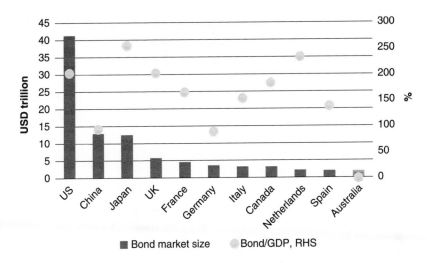

Figure 4.13   Global bond markets at a glance 2018.

Sources: BIS, World Bank, ANZ Research China Rates Primer 2019

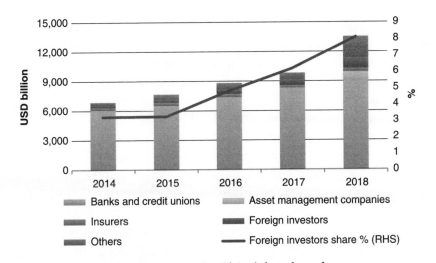

Figure 4.14   Foreign investment in China's bond market.

Sources: China Central Depository & Clearing, ANZ Research China Rates Primer 2019

conducive to attracting overseas investors to allocate assets denominated in RMB. On January 31, 2018, Bloomberg formally confirmed the inclusion of Chinese bonds into the Bloomberg Barclays

Global Composite Index from April 2019. On September 4, 2019, JP Morgan announced it would include China bonds into its Emerging Market Bond Indexes with a weight capped at 10%, effective on February 28, 2020.

China can attain dual goals by liberalizing foreign access to its domestic capital market. First, foreign entities typically need to convert their own currency (e.g. US dollar) into RMB for their China investment. The capital inflows can help stabilize the value of RMB, especially in the period when the trade war intensifies. Secondly, the yuan recycling process can utilize the idle RMB funds sitting in the offshore market. For emerging markets, having too much liquidity in the hands of offshore entities plants a financial risk because investors can use them to develop a speculative position. Tight liquidity means a higher cost for short positions and is important for exchange rate stability, which in turn, secures the confidence of long-term investors.

In 2018, China and many Belt and Road economies (as defined by the Chinese government) handled cross-border settlements of CNY 2.07 trillion, accounting for 13.1% of the total cross-border RMB settlements. Of the total, goods trade accounted for CNY 613.4 billion, direct investment for CNY 224.4 billion, other investment for CNY 333.1 billion, and cross-border financing for CNY 313.2 billion. By the end of 2018, China had signed bilateral local currency swap agreements with 21 Belt and Road countries. China also established RMB clearing arrangements in 8 countries and RQFII pilot programs with 6 countries. Anecdotally, some Belt and Road countries who are exporters to China have invested in China's bond market.

The three strategies we have reviewed seem to resemble the historic events that propelled the global position of the US dollar. However, the change in the global narrative towards deglobalization will limit the space for the yuan to tap the global market. It does not mean that the yuan cycling does not function. But the most optimistic scenario will be the one where the renminbi becomes a benchmark currency in a trade bloc China can get hold of. The RMB can be a major currency but not a replacement for the US dollar in the deglobalized era.

4.4 Reserve Diversification[10]

4.4.1 China's Holding of US Dollar Assets

A major reason for China and many other emerging economies to allocate a large share of foreign reserve in the US dollar is to buffer against external shocks, because most of the cross-border transactions are denominated in the US dollar. Reducing the dollar exposure in trade and investment via internationalization of the RMB can break the loop. Once this constraint is relaxed, reserve managers can diversify their portfolio and perhaps allocate more to non-USD assets, which can be yield enhancing.

Another reason for China and some countries to consider diversification or de-dollarization is sanctioned risk. The US Treasury has an explicit scheme to enforce economic and trade sanctions based on US foreign policy and national security goals versus specific countries and regimes, terrorists, international narcotics traffickers, those engaged in activities related to the proliferation of weapons of mass destruction, and other threats to the national security, foreign policy, or the US economy, according to the Office of Foreign Assets Control (OFAC). Countries and companies who want to trade with the US need to comply with a list of the US' political considerations. At the heart of its US-centric sanction scheme is the access to the US dollar and related financial assets.

In the context of the current geopolitical condition, China's dollar exposure thus poses risk to its economic and financial interests. Aside from the trade dispute and the ban on the tech giant Huawei, the *Washington Post* reported in June 2019 that a US federal judge was investigating if three large Chinese banks had violated sanctions against North Korea, an allegation denied by the banks.[11] No matter what the outcome of the investigations, such media reports can trigger market concerns not only about the impact of financial penalties on the alleged parties but also their ability to wire and clear their dollar exposure.

---

[10]This section draws many insights and data analyses published in *ANZ Research: China Insight* (October 11, 2019). I am indebted to my co-authors Khoon Goh and Xing Zhaopeng.

[11]*Washington Post*. In first, U.S. appeals court upholds contempt fines against three Chinese banks in North Korean sanctions probe (July 30, 2019).

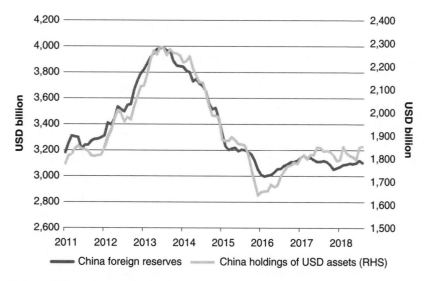

Figure 4.15 China's FX currency reserve and holdings of USD assets.
Sources: PBOC, TIC, ANZ Research China Insight, October 11, 2019

More recently, US officials were reportedly discussing ways to limit US portfolio flows into China. Although US Treasury officials have tried to curb speculation by suggesting that there are no concrete plans yet, such news headlines still present an event risk for financial market participants.

In July 2019, China's total FX reserves stood at USD 3.1 trillion (Figure 4.15). According to the data from the US Treasury, the holding of US Government securities by Mainland China was USD 1.1 trillion in the same month. This suggested that 35.8% of the total FX reserves was US Treasuries. However, this figure likely underestimated the total holding of China because the Chinese authorities also used overseas custodial accounts. ANZ Research (2019) found that the changes in China's FX reserves and the TIC data were weakly correlated statistically. Large monthly changes in China's reported UST holdings on some occasions also appeared at odds with the PBOC's net FX purchase figures or changes in the reserves (Figure 4.16).

To capture China's USD holding via an offshore custodian bank, market analysts also included Belgium's holdings as part of China's

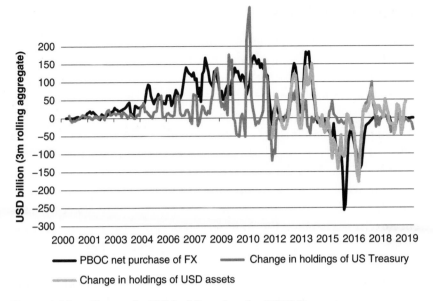

Figure 4.16   Change in FX holdings by the PBOC.
Sources: PBOC, ANZ Research: China Insight, October 11, 2019

portfolio. Brussels is where Euroclear Bank is located and is a key provider of securities settlement and custody services for State Administration of Foreign Exchange (SAFE). The US Treasury International Capital (TIC) holdings data showed that Belgium's holdings surged from USD 33.6 billion in June 2011 to USD 381.4 billion in the peak of March 2014, before a subsequent retreat. If the Belgian holdings of US Treasuries are added to China's reported direct holdings, total China's holdings of US debt should have been around 42.4% of its total FX reserves in July 2019. China also held other forms of long-term US securities, such as agency and corporate bonds, and possibly some equities. When these items were added to China's UST holdings as well as its official holdings of non-negotiable deposits and other US banking liabilities, the amount tracked the changes in the FX reserves very well. Total US dollar assets amounted to 59% of China's total FX reserves in June 2019. This figure was much lower than 79% in 1995. China's foreign reserve manager has clearly undergone a period of de-dollarization.

4.4.2 Alternative Assets

Sovereign wealth and foreign currency reserve are two separate concepts. In the case of China, the latter is a subset of the former. IMF guidelines only stipulate that the liquid foreign exchange assets of sovereign wealth funds or other separate investment entities controlled by the central government should be included in its data template on international reserves and foreign currency liquidity (IRFCL). Other foreign exchange activities are excluded, unless they pertain to the management of reserve assets. Also, the external assets have to be readily available to and controlled by monetary authorities for meeting balance of payments financing needs, for intervening in exchange markets to affect the currency exchange rate, and for other related purposes (such as maintaining confidence in the currency and the economy, and serving as a basis for foreign borrowing).

Investments made by the affiliates of China's SAFE could be more than liquid assets, but only liquid assets can be booked as reserve assets. SAFE has four investment entities overseas, commonly referred to as the four "Golden Flowers": Hua'an in Hong Kong, Huaxin in Singapore, Huaou in London, and Huamei in New York (Table 4.4). The State Council has allowed SAFE to invest no more than 5% of its reserves into equities. The four entities are reportedly affiliated with other offshore entities, such as Beryl Datura Investment, and Gingko Tree Investment which are involved in equity investment. In 2011, SAFE established a trading platform in Frankfurt, the year Belgium saw a jump in its UST holdings. Another relatively new investing vehicle is China Huaxin in Hong Kong, which reportedly made purchases of red-chip stocks in 2018. Based on public information, we could only identify USD 750 billion of invested funds. Since China's total foreign currency reserve was CNY 3.1 trillion, the rest should have been managed by other entities.

China's foreign currency reserve likely presented an incomplete picture of total foreign assets held by the government. China might still have reduced its US dollar holdings discreetly by moving its foreign holdings into alternative entities. China was experiencing net capital inflows via the current account, FDI, and net inflows of securities investment prior to 2015 (Figure 4.17). During that period, China's current account totaled USD 3.3 trillion, foreign direct investment comprised USD 1.85 trillion, and net inflows of securities investment reached USD

Table 4.4 Sources and investment of China's reserves in USD billions.

Investment		Source	
Beryl Datura Investment (曼陀罗: Cayman Islands)	150	Current account balance	3,270
Ginkgo Tree Investment (银杏树: UK)	unknown	Fixed direct investment (FDI)	1,843
SAFE Investment (华安公司: HK)	600	Securities investments	251
SAFE investment (华新公司: SG)	unknown	Other investments	−1,204
SAFE investment (华美公司: US)	unknown	Net errors and omissions	−1,058
SAFE investment (华欧公司: UK)	unknown		
SAFE Frankfort Office	unknown		
China Huaxin Investment (中国华馨: HK)	unknown		
Total	**3,102**	**Total**	**3,102**

Sources: Media, SAFE, ANZ Research: China Insight, October 11, 2019

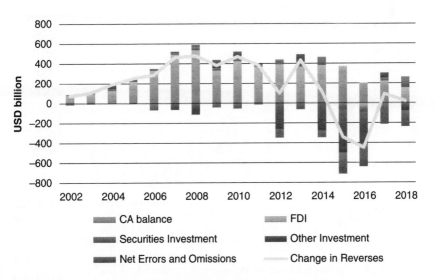

Figure 4.17 Changes in China's balance of payments.

Sources: SAFE, ANZ Research: China Insight, October 11, 2019

0.25 trillion. The sum of these three was USD 5.3 trillion. However, there were also two major outflows in the balance of payments: USD 1.2 trillion of "Other investments" and USD 1.1 trillion of "Net errors and omissions." When these two items were excluded from the gross total, the amount of accumulated FX reserves was USD 3.1 trillion, which coincided with the official foreign reserves figure (Figure 4.18).

It is possible that the USD 1.2 trillion of "Other investments" and USD 1.1 trillion of "Net errors and omissions" include some Chinese sovereign assets. In fact, deposits and loans accounted for the bulk of other investments in China's balance of payments. It may be related to China's engagement in multilateral development institutions (about USD 300 billion) and entrusted loans via state-owned banks, especially for Belt and Road (about USD 560 billion), because the years in which these outflows took place are 2012 and 2014–2016.

Aside from the above outflows, some offshore investments could also be categorized under "Net errors and omissions," especially as the below items are unclassifiable (see Table 4.5):

- Providing equity capitals for state-owned financial institutions via the Ministry of Finance (MOF). Since 2003, FX reserves have been

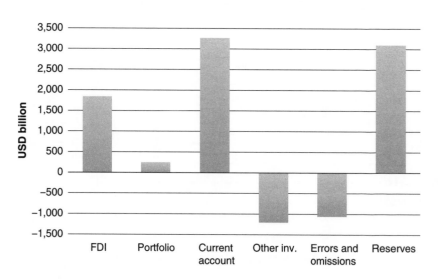

Figure 4.18 Accumulation of balance of payments 2001–2018.
Sources: SAFE, ANZ Research

Table 4.5 China's sovereign wealth.

Usage	Amount USD billion	Details
ASEAN 10+3 FX Reserves Repository	76.8	In 2009, China, Japan, South Korea, and ASEAN economies started a joint FX reserves repository of USD 120 billion, in which China contributed 32%. In 2012, the size of the repository doubled.
BRICS FX Reserves Repository	4.0	In 2013, BRICS established a joint reserves repository of USD 100 billion, in which China contributed USD 41 billion.
Inter-American Development Bank	0.35	In 2009, China joined the Inter-American Development Bank, with USD 0.35 billion shares.
IMF	93.0	In 2009 and 2012, China announced it bought IMF notes of USD 43 billion and USD 50 billion, respectively.
World Bank (WB)	16.0	In 2013, International Finance Corporation announced China participated in its Managed Co-Lending Portfolio Program with USD 3 billion. In 2015, China launched China-WB Partnership Fund of USD 50 million. In 2018, China increased its share in WB to 5.71%.
African Development Bank (AFDB)	2.6	China donated about USD 600 million to AFDB, ADF-11, and ADF-12. In 2014, PBOC signed the financing agreement with AFDB to establish the Africa Growing Together Fund of USD 2 billion.

(Continued)

Table 4.5   (Continued)

Usage	Amount USD billion	Details
China-Africa Development Fund	10.0	Started in 2007 with USD 5 billion. Increased to USD 10 billion in 2015.
China-LAC Cooperation Fund	10.0	Started in 2014 with USD 5 billion. Increased to USD 10 billion in 2015.
New Development Bank	20.0	In 2014, China provided USD 20 billion capital to NDB.
Asian Infrastructure Investment Bank	30.0	In 2015, China provided USD 30 billion capital to AIIB.
European Bank for Reconstruction and Development	2.4	As of 2017, China accounts 0.096% (EUR 1.7 billion) share of EBRC. It has contributed EUR 44 million to Chernobyl Shelter Fund and EUR 250 million to Equity Participation Fund.
Central Huijin	470.0	According to banks' financial statements, Central Huijin held equities worth USD 470 billion, as of 2017.
China Investment Corp	350.0	China injected USD 200 billion into CIC in 2007; USD 50 billion to CIC International in 2012; USD 100 billion into CIC Capital in 2015.
China-Africa and China-LAC Capacity Cooperation Funds	33.5	SAFE holds 80% and 85% of these two funds. They merged in 2019.
China Development Bank	48.0	In 2015, SAFE swapped part of its entrusted loans to equity.
EXIM Bank of China	45.0	In 2015, SAFE swapped part of its entrusted loans to equity.

Table 4.5 (Continued)

Silk Road Fund	6.5	In 2014, SAFE provided USD 6.5 billion as equity capital.
Buttonwood	7.5	As of 2018, Buttonwood and its subsidiaries Fengshan, Kunteng, and Jiyuan held domestic equity values of CNY 50 billion.
Hong Kong listed red-chips	8.4	As of June 2019, China Huaxin held HKD 65.1 billion of listed shares.
CNIC	29.97	As of 2017, CNIC has USD 33.3 billion assets in management; 90% belongs to China Huaxin.
FX entrusted loans	560	In 2019, PBOC announced Belt and Road investment had reached USD 90 billion of ODI and USD 600 billion of others. We assume 80% from SAFE.
Total	**1,861**	

Sources: Media, SAFE, ANZ Research China Insight, October 11, 2019

frequently injected into the balance sheets of state-owned banks, brokerages, and insurers, amounting to at least USD 470 billion as of 2018. In addition, the MOF established a high-profile sovereign entity, China Investment Corporation (CIC), with a capital of USD 200 billion in 2007. CIC's total assets under management rose to USD 940 billion in 2018.

- SAFE established Buttonwood, or Wutongshu Investment platform, in December 2014 and invested in China's Silk Road Fund. In August 2015, Buttonwood injected a combined USD 93 billion into China's two policy banks, including China Development Bank and the Export–Import Bank of China. The total market value of its holdings reached CNY50 billion by end-2018. However, Buttonwood also invested in the onshore stock market, which is not denominated in foreign currency.
- China Huaxin is the holding company (similar to Buttonwood) but focuses on the Hong Kong market.

These offshore investments can be called China's shadow reserves. The amount was estimated to be USD 1.86 trillion in historical value as of June 2019. This figure could explain partially the total amount in the "Other investments" and "Net errors and omissions" categories in China's balance of payments accounts, i.e. USD 2.2 trillion. However, it was still an explanation of the persistent discrepancy in China's balance of payment statistics, besides the usual suspect of underground outflows. The foreign investment position of the Chinese sovereign wealth (including SAFE, MOF, and other entities under the control of the State Council) was much larger than what the headline foreign currency reserves figure indicated.

These shadow reserves are not highly flexible or convertible, so they are not qualified FX reserves based on the IMF's definition. Undoubtedly, they will provide not only higher yields but also other powerful forms of reserves if the Chinese government liquidates them. Although we know very little about the geographical allocation of these investments, especially in equity, the ultimate asset holdings seem to be less in the US, but scattered across Europe, Hong Kong, and Belt and Road economies. From a broader perspective, the share of USD in China's sovereign wealth could be less than 59%.

There are several observations about China's reserve management. First, it has already maintained a lower share of US dollar assets compared with the world average. Moving away from dollar peg to a managed float exchange rate regime provides a greater flexibility in currency allocation. Secondly, China's sovereign wealth holding includes a large amount of non-liquid investments including equities and loans. These investments are often driven by strategic consideration rather than fulfilling balance of payments demand. Thirdly, China also uses its foreign reserve to support multinational organizations with a bias towards Belt and Road region. This seems to be motivated by a desire to lead the development of a trade bloc in the era of regionalization.

In the financial market, there has been a concern that China will reduce its holding of US Treasuries in order to retaliate against Trump's import tariff. However, our discussion in Chapter 2 offers another way to justify this action. China's investment in US dollar assets supports a factory-dollar recycling process that, in turn, results in the global imbalance. China's withdrawal from this loop will result in a positive adjustment of the US current account profile. If China and other countries buy fewer US Treasuries, the government will only rely on the Fed to make up the gap. By doing so, the Fed's balance sheet will expand. This accommodative monetary policy will likely press the US dollar to depreciate. Maybe this can help restore export competitiveness and close the current account deficits. Therefore, China's reserve diversification can be an alternative way to address China-US trade imbalance.

Chapter 5

A Race on the Digital Turf

5.1 Reform and Technology Independence

There is always a discrepancy between market perception of China's economic health and the Gross Domestic Product (GDP) number reported by the National Bureau of Statistics (NBS). The GDP figure is considered too smooth to reflect the corresponding changes in other economic statistics such as industrial value added. Many economists in the financial market decided to develop their own gauge of Chinese growth momentum. There is a slew of "China activity indices" published by research houses. Many indices are simply estimated by blending many high-frequency indicators through a principal component analysis or a regression. If there is a discrepancy between the index reading and GDP, analysts typically question the reliability of GDP data.

Price is supposed to reflect the underlying condition of supply–demand in economics. For a large economy like China, GDP data released 21 days after the quarter has ended is a poor gauge of economic activity. Instead, price movement can indicate if the economy is overheated or underutilized. In China, producer prices are largely determined by the free market, unlike many items of consumer price index (CPI), which are regulated by the government. In the past few years, the upturn and downturn of China's producer price index (PPI) certainly points to the movement of growth momentum. Statistically, the index is closely related to the Purchasing Managers Index (PMI), a monthly indicator gauging China's growth momentum cyclically.

China's impressive growth rate has become its own policy burden. In 2018, China celebrated the 40th anniversary of economic reforms. Between 1979 and 2018, the real GDP expanded at an annual average rate of 9.5%. In some years, China impressed the world with GDP growth as high as 15% (1984, 1992, 2007). Even in a gloomy year, China had still reported a growth rate of 3.8% (1990). Policymakers from the central government to the provincial governments used to believe in their obligation to deliver a good GDP number. In the advanced economies, central banks are often mandated to maintain price stability. In China, the government officials were expected to meet growth target. Local governments were accused of making up the growth number and affecting the quality of Chinese data (see Owyang and Shell 2017).

While data reliability is an endless topic in China research, the consensus view is that high-speed growth is no longer sustainable. An aggressive growth target is costly. China's consumption of natural resources in the post-global financial crisis (GFC) period has resulted in many social and environmental problems such as pollution. Excessive investments have turned into idle capacity. Deflationary pressure has been mounting. Lacking a major productivity breakthrough with a shrinking labor force, China could only boost growth through credit expansion. However, the rapid increase in debt combined with slowing marginal return would end up leading China into a financial crisis.

In view of population aging and overleveraging, productivity improvement is the only driver of growth. As the world enters an era of innovation and technology, China has also embraced the concept of German's Industry 4.0. The ambitious blueprint of Made in China 2025 has attracted much attention during the trade war.[1] The government

---

[1] Kania, E.B. (2019) Made in China 2025, explained. *The Diplomat*. February 1.

aims to lift the Chinese economy to a leading position by integrating all the emerging concepts like Big Data, 5G, robotics, and the Internet of Things into every economic sector. In 2012, the World Bank warned that China would fall into a middle-income trap. China must continue to push its tech capacity proactively.

The trade war puts China's tech push into an awkward situation. The US accuses China of forced technology transfer and stealing of intellectual property rights. Made in China 2025 is regarded by the US as a plan to acquire critical technology through unfair trade practice. But some observers fear that China would eventually rival the position of the United States, Germany, Japan, and Korea.[2] Meanwhile, China feels it has a right to develop technology and believes the US trade policy is to suppress China's rising. Hawkish measures by the US towards China's tech companies based on national security reasons have only reinforced China's belief in a "self-sufficiency" approach to tech development.

The reality is that China is wary of following the footsteps of Japan. The reform policy is to avoid a Chinese version of the Lost Decade. Indeed, many structural economic issues facing China today seem to replicate the Japanese situation in the 1990s: aging, Plaza Accord, property bubbles, inefficient Keiretsu, etc. Japan's loss of global leadership in memory chips following the semiconductor agreement with the US has taught China a lesson.[3] Since China sees the urgency to transform the economy before it is too late, the trade pressure from the US will only make China more determined to strive for "self-sufficiency" and tech-independence. To address the problem of structural economic slow-down, China is digitizing the country rapidly.

This chapter begins with a brief discussion of China's macroeconomic challenges. I argue that technological development is the only way for the country to beat the middle-income trap. I then provide an overview of China's push for digitizing the economy. This is a development strategy many countries are pushing through in order to stay competitive. China has already held a leading position in e-commerce and

---

[2] Laskai, L. (2018). Why does everyone hate Made in China 2025? [Blog post] Council on Foreign Relations Blog (March 28).

[3] Miller, C. (2019). A semiconducted tech war. *Foreign Policy.* July 1.

internet connectivity. Belt and Road becomes an opportunity to extend this connectivity globally. Along the theme of deglobalization and economic decoupling, this chapter concludes that the trade tension will inevitably become a technological rivalry between China and the US.

5.2 China's Structural Challenges

5.2.1 Demographic Challenge and Overleveraging

The financial market is currently learning a changing narrative of China's economic growth. The world's most populous country with 1.35 billion people used to have a nickname of "economic miracle." After the GFC, however, China's momentum has been fading too. The massive stimulus launched by the government had once boosted the GDP number for just a few years. But the growth rate has slowed in recent years. This is alarming, as China's GDP per capita still has a big gap compared with the advanced economies. As the guru in growth economics Robert Barro (2016) said, "From the perspective of conditional convergence, China's GDP growth rate since 1990 has been surprisingly high. However, China cannot deviate forever from the global historical experience, and the per capita growth rate is likely to fall soon from around 8% per year to a range of 3–4%."

Population used to be the foundation of China's economic success. When the country opened up its economy in 1979, the world was excited about the massive increase in labor supply. Influx of foreign capital began to support the industrialization story of the Chinese economy. In 1979, primary industry (e.g. agricultural and related) represented 31% of the total GDP. But the share declined to 7.2% in 2018. In the subsequent decades, rural lands were converted into industrial parks. Farmers were turned into factory or construction workers. Urbanization began in the Pearl River Delta and quickly expanded across the coastal provinces. After joining the World Trade Organization (WTO) in 2001, China's manufacturing sector further integrated into the global supply chains.

As the country enters the twenty-first century, the power of "population dividend" is running out of steam. In the past three years, the total labor force has continued to contract (Figure 5.1). The economy has increasingly felt the impact of the infamous one-child policy adopted in 1980. Fertility rates did not pick up despite the policy relaxation in 2016

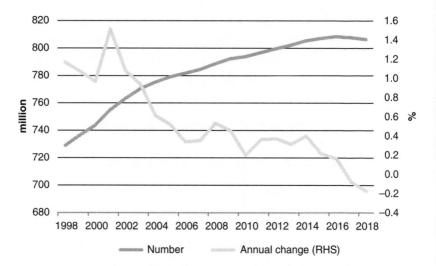

Figure 5.1   China's total labor force.

Source: National Bureau of Statistics

that allowed two children. China's demographic profile today resembles Japan's in early 2000s (Figure 5.2). This trend is irreversible. Wage rates have been rising quickly. According to the National Bureau of Statistics (NBS), the average wage of staff and workers reached CNY 76,121 in 2017, almost 100 times the level in 1980. China has passed the Lewis Turning Point where an economy no longer benefits from surplus rural labor (Das and N'Diaye 2013, Zhang et al. 2018).

Dissipation of the "population dividend" poses a challenge to China's conventional growth model. High national saving has been a unique characteristic of the Chinese economy. In the past, it was a key pillar to support its investment-led growth. However, according to the IMF's projection, China's savings rate will enter a declining track and will reach from the peak of 53% in 2008 to 40% by 2024 (Figure 5.3). This was the level before accession to the WTO. This trend has been closely related to the problem of aging population since 1980. While the fall in saving rate mirrors the increase in China's consumption economy, it also means China cannot push growth through massive investment.

Unfortunately, some policymakers continued to be enamored by previous success. The economic miracle of "double-digit" GDP growth rate became a curse in policymaking. Local officials and

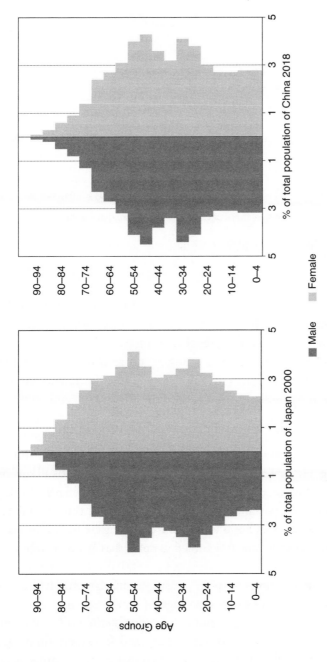

Figure 5.2 Population pyramid of China 2018 and Japan 2000.
Source: UN Population Statistics

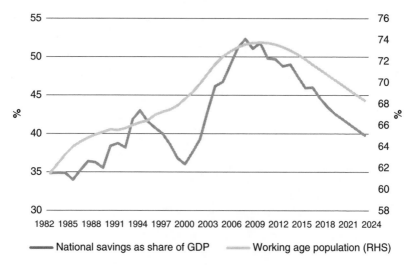

Figure 5.3 China's labor force and national saving rates.

Source: IMF projection

state-owned enterprises regarded the GDP "forecast" by political leaders as a hard target. There was a tendency for the government to exceed its growth forecast via a countercyclical policy.

The best way to illustrate this policy stance is to observe China's monetary policy decision. The reserve requirement ratio (RRR) of banks has been a popular policy tool of the PBOC because the country's monetary system has yet to come up with a single policy interest rate similar to the Fed fund rates in the United States. Cutting RRR effectively releases banks' liquidity and is a form of monetary policy easing. Historically, the PBOC lowered the RRR (Figure 5.4) when the gap between the actual GDP figure and the official target narrowed and vice versa. Same as other countries, the central bank tends to ease when there is an economic shortfall. But the obsession to high GDP growth rate has fueled a period of unstoppable credit expansion.

The flip side of monetary policy easing is debt growth. In 2009, the government launched a stimulus package of CNY 4 trillion in response to the sharp decline in growth momentum due to the GFC. Since then, the domestic banking system has seen a large and fast expansion of credit. According to BIS data, total credit to non-financial sector as a ratio of GDP has expanded from less than 150% in 2009 to 260% in 2019

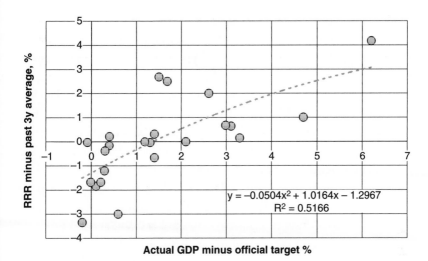

Figure 5.4 GDP growth gap and reserve requirement ratio (RRR).
Sources: NBS, PBOC

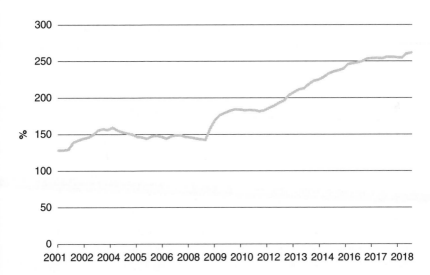

Figure 5.5 China's credit to non-financial sector as % of GDP.
Source: BIS

(Figure 5.5). This means that the growth rate of financial inputs has out-paced the increase in nominal GDP value. One yuan of additional credit has generated less and less nominal GDP. Since the nominal side lags behind the credit input, China is potentially falling into a liquidity trap.

Globally, a liquidity trap was often the consequence of a property sector collapse after a period of excessive investment (e.g. the US subprime crisis and Japan's Lost Decade). In China, the role of property investment in China's business cycle can be tracked by the close relationship between property prices and average inflation (as China's GDP data lacks variability). Monetary injection and loose housing policy inflated real estate value. Construction activity was vibrant. Wealth effect promoted household spending. Land sales revenue became a key source of local government revenue (about 40% share in 2018). Property investments became a key pillar of China's GDP growth. However, this property-led growth resulted in a mounting level of corporate and household debt. In 2018, total debt of Chinese households stood at 52.6% of GDP, 32 percentage points higher than in 2008 (Figure 5.6).

Excessive leveraging in an aging economy brews a perfect storm. As a result of the well-known economic event, the collapse of Japan's property market, the Lost Decade began in 1991. However, population aging and lack of growth driver resulted in a long period of low economic growth and deflation. Despite many years of aggressive monetary policy easing by Bank of Japan, the economy could not recover, and inflation failed to pick up, a phenomenon called liquidity trap. Lacking population

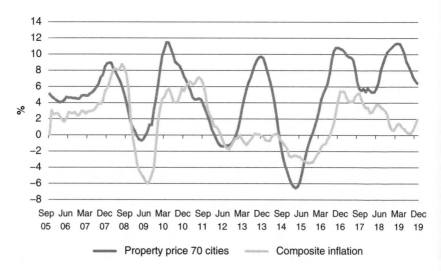

Figure 5.6   Inflation and property prices in China.

Source: National Bureau of Statistics

growth, house prices could not rebound. Since wages could not pick up, many households could not sustain their mortgage payments. Even though labor shortage could be considered a supply shock and can drive stagflation, i.e. slow growth, high inflation, the case of Japan suggests an aging population will likely engineer long-term deflation.

5.2.2 Supply-Side Structural Reforms

China was about to repeat the Japanese style of property collapse in 1991. In view of this, Xi Jinping's government kicked off a high-profile campaign of financial deleveraging by publishing an authoritative article in *People's Daily* on May 9, 2016. In 2015, the government began to adopt an economic policy package called supply-side structural reform (供给侧结构性改革), comprising five strategies to address the economic issues generated from the credit-fueled model: (1) Cutting production capacity; (2) reducing property inventory; (3) financial deleveraging; (4) cost saving; (5) fixing the weak segments – labeled in Chinese as "san qu yi jiang yi bu" (三去一降一补).

In a nutshell, the policy was to improve economic efficiency and abandon the old economic model. Cheap labor and easy credit became history. A financial intermediary was needed to make sure every yuan was invested into projects that could generate real value added. The authorities also launched a financial regulatory reform, aiming to tame the growing shadow banking activities, which were believed to have boosted financial bubbles. The whole package was not just a campaign of conventional economic tightening but a series of structural reforms.

This reform was consistent with Xi's call for changing the economy from quantity expansion to quality development. Under the Solow-Swan framework, we can interpret the policy preference of shifting from capital inputs to total factor productivity given the labor force constraint. Partly because of the US concern during the trade negotiation, the state's media replaced the name of Made in China 2025 with Created in China.[4] But the concept remains to upgrade the manufacturing sector, aiming to capture the high-value proportion of the chains that is currently dominated by the advanced economies.

---

[4] Xinhua, "From Made in China to Created in China", February 2, 2018 (http://www.xinhuanet.com/2018-02/02/c_1122359437.htm).

The shifting of a resource-driven approach to a technology-led development model is critical for China's sustainable growth. The World Bank warned that if the development model does not change, China could easily fall into a middle-income trap that will cap income growth (World Bank 2012). The Chinese Communist Party also set a goal to double GDP per capita in 2020 from the level in 2010. The political leadership remains keen to close the gap between China and the advanced economy. For China to beat the middle-income-ranking countries, bold reforms are needed to overcome the demographic challenge (Figure 5.7). Innovation and technology are key to break the trap.

In the nineteenth century, globalization was about the flows of goods. In the twentieth century, capital flows and labor mobility were a new phenomenon. But technological breakthrough in the last few decades has redefined the nature of the global value chain. Data flows become a hot property. As McKinsey (2016) wrote, "Soaring flows of data and information now generate more economic value than the global goods trade." In the digital era, data is a precious commodity. For China to repeat its recent success of e-commerce in manufacturing and even the agricultural industry, striving for critical technology that can master data business will define its global leadership. The path will be to

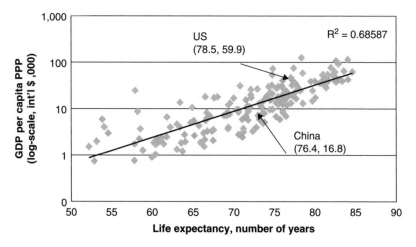

Figure 5.7 GDP per capita and life expectancy.
Source: World Bank

develop an economic infrastructure that enables automation and data exchange in manufacturing technologies and processes.

Made in China 2025 was evolved from the following backdrop. Launched by Premier Li Keqiang in 2015, this initiative was inspired by Germany's Industry 4.0 plan. But the Chinese version was put into a much broader macroeconomic context. Industry 4.0 is epitomized by the concept of a smart factory. At the micro level, the idea is to integrate information technology to manufacturing, using the Internet of Things to connect small and medium-sized firms along the global supply chain. The IoT can feed intelligence to producers, helping them customize products.

China escalates the idea to the national level, aiming to digitize the entire economy. Marr (2018) provided a "super easy explanation" of Industry 4.0: "When computers were introduced in Industry 3.0, it was disruptive thanks to the addition of an entirely new technology. Now, and into the future as Industry 4.0 unfolds, computers are connected and communicate with one another to ultimately make decisions without human involvement. A combination of cyber-physical systems, the Internet of Things and the Internet of Systems make Industry 4.0 possible and the smart factory a reality. As a result of the support of smart machines that keep getting smarter as they get access to more data, our factories will become more efficient and productive and less wasteful. Ultimately, it's the network of these machines that are digitally connected with one another and create and share information that results in the true power of Industry 4.0."

Made in China 2025 was an action plan to apply the smart factory concept in different industries. China planned to develop many innovative centers to support this development. One industry observer noted that the US government also established several Institutes for Manufacturing Innovation, a concept similar to Chinese innovation centers. In a sense, Made in China 2025, Industry 4.0, and America's National Network for Manufacturing Innovation (NNMI) all reflect government activism in their industrial policy.[5] From the Chinese perspective, proactive industrial policy is the best way to address the structural problem facing the economy.

---

[5] MAPI Foundation. The Internet of Things: Industrie 4.0 vs. the Industrial Internet (July 23, 2015). (https://mapifoundation.org/economic/2015/7/23/the-internet-of-things-industrie-40-vs-the-industrial-internet).

5.3 China's Digital Economy

5.3.1 Digitalization and Structural Rebalancing

China is seeing digitalization as an opportunity for its structural reforms in two ways. First, rapid adoption of Industry 4.0 across all sectors will enhance the total factor productivity of the economy. Data flows will drive not only massive gain in cost efficiency but also quality improvement via customized solution on a need basis. For example, Chinese mobile phone shoppers can order customized T-shirts with door-to-door delivery within 48 hours or even quicker. Second, the size of China's market facilitates a scale advantage for the development of technology industry. This applies not only to the famous Internet giants, i.e. Baidu, Alibaba, Tencent (BAT), but also device makers (e.g. Huawei, Xiaomi) and telecommunication service providers (e.g. China Mobile, Unicom). Scale is China's digital advantage.

Interestingly, China's digital success contrasts its ranking in some global league tables. The World Bank's Digital Adoption Index ranks China 50th out of 131 countries in 2016 and 36th out of 62 in the Fletcher School Digital Evolution Index in 2017. Another league table, the World Economic Forum's Networked Readiness Index, placed China 59th out of 139 economies in 2016. This mediocre ranking contrasts the general perception of the world's biggest cashless country in which the daily lives of a plumber in Beijing and a farmer in Henan already relies on their handheld devices. With the 5G mobile network rolling out across the country, perhaps China's ranking will have climbed.

The digital economy has been growing fast. Penetration of mobile devices in the Chinese population can be a good proxy measure (Figure 5.8). According to the estimation of China Academy of Information and Communications Technology (CAICT), the size of digital economy reached CNY 31.3 trillion in 2018 with an annual growth rate of 15.1% in nominal terms. Its share in GDP rose to 34.8% from 32.9%.[6] A report by the IMF (Zhang and Chen 2019) showed that this

---

[6] China Academy of Information Communication and Technology. White Paper on China's digital economic and employment development (中国数字经济发展与就业白皮书2019年).

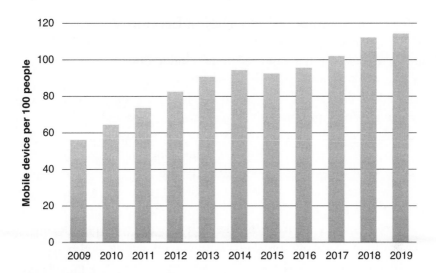

Figure 5.8 Mobile device penetration in China.

Source: Ministry of Industry and Information Technology

level of digitalization was still below the level of the U.S. (59%) and Japan (46%). However, a US Bureau of Economic Analysis (BEA) report estimated that the size of digital economy was only 6.7% of the US GDP. Apparently, there lacks a global standard for measuring the size of digital economy. International comparison remains difficult and controversial.

The digital economy can be narrowly measured as the direct contribution of digital-related industries, comprising software, hardware, and ICT services, or the organic growth of these industries as a sector. In 2018, the value of this sector was CNY 6.41 trillion, just 4% higher than the figure in 2017, according to CAICT's estimate. Telecommunication revenue, for example, was underperforming, registering only 3% increase in revenue. Measured in terms of data transmission, however, the growth was spectacular. Mobile internet traffic was 71.1 GB, up by 189.1%. In manufacturing, the value added of ICT products rose 13.1%, much higher than total industrial value added of 6.9%. Since the export of electronic products was affected by the ongoing trade war, the outlook of hardware manufacturing was seen to have limited upside in the near term.

Expressed in GDP, the value added of digital industry was outperforming. By industry breakdown, the GDP of Information Communication,

Software and Information Technology Services rose 30.7% in real terms in 2018, representing 3.6% of China's total GDP. In fact, the GDP figure of this sector has reported double-digit growth in recent years. In secondary industry, Electronics and ICT Manufacturing registered a value added increase of 13.1% in 2018. This figure comprised the manufacturing of ICT products (13.8%), electronic parts and semiconductor (13.2%), electronic products (14.5%), and computers (9.5%). All these growth rates were expressed in real value added and were higher than China's GDP growth of 6.6% in 2018 (Figure 5.9).

If we take a broader perspective, the digital economy also includes the level of technological adoption and commercialization in conventional industries. CAICT estimates that the technological content is the biggest driver of China's economic digitalization, representing almost 79.5% of the total in 2018. In 2018, shares of digital economy by segments were 18.3% in manufacturing, 35.9% in services, and 7.3% in agriculture. In fact, shares in the service sector rose more quickly than the secondary industry and agriculture in 2018 with the respective figures of 3.3ppt, 1.1ppt, and 0.7ppt, consistent with the view that e-commerce and fintech are the strength of China's digitalization.

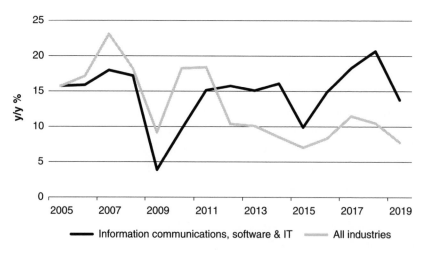

Figure 5.9   GDP of IT industry.

Source: NBS

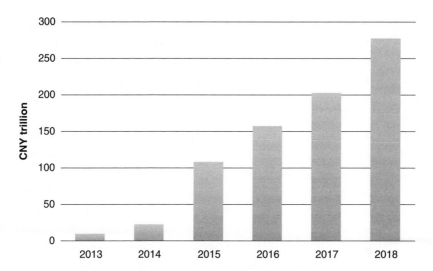

Figure 5.10 China's electronic payments via mobile devices.

Source: PBOC

According to McKinsey (2019), China's online retail sales was estimated to have reached USD 1.5 trillion in 2019, compared with USD 600 billion of the US. The size was larger than the next 10 markets combined. Alibaba announced a better-than-expected sales revenue of USD 16.7 billion in Q3 2019, up 40% from the previous year.[7] A comparison with its global rival Amazon indicated that Alibaba's commerce revenue has been catching up closely with the US-based global giant.[8]

Fintech has been an enabler of digital services in China. Mobile payments have taken the center stage. According to the PBOC, transaction volume of mobile payments reached CNY 277.4 trillion (USD 41.51 trillion) in 2018, increased by more than 28 times from the level in 2013 (Figure 5.10). By the end of 2018, 424 commercial banks and 115 payment institutions were connected to NetsUnion Clearing Corp., an online clearing platform backed by the central bank.

---

[7] *Nikkei Asia Review.* November 6, 2019 (https://asia.nikkei.com/Business/China-tech/Alibaba-defends-No.1-position-in-China-s-e-commerce-market).

[8] *Forbes.* September 24, 2019. (https://www.forbes.com/sites/greatspeculations/2019/09/24/is-alibaba-really-the-amazon-of-china/#2841456612c0).

E-commerce has been a driver of China's consumption. The NBS data showed that online retail sales reached CNY 9 trillion or USD 1.33 trillion in 2018, an increase of 24% compared with 2017. About 24% of total retail sales in China was done online in 2018. As a comparison, the US Department of Commerce data indicated that consumers spent USD 534 billion online in 2018, an increase of 13.6% from 2017. The share of e-commerce in total retail sales in the US was only 9.9% in 2018. In the same year, China's total retail sales grew 9.0%, compared with the US annual growth of 4.7%. This suggested that the online platforms drove the outperformance of China's total consumption. From a macroeconomic perspective, digitalization facilitated China's transformation from an investment-led to a consumption-led economy.

One unique advantage in China's digital transformation is scale. According to the data of a pseudo government organization, China had 854 million internet users as of June 2019.[9] This translated into the internet penetration rate of 61.2%. Mobile phone users accounted for 99.1% of internet users, up 0.5ppt. The scale advantage of China is also magnified by economy of scope in the "digital ecosystems." Social media platforms like WeChat play a central role. Consumer analytics teams can monetize the behavioral and transaction data into valuable insight. According to the 2017 McKinsey Chinese iConsumer Survey, 31% of WeChat users shopped on the platform in 2017, more than doubling the level in 2015 (13%) and 83% of internet users used online to offline (O2O) services doubling that in 2015 (41%).

E-commerce business benefits from big data. According to an interview with Tencent senior executives, the social media giant can identify "what type of celebrities does an individual follow, what stores do they prefer, what games are they a fan of, which sports teams are they passionate about, which news topics matter to them, and so on. These tags then enable a more detailed understanding of a consumer's entire life. Unlike survey-based data, which is based on what consumers say, this first-party data enables companies to understand actual behavior."[10]

---

[9] Xinhua. August 30, 2019. (http://www.xinhuanet.com/english/2019-08/30/c_138351278.htm).

[10] *Forbes.* January 9, 2018. (https://www.forbes.com/sites/kimberlywhitler/2018/01/09/how-tencent-is-using-closed-loop-data-to-drive-better-insight-and-engagement/#84b47391f0dd).

Continuous urbanization in China offers a promising outlook for China's digitalization. Densely populated cities provide further spatial advantage for digital service. At present, 60% of the population live in urban areas. Instead of expanding the megacities, China is adopting a new urbanization strategy called city clustering. That is, the government plans to bundle a group of cities by building efficient transportation. Famous city clustering plans in the pipeline are Beijing–Tianjin–Hebei, Shanghai–Jiangsu–Zhejiang–Anhui, and Greater Bay Area in Guangdong–Hong Kong–Macau. These projects are expected to expand city lifestyle to surrounding countries. The expanded scale of urban will boost the online-to-offline (O2O) consumption model.

The strength of manufacturing industry provides external benefits to the national development of digitalization. China's factory can produce handheld devices quickly and cheaply. Besides the global names like Huawei or Xiaomi, there are also other domestic brands that can offer low-cost options for average households. This enables China to increase the penetration of mobile data services. According to GSMA Intelligence, an industry research organization, the number of smartphone connections in China surpassed 1 billion at the end of 2018.[11] Thanks to the trade tension with the US, the rise of nationalism boosted the sales of local brands, which were price competitive. Huawei alone was targeting 50% of mobile phone market share domestically.[12]

Within China, CAICT found a positive correlation between the growth of digital economy and GDP growth. This finding suggests that digitalization can be used to address regional inequalities. Guizhou is an example. This province used to be one of the poorest in China. But the province has felt the government's promotion of the digital economy with very proactive investment policy. In 2018, the province registered a GDP growth of more than 9% with the growth of digital economy expanding 24%. Big data has contributed more than 20% of

---

[11] GSMA. The Mobile Economy China 2019. March 2019. (https://www.gsma.com/mobileeconomy/china/).

[12] *South China Morning Post.* March 15, 2019. (https://www.scmp.com/tech/big-tech/article/3001799/huawei-targets-50-cent-smartphone-market-share-china-way-wresting).

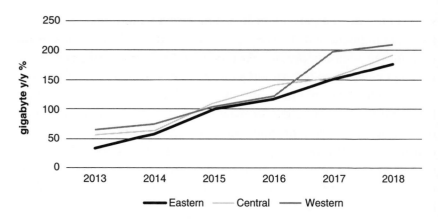

Figure 5.11   Data traffic of mobile network by region in China.
Source: Data from MIIT

Guizhou's economic growth with over 9,500 big data-related enterprises operating in the province, including global names like Apple, Microsoft, Dell, Alibaba, Huawei, Tencent, and China News Service.[13] Guizhou is attractive to data center investors because of its stable temperature, offering a hardware-friendly environment to the operation of data centers. Data traffic in the western region has grown faster than other regions in recent years, suggesting the faster growth of IT-related activity in the western region (Figure 5.11). This development can help improve the income gap between poorer provinces and the richer coastal region.

China's manufacturing sector has been hit by the trade war, leading to an increasing concern about the employment situation. However, digitalization seems to provide a timely solution to alleviate the job pressure. The digital economy sustained 191 million jobs in China, representing 24.6% of total employment and an annual increase of 11.5%. The increase in digitalization is associated with employment creation in primary, secondary and tertiary sectors. In particular, the rising digitalization added 16.6% of jobs in the services sector and 20.9% in the primary sector in 2018. The faster rate of job creation in these two

---

[13] *China Daily.* June 24, 2019. (http://www.chinadaily.com.cn/a/201906/24/WS5d1099a9a3103dbf14329ed2.html).

sectors increases the capacity to absorb the surplus labor from the manufacturing industry, which has been affected by the trade war. This trend is consistent with the overall theme of structural rebalancing in China, i.e. building a larger share of service sector in the economy.

There has been an impression that digitalization will replace human labor and is negative to employment. Bloom et al. (2018) studied the outlook of global employment through to 2030 and expressed some concerns about the impact of digitalization. Industrial robotic, 3D printers and diagnostic tools based on machine learning, algorithms that write reports and newsflashes, and robots in the service sector are all likely to have an effect on future employment. The negative impact would be bigger in advanced economies as higher wages and an aging population have motivated the automation. Similar to the "downside" of globalization, this substitution effect brought by technological development could trigger protectionism.

However, this era of digitalization likely differs from previous substitution between human and machine. This new form of data-driven transformation is not solely a cost reduction scheme but also a way to create new demand, representing an "income effect." Many products and services that were previously unavailable and unfathomable to society, are now made possible. Modern e-commerce establishes an ecosystem that facilitates the participation of SMEs and freelance. *China Daily* states: "Renmin University estimated that Alibaba created about 40.82 million jobs in 2018, representing an annual increase of 10.9%. The job growth from its e-commerce platforms provided about 15.58 million jobs." It also increased the demand for professionals in upstream and downstream sectors like R&D, design, manufacturing, and logistics, estimated to be about 25.24 million.[14]

Compared with the manufacturing industry, the service sector has a higher level of digitalization in China (Figure 5.12). Insurance tops the list with 56.4%, followed by the movie and entertainment industries. Insurance companies are actively exploring opportunities to employ big data technology in underwriting. Mobile technology also makes the claim procedure more efficient. For example, the Ping An insurance

---

[14] *China Daily.* February 28, 2019. (http://www.chinadaily.com.cn/a/201902/28/WS5c774c6da3106c65c34ebee3.html).

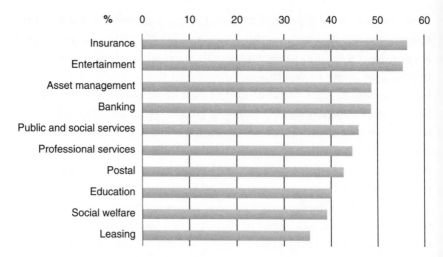

Figure 5.12 Digitalization level in different services industries in China 2018.

Source: Data from CAICT

company can provide an almost real-time estimate of indemnity for a damaged vehicle.[15] Compared with primary and secondary industries, financial industry can reap the benefit of information communications easily because it does not require physical delivery. Digitalization addresses some structural inefficiencies in many service industries and to some extent benefits the macroeconomic reforms.

The intrusion of fintech into banking is another example. In the past, China's banking system was criticized as a protected industry. Prior to the interest rate liberalization of which deposit and lending interest rates were fixed by the PBOC, banks enjoyed a guaranteed net interest margin. Depositors were looking for alternative investment such as property investment or accepting a low deposit interest rate.

Alibaba offered a business model that took advantage of this inefficiency, and launched Yu'ebao in June 2013, providing yield enhancing services for retail consumers linking to Alibaba's Taobao and other e-commerce platforms. By collecting a mass of small amounts retained in Alipay's mobile wallets, Yu'ebao quickly became a large money market

---

[15] *Fortune.* July 22, 2019 (https://fortune.com/longform/ping-an-big-data/).

fund, named the Tianhong Fund, and offered a higher return to the online investors. Within a month after its launching, the fund had already accumulated 4 million investors with an aggregate fund size of CNY10 billion. The assets under management (AUM) of Tianhong Yu'E Bao hit an historical high of USD 250 billion in March 2018, one of the world's largest money market funds by AUM. The rapid growth of fund size triggered regulatory concern. In subsequent years, China's financial authorities tightened the regulation and released some macroprudential measures. The AUM under Tianhong declined to USD 168 billion by the end of 2018.

Digitalization in the service sector also helps lift worker productivity subtly. Didi Kuaidi, which is a merged entity of two previously separate taxi-hailing applications, Didi Dache and Kuaidi Dache, offers a new business model that can increase worker productivity. According to the study of this ride-hailing application company, white-collar workers living in China's megacities, namely Beijing, Guangzhou, Shenzhen, and Shanghai, lost a lot of work time due to traffic congestion. The cost ranged between CNY 7,972 and CNY 6,324 per person in the four cities.[16] In another study, the traffic jams were costing Beijing CNY 70 billion per year in lost productivity. The ride-sharing and bicycle-sharing business models can reduce the number of cars on the road and improve traffic.

5.3.2 China's Tech Policy

In October 2017, Xi Jinping elaborated his "Thought on Socialism with Chinese Characteristics for a New Era" at the 19th Congress of the Communist Party of China (CPC).[17] According to his plan, China should realize socialist modernization in the first stage from 2020 to 2035, before developing China into a "great modern socialist country" that is "prosperous, strong, democratic, culturally advanced, harmonious and beautiful" after another 15 years. There are a set of social and economic goals

---

[16] *China Daily*. January 20, 2016. (https://www.chinadaily.com.cn/china/2016-01/20/content_23169275.htm).

[17] Xinhua. October 18, 2017. (http://www.xinhuanet.com/english/2017-10/18/c_136688933.htm).

Xi wants China to achieve by 2035. Specifically, he envisaged that "China's economic and technological strength has increased significantly. . . . China has become a global leader in innovation." In the second phase, the goal is for China "to reach a new height in every dimension of material, political, cultural and ethical, social, and ecological advancement by the middle of the 21st century. China has become a global leader in terms of composite national strength and international influence."

This New Era plan attempts to chart a course for China to attain a stage similar to the US today or the UK in the nineteenth century. The plan is ambitious but is not impossible. First, China has the track record of being a fast-growing country. It took just four decades growing from one of the poorest countries to the second-largest economy in the world. Another 30 years seems to be a reasonable timeframe by linear projection. Secondly, the US also took over the helm from Great Britain during the interwar period. The former was number two in the world setting. The number two today should also be the next in the pecking order.

The "China Dream" is to boost China's innovative capacity and technology leadership. The blueprint is more ambitious than just a plan for building bigger e-commerce. China has firmly established its position as the world factory that can deliver quality product in scale. But it is still largely a contracted manufacturer. Digitalization in the secondary industry is still lagging behind. Of 126 economies, China ranked 17th in the Global Innovation Index in 2018.[18] However, in the Innovation Input sub-index, the ranking was 27th, lower than its Asian tech peers, namely, Japan (12th) and Korea (14th). In the global supply chain, China is unequivocally strong in the downstream. But it has yet to find a position in the upstream.

The Chinese government is actively preparing the country to strive for digital leadership. Many local governments have also drafted plans to boost their digital economy (Table 5.1). Twenty-one provinces have already launched relevant documents on digital developments. Many local government plans are working around the timeframe of Made in China 2025. Several local authorities are coordinating their efforts to develop digital economy at the regional level. For instance, Beijing–Tianjin–Hebei are developing a Comprehensive Pilot Zone for big

---

[18] World Intellectual Property Organization. Global Innovation Index 2018. (https://www.wipo.int/edocs/pubdocs/en/wipo_pub_gii_2018.pdf).

Table 5.1   Local government plans for developing the digital economy.

	Date	Latest major provincial / city government documents
Inner Mongolia	Jan 11, 2019	Digital Inner Mongolia Construction and Development Plan 2018–25 (Consultation paper)
Jilin	July 7, 2018	Opinion on Digital-led Industrial Transformation to Promote High Quality Development
Zhejiang	Sep 14, 2018	A Plan for Doubling Digital Economy in Five Years
Anhui	Oct 23, 2018	Notification of Supporting Measures for the Development of Digital Economy
Fujian	Sep 21, 2018	Administration Measures for Designated Fund for the Development of Digital Economy
Jiangxi	Feb 18, 2019	Opinion on Digital Economy Development Strategy
Shandong	Mar 13, 2019	Digital Shandong Action Plan 2019
Guangdong	Apr 10, 2018	Digital Economy Development Plan 2018–25 (Consultation paper)
Guangxi	Sep 17, 2018	Digital Economy Development Plan 2018–25
Sichuan	Nov 16, 2018	Opinion on Expediting Deep Integration of Digital Economy and Real Economy
Guizhou	Jun 21, 2018	Opinion on Expediting Digital Guizhou Through Big Data, Cloud Computing, AI Innovation Development
Yunnan	Feb 19, 2019	Notification of the Establishing the Office for Digital Yunnan
Shannxi	Apr 17, 2018	Key Measures for Digital Economy 2018
Gansu	Jun 1, 2018	Dedicated Action Plan for the Development of Information Technology Industry

(Continued)

Table 5.1   (Continued)

	Date	Latest major provincial / city government documents
Qinghai	Oct 16, 2018	Taskforce for Digital Economy in Qinghai
Changchun	Jul 27, 2018	Opinion on Promoting Digital Economy for Reviving Rusty Industry
Hangzhou	Oct 9, 2018	Action Plan for Three Digital Integrations for Pushing Hanzhou Country's Leading Position in Digital Economy 2018–22
Fuzhou	Jul 10, 2018	Seven Measures to Develop Digital Economy
Jinan	Jan 9, 2019	Measures to Promote Advanced Manufacturing and Digital Economy
Nanning	Nov 23, 2018	Digital Economy Development Plan 2018–20
Chengdu	Mar 1, 2018	Implementation Plan for Developing Digital Economy

Source: CAICT

data. In the Yangtze River Delta, Shanghai, Jiangsu, Zhejiang, and Anhui have agreed to develop IoT, big data, AI, and the semiconductor industry under the roof of the Action Plan for Yangtze River Delta (YRD) Regional Integration 2018–20. There is a plan to develop a regional coverage of 5G network, which will be a critical infrastructure for high-volume data transmission. In fact, the Yangtze River Delta Economic Region is the largest digital economy within China with a size of CNY 8.6 trillion, followed by Pearl River Delta Region of CNY 4.3 trillion.

China is also seen to have boosted research and development, with spending 70% higher in 2017 than in 2012. In fact, 86% of China's "unicorns" appeared between 2014 and 2017 and a vast sum of venture capital was pledged into the tech sector during the same period.[19] Tech giants are investing heavily in research centers, laboratories, and

---

[19] Matthews Asia. China's Growing Stable of Unicorns. November 2018. (https://us.matthewsasia.com/resources/docs/pdf/Perspectives/Unicorns.pdf).

incubators focusing on artificial intelligence, robotics, and big data. Abundant financial resources enable high-value businesses being funded faster than anywhere else in the world. As of February 2018, China ranked second behind the US in terms of its number of unicorns – privately held startup companies valued at USD 1 billion or more. McKinsey (2017) also cites China's activism in tech acquisition offshore. Outbound venture capital totaled USD 38 billion in 2014–16, representing 14% of global total excluding China, up from 4% in 2011–13. About 80% of investment went to advanced economies, and approximately 75% was spent on digital-related sectors. China's influence in the global startup market has grown rapidly.

The term 5G has been repeatedly mentioned in the discussion of digitalization. 5G is the fifth generation of mobile broadband that will eventually replace the current standard of 4G LTE connection. 5G is expected to push the speed of data transmission 100 times faster than 4G. The technology also reduces network latency, which is the time for devices to respond. Reducing latency has great impact on the velocity of data transmission. 5G reduces the time of inter-device connectivity. This upgraded network will enable faster download and upload speeds. Therefore, 5G can support instant access to many more services and applications that are not available today. According to the Global System for Mobile Communications Association (GSMA), global 5G coverage is projected to reach 15% by 2025 (Figure 5.13). CCS Insight projects that China is set to take an early lead in 5G. By 2025, it will account for more than 40% of global total 5G connections.[20]

5G will spur a quantum jump of mobile network transmission and generate a tremendous amount of economic value. IHS Markit (2017) described 5G as a new class of technology similar to steam engine and electricity that will transform different industries profoundly (see Figure 5.14). The 5G value chain will generate USD 3.5 trillion in output and 22 million jobs in 2035. From 2020 to 2035, the economic contribution of 5G to the world economy will be equivalent to the size

---

[20] CCS Insight. Press release October 18, 2017 (https://www.ccsinsight.com/press/company-news/3240-ccs-insight-predicts-1-billion-users-of-5g-by-2023-with-more-than-half-in-china/).

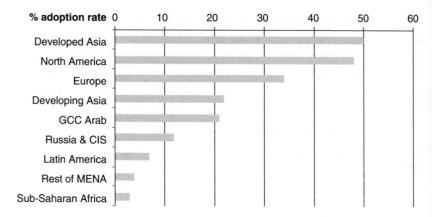

Figure 5.13 Projected 5G connections in the world by 2025.
Source: GSMA

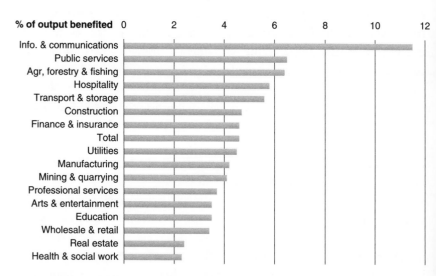

Figure 5.14 Impact of 5G on different industries 2035.
Source: IHS 2017

of India's GDP. By 2035, 4.6% of global real output will be associated with 5G deployment.

The economics of 5G follows the strand of study on technology adoption in the presence of network externalities (Katz and Shapiro 1986).

The positive (or negative) network effect means that an additional user of goods or services can increase (or decrease) the value of other members in the network. This concept is a variation of increasing return to scale, which is based on an additional unit of the same input. Network externalities creates value through bringing in new members. The value of a national mobile network increases at an increasing rate as more countries are covered. Empirically, researchers also find that positive externalities are present in central clearing service for electronic payments (Gowrisankaran and Satvins 2004).

China appears to take a leading position in 5G network. CAICT estimates that 5G will directly generate CNY 6.3 trillion of output or CNY 2.9 trillion in value added terms by 2030. The indirect economic value-added is estimated to be CNY 3.6 trillion. One observer sees that "The rollout of 5G networks will mean a very different Internet. 5G or fifth generation mobile telecommunications is set to connect a vast global network of sensors, robots, and autonomous vehicles through sophisticated artificial intelligence (AI) and machine learning. Underlying the story of 5G is the rise of Asia and particularly China in the broad transformation of the post-American world."[21]

China's 5G plan reflects the government's belief in connectivity as a source of economic growth. The country is proud of its national coverage of high-speed train network. Since 2008, China has put into operation over 25,000 kilometers of dedicated high-speed railway lines, far more than the total high-speed lines operating in the rest of the world. The World Bank has studied the economic benefit of this project in China and found that "The rate of return of China's network as of 2015 is estimated at 8%, well above the opportunity cost of capital in China and most other countries for major long-term infrastructure investments. Benefits include shortened travel times, improved safety and facilitation of labor mobility, and tourism. High-speed networks also reduce operating costs, accidents, highway congestion, and greenhouse gas emissions as some air and auto travelers switch to rail." High-speed

---

[21] *Forbes.* April 5, 2019. (https://www.forbes.com/sites/danielaraya/2019/04/05/huaweis-5g-dominance-in-the-post-american-world/#5972d14c48f7).

railway network is an important infrastructure promoting people or human capital flows. Likewise, 5G is expected to enhance productivity growth through a super network for data flows.

Data connectivity also echoes Xi Jinping's Belt and Road initiative that emphasizes an inclusive economic cooperation with a network of countries.[22] The official release states that "The initiative aims to promote orderly and free flow of economic factors, highly efficient allocation of resources and deep integration of markets by enhancing connectivity of Asian, European and African continents and their adjacent seas.... The plan called for policy coordination, facilities connectivity, unimpeded trade, financial integration and people-to-people bonds to make complementary use of participating countries' unique resource advantages through multilateral mechanisms and multilevel platforms."

Some Western-based think tanks are worried about China's increasing spending on Digital Silk Road from a national security perspective (Figure 5.15). Mercator Institute of China Studies (2019) pointed out that Chinese entities have provided more than USD 17 billion for Digital Silk Road projects completed since 2013, comprising USD 7 billion in fiber-optic and telecommunication network and USD 10 billion in e-commerce and mobile payment deals. In late 2017, Huawei Marine partnered with the Pakistani authorities to start a project called the Pakistan East Africa Cable Express, which will connect Pakistan to Kenya and Djibouti.[23] Chinese tech firms are spearheading efforts to develop 5G networks and cloud computing intended for Southeast Asian markets, citing that Huawei launched its 5G test bed in Thailand, the first one in Southeast Asia,[24] and Alibaba Cloud opened a second data center in Indonesia.[25]

---

[22] China Government. Press release (March 28, 2015).

[23] Chan, J.H. (2019). China's Digital Silk Road: A game changer for Asian economies. *The Diplomat*. April 30.

[24] *South China Morning Post*. February 8, 2019. (https://www.scmp.com/news/asia/southeast-asia/article/2185465/thailand-launches-huawei-5g-test-bed-despite--us-calls).

[25] Stratfor. August 16, 2019. (https://worldview.stratfor.com/article/follow-digital--silk-road-5g-china-vietnam).

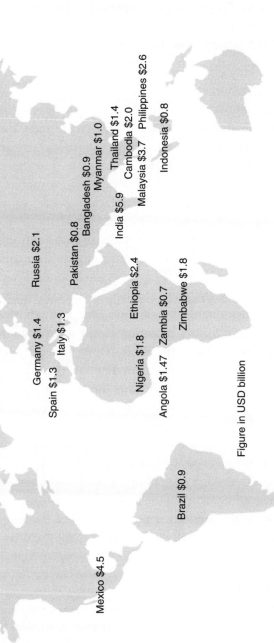

Figure 5.15 China's spending on Digital Silk Road estimated by RWR.
Source: Bloomberg Businessweek, January 10, 2019, citing data of RWR Advisory Group

5.4 The Tech Rush and the Little Chips

5.4.1 Forced Technology Transfer

China's proactive stance in developing the digital economy has obviously drawn much attention from the Western media. In June 2019, UK's BBC produced a video called "How a trade war became a tech war," describing how the rivalry of the United States and China in economic supremacy has shifted to attacking each other's tech industries.[26] The *South China Morning Post*, a Hong Kong-based newspaper, wrote that "The United States and China are competing for supremacy in the suite of advanced technologies that will affect the means of future economic production. The US efforts to curtail China's access to American technology are threatening to unravel decades of globalization and interdependent supply chains and raising the risk of a confrontation that has been likened to a new cold war."[27]

At the beginning of the trade conflict, the official media in China was very careful in wording the event. After several rounds of unsuccessful negotiation, the authorities began to accept this common description. "Trade war" was used in the White Paper issued by Ministry of Commerce issued in June 2019[28] when Trump's government decided to escalate the conflict by compiling the "Entity List," i.e. prohibiting US companies from transactions with the companies on the list. In the technology issue, the Chinese government has downplayed the issue of Huawei during the trade negotiation. The authorities were still cautious in positioning the technological relationship with the United States.

In the trade war, the US alleged that China was practicing "forced technology transfer," i.e. foreign companies investing in China were required to share their intellectual property with a Chinese domestic partner. The US complained that China's FDI policy and laws enabled

---

[26] BBC. June 20, 2019. (https://www.bbc.com/news/av/business-48708491/how-a-trade-war-became-a-tech-war).

[27] *South China Morning Post*. February 29, 2019. (https://www.scmp.com/topics/us-china-tech-war).

[28] China Ministry of Commerce. Press release. June 5, 2019. (http://images.mofcom.gov.cn/lgj/201906/20190605184244727.pdf).

the local partners to steal foreign advanced technology. In the language of the WTO, the question is whether the Chinese government exercises any measure that mandates the sharing of intellectual property in a way that violates WTO rules, as technology transfer is an issue under The Agreement on Trade-Related Aspects of Intellectual Property Rights (TRIPS). Article 7 of the TRIPS Agreement states that "the protection and enforcement of intellectual property rights should contribute to the promotion of technological innovation and to the transfer and dissemination of technology, to the mutual advantage of producers and users of technological knowledge and in a manner conducive to social and economic welfare, and to a balance of rights and obligations."[29]

In August 2017, the US kicked off a Section 301 investigation into "whether China's acts, policies, and practices related to technology transfer, intellectual property, and innovation are unreasonable, unjustifiable, or discriminatory and burden or restrict U.S. commerce." Under the US Trade Act of 1974, the US can conduct investigations into allegedly unfair trade practices of other countries and form a procedural basis for further actions. Based on the investigation result on China's trade practice, Trump's administration endorsed a series of proposed Section 301 actions in March 2018, including the first round of tariffs on products from certain industries, such as aerospace and information and communication technology. At the same time, the United States Trade Representative (USTR) filed a complaint at the WTO (DS542).[30] Ahead of the meeting between Xi and Trump at G20 in June 2019, the US requested the panel to suspend its proceedings until December 31, 2019.

On June 1, 2018, the EU also submitted its own WTO consultations request on China's laws and regulations on foreign technology transfer (DS549).[31] On June 8, 2018, Japan requested to join the consultations. On June 14, 2018, the US requested to join the consultations. On June 15, 2018, Chinese Taipei requested to join the consultations. The EU's

[29] WTO. Technology Transfer. (https://www.wto.org/english/tratop_e/trips_e/techtransfer_e.htm).

[30] WTO.DS542. (https://www.wto.org/english/tratop_e/dispu_e/cases_e/ds542_e.htm).

[31] WTO.DS549. (https://www.wto.org/english/tratop_e/dispu_e/cases_e/ds549_e.htm).

concern focused on Chinese regulation on the approval of investments for electric vehicles and biotechnology and the approval of joint ventures across sectors. Specifically, the EU complained that China forced foreign companies to transfer technology to their Chinese JV partners in exchange for the necessary administrative approvals by the Chinese authorities. In addition, the EU also expressed concern in a 2018 Commission Staff Working Document on intellectual property rights protections and enforcement, saying that many Chinese procurement proceedings require technology transfers or know-how disclosure from foreign companies.

At the National People's Congress in March 2019, China passed a new foreign investment law to relieve the concern of IPR and technology transfer. Effective on January 1, 2020, the new foreign investment law contains a relevant provision:

> Clause 22: Technology cooperation between foreign and Chinese entities shall be undertaken voluntarily based on commercial rules. The terms and conditions for such cooperation shall be negotiated by the entities themselves. All levels of government and their officials are prohibited from forcing technology transfer through administrative means.

The change at least reflected that the Chinese government was willing to address the concerns of the Western countries. The launching of this new FDI law was also consistent with Xi Jinping's repeated pledges to open up the economy further. Foreign investors seemed to appreciate the wording of the new law.[32]

5.4.2 The Little Chips

While "forced technology transfer" may be an official reason for the US government pressing China to change its trade practice, from the Chinese perspective, the export control imposed on Chinese companies via the Entity List may also be a measure that the US attempted to contain China's technology development. In addition, the sanction imposed

---

[32] CNBC. October 21, 2019. (https://www.cnbc.com/2019/10/21/eu-chamber-chinas-foreign-investment-law-is-surprisingly-accommodating.html).

on two Chinese mobile phone giants ZTE and Huawei had created a massive supply shock to their production. The two incidents highlight that China's electronic industries have yet to become self-sufficient, as the US continues to retain many critical technologies.

The case of ZTE revealed that China has yet to master the semiconductor industry. ZTE purchased most of its smartphone chips from US chipmaker Qualcomm. In March 2017, the Commerce Department banned American firms from selling to ZTE after finding out that ZTE had been exporting products containing US components to Iran and North Korea.[33] These transactions violated the US sanctions against these two countries. In April 2018, the US government prohibited American companies from doing business with ZTE. Due to the lack of critical supplies, ZTE had to shut down most of its production lines. This ZTE event prompted China's Foreign Ministry to warn the US government "about turning the tide in Sino-US relations."[34] In July, the US government entered a deal with ZTE, fining the company USD 1 billion. ZTE also needed to overhaul its management and allowed a team of compliance monitors to be installed inside the company for 10 years.

A similar case happened to Huawei. In February 2018, six US intelligence agencies including the FBI, CIA, and the NSA openly advised US citizens against using Huawei smartphones. The officials were particularly concerned with Huawei's close relationship with the Chinese military and feared that the phone could be a tool for China to access US consumer data. On May 15, 2019, Trump issued an executive order and ".... declares a national emergency with respect to the threats against information and communications technology and services in the United States and delegates authority to the Secretary of Commerce to prohibit transactions posing an unacceptable risk to the national security of the United States or the security and safety of United States persons." Although the order did not explicitly mention its name, Huawei was obviously a target. On May 20, the US government eased restrictions on Huawei by granting it a temporary license to "provide service and support, including

---

[33] Reuters. April 17, 2018. (https://www.reuters.com/article/us-china-zte-qualcomm-analysis-idUSKBN1HO0XT).

[34] *South China Morning Post.* April 20, 2018. (https://www.scmp.com/tech/article/2142557/zte-calls-us-government-ban-extremely-unfair-vows-fight-its-rights).

software updates or patches, to its handsets that were available to the public on or before May 16, 2019." This event affected Huawei's sourcing of chips, i.e. Intel, Qualcomm, Micron, and operating systems, i.e. Android.

The ZTE and Huawei events highlighted the risk of "short circuits" in the supply chain of integrated circuits. After learning this lesson, China strengthened its involvement from merely packaging and testing chips to R&D and IC design of memory chips and compound semiconductors. China is a net buyer in the semiconductor industry (Figure 5.16). Its semiconductor consumption is 58.5% of the world's total. The US dominates the upstream process in terms of R&D and intellectual property ownership while China has only 4% on the supply side. Chip production is very sophisticated. China's involvement in the value chain has been at the low end. Up until 2015, it had little involvement in high- value-added activities but small share of global revenue in fabless (10%), foundry (7%), and outsourced semiconductor assembling and testing (OSAT) (12%). There are signs that China is increasingly getting itself involved in design and less on packaging/testing.

Semiconductors have taken center stage in the digital era. As the volume of data flows rises exponentially under 5G standard, demand for

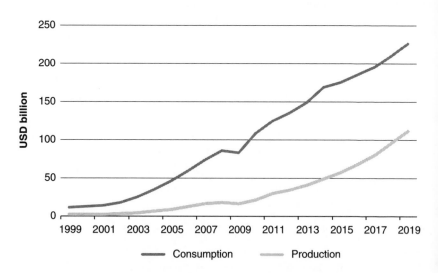

Figure 5.16 China's semiconductor market by consumption and production.
Source: PWC

Table 5.2 Top suppliers of semiconductors 2018.

Company	Operating model	2018 sales forecast, USD billion
Samsung	IDM	65.9
Intel	IDM	61.7
TSMC	Foundry	32.2
SK Hynix	IDM	26.7
Micron	IDM	23.9
Broadcom	Fabless	17.8
Qualcomm	Fabless	17.0
Texas Instruments	IDM	13.9
Toshiba	IDM	13.3
Nvidia	Fabless	9.4
NXP	IDM	9.3
STMicroelectronics	IDM	8.3
Infineon	IDM	8.1
Sony	IDM	7.9
Western Digital / Sandisk	IDM	7.8

Source: IC Insights, "Nine Top-15 2018 Semi Suppliers Forecast to Post Double-Digit Gains," November 12, 2018

chips will only continue to expand. The growth of 5G will also have a more direct impact on chip sales.[35] As the largest buyer of the semiconductors, China's production of mobile devices will jump on the implementation of 5G, creating a wall of semiconductor demand from major segments, including industrial, automotive, computing and consumer electronics. Analysts at Bank of America/Merrill Lynch (March 2019) estimate the market for 5G semiconductors will boom to nearly USD 19 billion by 2022, up from USD 593 million in 2018 (see Table 5.2).

---

[35] IHS. Press release. October 8, 2019. (https://technology.ihs.com/618002/5gs-rise-set-to-break-the-semiconductor-markets-fall-in-2020).

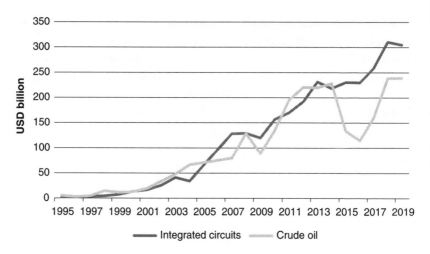

Figure 5.17   China's imports of oil vs. semiconductors.
Source: WIND

As the semiconductor is a critical technology to define the long-term competitiveness of China, the government is eager to strive for chip independence. Made in China 2025 has already stated it will produce 40% of the chips it uses by 2020 and 70% by 2025. The case of Huawei and ZTE simply reinforced this belief. Following the events, the government announced tax breaks for homegrown semiconductor companies and software developers. Huawei's subsidiary HiSilicon has developed its own "Kirin" series of processors for its smartphones and a 5G modem that can allow devices to connect to the newest version of the mobile internet. Xiaomi and Alibaba are also looking to develop a chip that could power AI products.[36] Trade pressure from the US turned out to be a great motivator for China's chip development. The previous worry about Made in China 2025 fueled a bigger worry about Created in China. To the US chip makers, "[China] is a large market that US companies need access to, together with being what will become a major technical competitor. We have never faced that."[37]

---

[36] CNBC. June 4, 2019. (https://www.cnbc.com/2019/06/04/china-ramps-up--own-semiconductor-industry-amid-the-trade-war.html).

[37] IEEE. October 10, 2019. (https://spectrum.ieee.org/view-from-the-valley/semiconductors/devices/semiconductor-industry-veterans-keep-wary-eyes-on-china).

With digitalization, global competition will take place in a new battlefield. In the eighteenth and nineteenth centuries, the Gold Rush defined the wealth of nations. In the twentieth century, petroleum stood as the working capital in postwar industrialization. In the digital age, data flows, processing speed, and smart learning depend on the capacity to develop and manufacture semi-conductors. Countries prefer chips than fish. Integrated circuits are more valuable than crude oil (Figure 5.17). The game plan of the new globalization will be very different from the previous ones. The driver of national wealth is redefined, and inevitably, so is the nature of trade disputes in the future.

Chapter 6

Cryptocurrency and the People's Money

6.1 Deglobalization in the Digital Time

A key feature of the postwar globalization has been the booming of international finance. Not only have we seen booming payment flows on the back of growing trade financing but also a surge of the capital mobility induced by portfolio investments. Multinational corporations (MNCs) and financial institutions are managing their balance sheets globally. They can profit from carry trades that involve borrowing low-cost currency for high-yield investments, resulting in surging financial activities. Financial institutions are active in settling payment flows associated with their activities in debt and equity capital market, FX, and interest rate hedging as well as securities trading. The global might of cross-border finance distinguishes the contemporary version of globalization from that of the nineteenth century.

The world has been following the doctrine of international capital mobility for a few decades. As the Vatican of the international monetary system, the IMF has been pressing many economies to liberalize their capital and financial accounts. As an accomplice, the WTO has been promoting market access of financial institutions in other countries. US banks with access to US dollar liquidity were riding the tide of globalization. The ability to convert local currency into US dollar became the passport for participating in globalization. The New York Fed provided custodian services for many central banks, which supported the foreign currency needs of exporters and importers in their countries. All countries needed to comply with the US sanction rule. Modern international finance became a US-centric regime.

Deglobalization mirrors a regime shift from economic interdependence to independence. Protectionism is replacing multilateralism. Countries are beginning to question or ignore the central authority of supranational organizations. Rules and standards that were functioning well for a large group of countries in the past no longer appeal to political leaders of individual countries. Bilateral agreements have increasingly become a preferred trade policy option. When country A and country B find a win-win between them, they are willing to cut ties with country C even if a common deal for A-B-C generates a bigger gain in total. In a deglobalizing regime, the policy preference is to go peer-to-peer (P2P).

The concept of P2P transactions is shaping the recent development in the digital economy. Blockchain provides a new path for organizing payment systems on an electronic platform. The concept of distributed ledgers for processing bilateral payment flows contrasts the conventional model of a trusted intermediary. In blockchain, there is no single and central authority in governing the payment system. Participants share the power to book and validate transactions. This development challenges the authority of central banks and financial franchises at a time when society has begun to question the reputation of regulatory authorities and financial institutions in the aftermath of the global financial crisis (GFC).

With blockchain disrupting the architecture of global finance, cryptocurrency challenges the regime of fiat money. Proponents of cryptocurrencies suggest their inventions can replace trusted intermediaries and hence provide a cost saving to the economy (Bitcoin[1]). They claim that the system can improve financial access of underprivileged populations and small- and medium-sized enterprises (SMEs) (Libra[2]). Blockchain participants who help validate a block of transactions are rewarded with a new coin. Hence, the value previously enjoyed by licensed providers of financial services is shared amongst the participants. The system creates "money" when Bitcoin miners can prove their work. The idea that anyone can create the money is in stark contrast to our current regime, which relies on central banks to issue paper notes.

With the economy deglobalizing and decentralizing, the world is also looking for a consistent currency option. Prior to the twentieth century, the international monetary regime was not institutionalized. During that time, physical gold was widely accepted in the physical economy. It was apolitical and did not require a government to issue (although it did need an authoritative gold mint for quality assurance). As the global economy becomes more digital than physical, there is a quest for a compatible regime. Admittedly, none of the existing cryptocurrencies in the market have become common means for legitimate and genuine economic transactions. Bitcoin and Ether remain a special interest of speculative investors. Calling cryptocurrency money remains premature.

This chapter serves three purposes. First, it reviews the development of digital currencies. Our discussion will stay conceptual rather than technical. I also describe the recent development of the cryptocurrency market. Secondly, I attempt to assess whether cryptocurrency can be a qualified form of money. It is an important question. If cryptocurrency cannot perform the function of a medium of exchange, it will not be useful to denominate transactions. Lastly, we examine the implication of cryptocurrency on monetary policy. The conclusion in this chapter will help answer the question of whether cryptocurrency will be a global reserve currency, which will be the focus of the next chapter.

---

[1] Bitcoin.org. (https://Bitcoin.org/Bitcoin.pdf).

[2] Libra.org. (https://libra.org/en-US/wp-content/uploads/sites/23/2019/06/Libra WhitePaper_en_US.pdf).

6.2 Bitcoin and Distributed Ledgers

6.2.1 The Basics of Blockchain

The past few decades have seen an explosive amount of research and development of financial technology. Fintech is already an acceptable term in the English dictionary.[3] Blockchain, Bitcoin, distributed ledgers, and cryptocurrencies are all said to be disruptive and urge the financial industry to rethink their prevailing business model. Traditional models of financial intermediaries, including banking, insurance, wealth management, and securities trading, are being tested. On one hand, governments are assessing the risks and regulatory challenges brought by cryptocurrency; on the other, they see blockchain as an opportunity to transform public service delivery (David et al. 2019). Against the backdrop of the China–US trade war, the two countries are also perceived to compete on their leadership in disruptive technology.[4] Their digital rivalry we postulated in the previous chapter is consistent with the overall theme of de-dollarization.

The reality is that it has taken almost a decade for the business community to consider blockchain in formulating their business strategy. In a global survey of 1,386 senior executives with sizeable companies in 2019, Deloitte found that more than half of respondents had considered blockchain a top-five strategic priority, 10 percentage points higher than in 2018 (Figure 6.1).[5] In another executive survey by PwC, 84% of respondents said their companies were actively involved with blockchain.[6] IDC, an international technology research firm, forecasted that total corporate and government spending on blockchain could reach USD 2.9 billion in 2019, led by investment by financial institutions of

---

[3] https://www.merriam-webster.com/dictionary/fintech.

[4] *Washington Post*. March 7, 2019. (https://www.washingtonpost.com/opinions/global-opinions/china-is-racing-ahead-of-the-united-states-on-blockchain/2019/03/07/c1e7776a-4116-11e9-9361-301ffb5bd5e6_story.html).

[5] Deloitte. 2019 Global Blockchain Survey. (https://www2.deloitte.com/content/dam/Deloitte/se/Documents/risk/DI_2019-global-blockchain-survey.pdf).

[6] PWC. Blockchain in Business. (https://www.pwc.com/gx/en/issues/blockchain/blockchain-in-business.html).

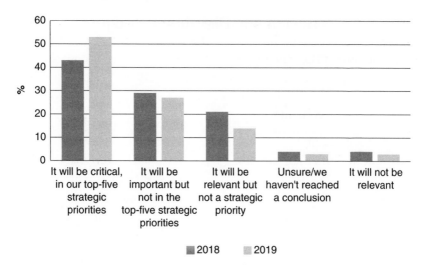

Figure 6.1 Business executive survey on blockchain.

Source: Deloitte

USD 1.1 billion. With an annual increase of 89% in 2018, the amount of investment is projected to surge tremendously to USD 12.4 billion by 2022.[7]

What is blockchain? Since Nakamoto (2008) laid the concept in the seminal Bitcoin paper, there have been tons of explanations of this concept. A good starting point is, in fact, the original objective stated in the whitepaper:

> What is needed is an electronic payment system based on cryptographic proof instead of trust, allowing any two willing parties to transact directly with each other without the need for a trusted third party.

The current architecture of the financial system is based on a trusted intermediary. If we want to transfer an amount of money to another entity, we can proceed in one of two ways. The most direct way is to draw real cash physically from our bank (or for some people, their basement),

---

[7] IDC. Worldwide Blockchain Spending Guide. March 4, 2019. (https://www.idc.com/getdoc.jsp?containerId=prUS44898819).

carry the paper notes in a suitcase (or an armored vehicle) and pass the money to the recipient. In this case, the trusted party is the central bank that issued the IOU. The risk is counterfeit money. In Hollywood movies, drug dealers also need to hire experts to validate the cash.

Another way is to instruct a bank to transfer the funds to a recipient bank. The two banks can be the same bank or different banks. But they are the trusted parties in between. We trust them because they are licensed and regulated by the governments. There is also an additional level of trust required for interbank payments, as any bank will assess the counterparty risk of another one, especially for cross-border transactions involving different time zones. A delivery risk called "Herstatt risk" could also result in a systemic collapse in payment chain.[8]

Blockchain is a conceptual model that can potentially bypass the trusted third party. The World Bank defines blockchain as "a particular type of data structure used in some distributed ledgers which stores and transmits data in packages called blocks that are connected to each other in a digital 'chain'. Blockchain employs cryptographic and algorithmic methods to record and synchronize data across a network in an immutable manner."[9] Akin but not exactly the same as money supply, a digital coin is created through developing a chain of blocks. The number of transactions per block is a few thousand.[10]

Blockchain enables the development of distributed ledger technology (DLT), which challenges the conventional model of financial transactions (Figure 6.2). Currently, the financial sector is built on a centralized model. Banks, exchanges, and other financial institutions pool and settle financial transactions of multiple parties. Based on trust (or

---

[8] On June 26, 1974, counterparty banks around the world paid Deutsche Marks to Herstatt in Cologne, expecting Herstatt to reciprocate and pay out USD during local banking hours in the US. But Herstatt declared bankruptcy that day and never fulfilled its leg of these FX transactions, leaving numerous institutions with huge losses.

[9] World Bank. (2017). Distributed Ledger Technology (DLT) and Blockchain. Fintech note no.1.

[10] The number of transactions per block can be viewed on https://www.blockchain.com/charts/avg-block-size?.

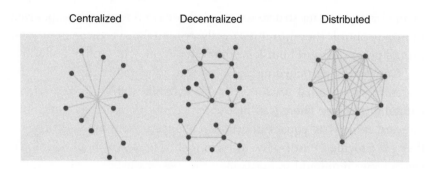

Figure 6.2   Network arrangement – Centralized, decentralized, and distributed.

Source: Author, Blockgeeks

capacity to absorb loss through a capital buffer), these institutions act as an independent intermediary serving multiple parties. In contrast, a distributed system enables peer-to-peer transactions directly. In the context of blockchain, all individual parties are informed of the history of bilateral transactions of the whole system. A distributed ledger system also requires the individual to take responsibility for validating the transactions. Even though a blockchain distributed system does not require all nodes to verify every transaction, it does require a consensus based on a majority rule to approve the history. In DLT, the duties performed by banks and central banks are decentralized to the members.

In discussing the meaning of distributed ledger, many bloggers differentiate between a decentralized system and a distributed system. The consensus is that as long as there is no single node taking full control, the system is decentralized. DLT is just an extreme case in which all individuals have the same level of authority. Vitalik Buterin, the founder of Ethereum, proposed three dimensions to describe the distribution system: architectural, political, and logical (de)centralization.[11] Basically, architectural decentralization is about the arrangement of physical computers in the network. Political decentralization concerns the level of control in the network. Logical decentralization examines the uniformity

---

[11] Vitalik Buterin. (2017) (https://medium.com/@VitalikButerin/the-meaning-of-decentralization-a0c92b76a274).

of interface and data structures. Blockchain is politically decentralized (no one controls them), architecturally decentralized (no infrastructural central point of failure) but logically centralized.

Computers participating in a blockchain network are called the nodes. In the original version of blockchain, all nodes play the role of trusted third party. There is no need to have a bank to act as a custodian, as every miner has equal opportunity to create the money as long as they can provide a proof-of-work. In our current world, the central bank prints paper notes and stamps a serial number. In blockchain, everyone has a chance to create money if all (or a sufficient number of) nodes confirm it is not counterfeit, i.e. double-spending. It is similar to having two pieces of notes with the same serial number. Instead of having a central authority to verify the previous transactions, the approach is to publicly announce the transaction history and allow all nodes to agree on a unique history (Figure 6.3).

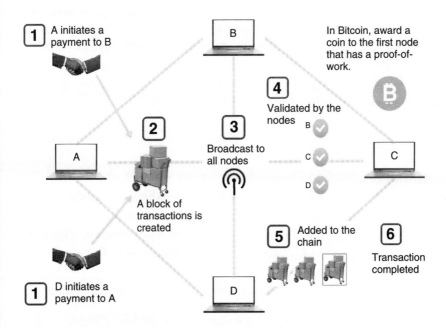

Figure 6.3   Transaction process in blockchain.
Source: Author

Nakamoto (2008) outlined the steps of creating a block, i.e. an electronic coin:

1. New transactions are broadcast to all nodes.
2. Each node collects new transactions into a block.
3. Each node works on finding a difficult proof-of-work for its block.
4. When a node finds a proof-of-work, it broadcasts the block to all nodes.
5. Nodes accept the block only if all transactions in it are valid and not already spent.
6. Nodes express their acceptance of the block by working on creating the next block in the chain, using the hash of the accepted block as the previous hash.

Validating the history of transactions is the most critical element in blockchain because this is a step to avoid counterfeit, which could have been done by changing the history of transactions. In Bitcoin, changing the history is difficult because the proof-of-work system is based on the Hashcash system. A hash is an output from the Secure Hash Algorithm-256 system, a unique and complex string of numbers produced from the algorithm. Only this 256-bit alphanumeric string is visible but not the original data. A nonce is added to a verified block. A miner needs to hash a block's header in such a way that is less than or equal to a target number of 4 leading zeros in the string (the last line below):

```
"Hello, world!0" =>
1312af178c253f84028d480a6adc1e25e81caa44c749e-
c81976192e2ec934c64 = 2^252.253458683

"Hello, world!1" => e9afc424b79e4f6ab42d99c-
81156d3a17228d6e1eef4139be78e948a9332a7d8 =
2^255.868431117

"Hello, world!2" => ae37343a357a8297591625e-
7134cbea22f5928be8ca2a32aa475cf05fd4266b7 =
2^255.444730341

...

"Hello, world!4248" => 6e110d98b388e77e9c-
6f042ac6b497cec46660deef75a55ebc7cfdf65cc0b965
= 2^254.782233115
```

```
"Hello, world!4249" => c004190b822f1669cac8d-
c37e761cb73652e7832fb814565702245cf26ebb9e6 =
2^255.585082774
```

**"Hello, world!4250" => 0000c3af42fc31103f1fd-
c0151fa747ff87349a4714df7cc52ea464e12dcd4e9 =
2^239.61238653**

In this example, the process requires 4,251 attempts. As the blockchain continues to build up, the number of zeros required increases. Since all nodes receive information on the development in the network, they will consider the longest chain to be the correct chain and they will attempt to extend it. Any tie will be broken quickly as the next proof-of-work is found. When one branch becomes longer, the nodes that are working on the other branch will then switch to the longer one. This proof-of-work process requires expensive computational time and power. The miners who spend time on this proof-of-work process are rewarded with coins. Since the coins are created when the zero bits meet the specified target, it is called Bitcoin.

The genesis block of Bitcoin began in January 2009. The nodes continue to build up as the network continues to validate subsequent transactions. This process is still ongoing at the time of the publishing of this book. According to Blockchain.info, the Bitcoin blockchain approached 256GB at the end of 2019, equivalent to 18.1 million of Bitcoin. This figure equals the total size of all block headers and transactions accumulated so far. The design of Nakamoto is to limit the total supply to 21 million coins. The block reward began at 50 coins per block and was then halved every 210,000 blocks. This means that each block up until block 210,000 will reward 50 coins, but block 210,001 will reward just 25. The difficulty of solving the equation also changes every 2,016 blocks, i.e. two weeks/10 minutes. With an average of 10 minutes per block, a block halving occurs every four years.

Bitcoin is not the only blockchain coin. The genesis block of another cryptocurrency called Ethereum began in July 2015, generating a coin called Ether. Compared with Bitcoin, Ether seems to have enhanced some features. One particular breakthrough is smart contracts, which enable a wider range of applications beyond financial transactions.[12]

---

[12] Ethereum.org. (https://ethereum.org/).

The idea was originally developed by Nick Szabo in 1997, proposing that a computer algorithm of cryptographic security function can enforce predefined legal obligations.[13] Szabo's famous analogy is the vending machine: "Anybody with coins can participate in an exchange with the vendor. The lockbox and other security mechanisms protect the stored coins and contents from attackers, sufficiently to allow profitable deployment of vending machines in a wide variety of areas." Similar to Bitcoin, new Ethers are created via the mining process but Ethereum does not set a maximum total number of Ethers. The reward rate is 5 Ethers per block and remains constant without decaying. Ethereum block times are in seconds, compared to Bitcoin's 10 minutes.

6.2.2 Cryptocurrency Market

Bitcoin gains its novelty as an application of blockchain technique. But blockchain is only one type of DLT. Broadly, DLT shares and synchronizes digital payment records across the network without a central administrator. There have been other types of DLT being developed since Nakamoto's introduction of the Bitcoin's version. Cryptocurrencies can enter circulation in different ways. In the case of Bitcoin, participants of the DLT system validate previous transactions. Whoever finishes the job first is rewarded with a new coin. For other cryptocurrencies, new coins are often sold via an initial coin offering (ICO), a virtual version of an IPO for fund raising. Cryptocurrency exchanges provide the buying and selling of cryptocurrencies in the secondary market. Similar to the "real world," not all cryptocurrencies are listed for trading.

Since the birth of Bitcoin in 2008, a large number of alternative digital tokens have been created via ICOs. Many versions are essentially a variation or improvement of Bitcoin. For example, Ether retains the blockchain feature of Bitcoin, but the speed of validation is much faster due to a different hashing algorithm. Unlike Bitcoin, which aims to be an alternative electronic payment system, the primary purpose of Ethereum is to facilitate the operation of smart contracts and decentralized application platform called "dapp," claiming that a programmable

---

[13] Szabo, N. (1997) Formalizing and securing relationships on public network. First Monday 9(1). September.

feature can facilitate developments of other fintech applications for borrowing, lending, and investing digital assets. In essence, Ethereum is a technology for secured obligations.

Although the first 10 years of cryptocurrency history has not fulfilled the original promise as an electronic payment currency, it has attracted massive speculative investment into this new asset class. Many crypto-assets have a short life cycle. Many different versions are created but do not have a high survival rate. Of almost 5,000 cryptocurrencies included on CoinMarketCap in December 2019, the top 10 accounted for more than 89% of the total market capitalization.[14] Dark et al. (2019) cited that only around half of all cryptocurrencies included on CoinMarketCap have existed for more than one year. Bitcoin remained the dominant "currency" in the virtual market (see Table 6.1).

The short lifespan of many cryptocurrencies suggests that the digital currency world may follow in the footsteps of the real world and see a dominant global currency. The USD can maintain its dominance as

Table 6.1 Top 10 cryptocurrencies by market capitalization.

Name	Symbol	Circulating unit	Market cap, USD
Bitcoin	BTC	18,106,162	119,758,064,814
Ethereum	ETH	108,948,312	13,319,828,635
XRP	XRP	43,310,265,523	7,942,061,755
Tether	USDT	4,108,044,456	4,108,917,575
Bitcoin Cash	BCH	18,172,500	3,210,767,747
Litecoin	LTC	63,654,657	2,356,845,291
EOS	EOS	944,783,744	2,074,196,391
Binance Coin	BNB	155,536,713	1,920,564,553
Bitcoin SV	BSV	18,068,415	1,458,706,058
Tezos	XTZ	660,373,612	1,011,603,126

Source: Coinmarketcap.com, December 18, 2019

---

[14] CoinMarketCap.com. (https://coinmarketcap.com/).

the global reserve and payment currency despite concerted efforts of the euro and the Japanese yen in the past few decades. The transaction volume of Bitcoin in the secondary market is normally 30% of the total, according to CoinMarketCap. Just as many investors prefer the liquidity of US dollar assets, participants in the cryptocurrency market are also cautious about the uncertainty of new coins. In addition, many other coins are simply a slight variation of Bitcoin. Lack of differentiation means low motivation for investors to support new listings.

As an emerging asset class, the price of cryptocurrency is volatile, similar to the exchange rate of emerging market currencies in the financial market. At one point, the value of Bitcoin reached USD 20,089 per unit on December 17, 2017, compared with USD 785 the same date in 2016. But the boom did not last long, as the price tumbled to a low of USD 3242 on December 15, 2018 (Figure 6.4).

Price volatility has been a major obstacle for cryptocurrencies to perform the economic functions of conventional sovereign-backed money as (1) a means of payment, (2) a unit of account, and (3) a store of value. As the value is unstable, only speculative investors have an intention to hold a position. Genuine use of cryptocurrencies as a means of payment becomes very difficult.

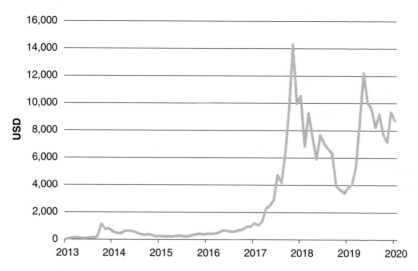

Figure 6.4 Bitcoin price -monthly average.
Source: CoinMarketCap

To improve price stability, developers proposed a new form of cryptocurrency called stablecoins. There are two ways to do this. The most straightforward way is to anchor the value of digital coins to real-world assets, i.e. asset-backed stablecoins (ABSs). The other way is to regulate the supply and demand of coins through an algorithm.

ABSs attempt to improve price stability through pegging with financial assets in the real world. Just as some real-world currencies that are issued only if there is a corresponding increase in collateral (e.g. Hong Kong Dollar Currency Board System), stablecoins are created if there is an inflow of assets of the same value. The coins can be redeemed at a fixed price by selling these assets. The most popular ABS is Tether, having a code of USDT. It is backed by US dollar and has a stable value of USD 1 for each USDT. Price stability seems to secure the confidence of cryptocurrency investors. The trading volume of Tether is amongst the top of all listings on CoinMarketCap, even though its market cap is only 3% of that of Bitcoin.

ABSs actually derive price stability from sovereign currencies as opposed to DLT design itself. In principle, this method relies on the guarantee from central banks and seems to defeat the original motivation of blockchain. But the rationale is also in line with the story of many emerging market (EM) currencies. Typically, the EM currency crisis ended up with some international assistance through facilities from the IMF. In the aftermath of the Nixon shock, the US dollar became a fiat money without gold convertibility. The greenback also went through a period of turbulence and eventually got stabilized through an implicit anchor to petroleum (see Chapter 2 for detailed discussion about petrodollar recycling).

However, the problem of ABSs is the governance of reserve management. In April 2019, it was reported that Tether was not fully collateralized. Instead, only 74% of USDT were backed by cash and cash equivalents.[15] Even though technically a currency did not need to be 100% collateralized, it raised the question about credibility.[16] In addition, it was reported that Tether's sister company Bitfinex took a loan of

---

[15] Bloomberg. April 30, 2019. (https://www.bloomberg.com/news/articles/2019-04-30/tether-says-stablecoin-is-only-backed-74-by-cash-securities).

[16] *Forbes*. March 14, 2019. (https://www.forbes.com/sites/francescoppola/2019/03/14/tethers-u-s-dollar-peg-is-no-longer-credible/#7c3fb4e3451b).

USD 850 million from Tether.[17] On November 20, 2018, Bloomberg reported that US federal prosecutors investigated whether Tether was used to manipulate the price of Bitcoin.[18]

One way to improve investor confidence in ABSs is to partner with established financial institutions or engaged regulators. An example is TrueUSD.[19] The developer TrustToken collaborated with an accounting firm, which provided a real-time, third-party view of TUSD in circulation and their related collateralized fiat funds.[20] They connected with an escrow bank, which looks after the holding of the US dollar collateral, as well as running Ethereum nodes to monitor TUSD supply. However, the use of an escrow bank in the case of TrueUSD is inconsistent with the original spirit of disintermediation. Improving governance involves some sacrifice of decentralization.

In 2019, Facebook also attempted to develop an ABS, called Libra.[21] To drive the development of this cryptocurrency, they led a Geneva-based organization with many institutional members from both the financial and technology sectors. The idea of Libra is no different from an ABS as it is backed by a reserve comprised of a basket of bank deposits and short-term government securities denominated in a range of national currencies. In September 2019, Facebook announced that the reserve basket would be made up of 50% US dollar, 18% euro, 14% Japanese yen, 11% pound sterling, and 7% Singapore dollar.

Although linking to sovereign currencies should have relieved the concern of price volatility, regulators still cast doubt on the potential impact on financial stability given Facebook's massive penetration

---

[17] Brave NewCoin. October 10, 2019. (https://bravenewcoin.com/insights/stablecoin-battle-heats-up-with-class-action-lawsuit-filed-against-tether).

[18] Bloomberg. November 20, 2018. (https://www.bloomberg.com/news/articles/2018-11-20/Bitcoin-rigging-criminal-probe-is-said-to-focus-on-tie-to-tether).

[19] TrustToken.com. (https://www.trusttoken.com/trueusd).

[20] CoinDesk. March 5, 2019. (https://www.coindesk.com/trueusd-stablecoin-soon-to-have-real-time-monitoring-of-dollar-backing).

[21] Libra. (2019). Libra White Paper. (https://libra.org/en-US/wp-content/uploads/sites/23/2019/06/LibraWhitePaper_en_US.pdf).

globally.[22] Some members of the Libra Association, like PayPal, decided to opt out of the project.[23] Without sufficient presence of household names in the financial service industry, it is still difficult to boost confidence in the ABS. Forming a membership organization of credible entities is akin to leveraging the franchise value of an escrow in the case of TrueUSD. The bottleneck is still the transfer of the value of trusts from regulated financial institutions to the hands of decentralized community.

Another way to address price instability without a trusted third party is to develop a protocol that can reduce price volatility. This is the approach of algorithmic stablecoins. This type of stablecoin relies on a protocol to manage the excess supply/demand in the market and attempts to smooth the market price. There are two types of algorithm. The first is built-in market intervention. The algorithm adds or removes coins from circulation. However, the automatic regulator intervenes the market by declaring some coins inactive. While algorithmic intervention is very innovative, there has not been a successful example to date, as noted in a comprehensive report by Bullmann et al. (2019).

The second type of stabilization scheme is to mimic the operation of a central bank in the real world. The model develops a program to conduct "open market operation." If there is an excess supply of coins, the value of coins drops. The stablecoin algorithm will issue a bond at a discount to purchase and destroy the surplus coins. If demand exceeds supply, the algorithm will instruct a repo to redeem the liability from the bond holders.

However, early experience of this algorithm approach has not been convincing. NuBits was one of the early generations of algorithmic stablecoins dating back to 2014. The design was to rely on creating a market force so that people were willing to "arbitrage" or lock up their NuBits in a bond-like instrument. This scheme attempted to establish an interest rate parity so that the value could reach the equilibrium. However, with the lack of confidence in the future value of NuBits, very few participants were willing to lock up in the bond, crippling the price

---

[22] Bloomberg. December 18, 2019. (https://www.bloomberg.com/news/articles/2019-12-18/fed-s-brainard-raises-red-flags-over-facebook-s-libra-project).

[23] *Fortune*. November 20, 2019. (https://fortune.com/2019/11/20/paypal-ceo-dan-schulman-libra/).

adjustment mechanism. The price of NuBits could not recover and the project was ceased.[24]

6.2.3 Decentralization, Scalability, and Forks

Bitcoin was only a beta version of blockchain. Despite all the promises it offered, the technology was still premature. There are still some technical issues to be addressed for cryptocurrencies to be a genuine payment currency. Particularly, there is a famous scalability trilemma. This trilemma was modified and discussed in the economics literature recently, labeled as blockchain trilemma (Abadi and Brunnermeier 2018).

The Scalability Trilemma is a terminology coined by Vitalik Buterin, the founder of Ethereum (Figure 6.5). He suggested that there existed some tradeoffs underlying the architecture of blockchain. Developers need to strive for an optimal design and juggle three components: decentralization, security, and scalability. Blockchain can build a decentralized and secure ledger system. These two elements should be complementary because there are always backup nodes in the system to retain true information. In a nutshell, DLT reduces the risk of a central point of failure. In our current financial system, if a central clearing house is hacked or comes across an operational failure, the whole system may collapse without a business continuity plan. In an

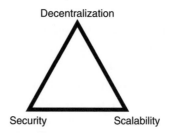

Figure 6.5   The Scalability Trilemma.
Source: Vitalik Buterin

---

[24] Coin Telegraph. December 13, 2018. (https://cointelegraph.com/news/major-stablecoin-basis-to-close-return-funds-to-investors-sources).

extreme case where all participants perform the same clearing functions, all members effectively ensure a backup in real time for the whole system.

The tech community pointed out a number of security risks that threatened distributed ledgers. Saad et al. (2019) provided a comprehensive review of different attacks facing public blockchains:

- Monopolizing or collusion: one or a set of entities that owns more than 50% of the total tokens outstanding, effectively owns the network. They could perform some malicious operation(s) on the network;
- Sybil attack or pseudonymous threat: one or a set of entities could forge multiple identities on a P2P system in order to effectively control a significant stake in ownership and/or decision making of the network;
- Penny spend or Distributed Denial of Service (DDoS) Attack— flood the network with low-value or malicious transactions in order to stop the network from running.

Of the three types of risks, the last two are general cybersecurity risks facing all network systems. Identity threat and Penny attack can happen in any electronic financial system. It is the first one the DLT needs to tackle. Ultimately, the degree of decentralization is the inverse of monopolization. Since having multiple nodes can reduce the chance of these attacks, decentralization can improve security.

However, decentralization in blockchain is costly as the network expands. Since decentralization and security are complementary, this trilemma can also be reduced to a tradeoff between the scalability and decentralization. The design of Bitcoin blockchain is scale-constrained because the protocol

1. Imposes a limit on the amount of information they can contain, i.e. the restrictions that fewer than 10 transactions or one megabyte per second; and
2. Takes roughly 10 minutes to validate a block.

This scalability limit began to constrain and become costly when high Bitcoin prices drew massive mining activities in the network in late 2017. When many miners raced for nominating new blocks, the network spent time on addressing the issue of orphan blocks, i.e. blocks already verified but had not been accepted by the network, resulting in a time lag. Given this time lag, many miners were still solving the mathematical problems for the same blocks without knowing the blocks had been solved.

Some developers have attempted to develop alternative consensus algorithms to reduce the burden stemming from proof-of-work. For example, in a proof-of-stake algorithm a new block is chosen, instead of solving the computationally expensive mining problem, based on combinations of random selection and other attributes, such as the coin age, i.e. the number of days the coins have been held.[25] However, proof-of-stake seems to be more centralized than proof-of-work as the validation tends to favor blocks in nodes that have larger stakes, rather than giving equal chance to all nodes. These alternative consensus algorithms could increase the throughput significantly but involve a tradeoff between centralization and scalability.

Another way to address the scalability problem is to alter the protocol in order to relax the constraint on transaction requirement for a block formation. Since there is an inherited inefficiency built within the Bitcoin model, changes in protocol are required to reduce the welfare loss (Chiu and Koeppl 2018, Kang and Lee 2019). In August 2017, the Bitcoin community came up with an upgrade in protocol called Segregated Witness (SegWit), which aimed at increasing the scale while keeping the existing chain preserved.[26] It was named SegWit because the proposal involved removing the unlocking signature ("witness" data) from the original portion and appending it as a separate structure at the end. This SegWit plan was meant to enable another payment solution called Lightning Network, a "Layer 2" payment protocol on top of Bitcoin for faster and cheaper micropayments bilaterally in a P2P network.[27] Some cryptocurrencies like Litecoin tapped this architecture.

---

[25] https://blackcoin.org/blackcoin-pos-protocol-v2-whitepaper.pdf.

[26] https://github.com/Bitcoin/bips/blob/master/bip-0141.mediawiki.

[27] Bloomberg. March 15, 2018. (https://www.bloomberg.com/news/articles/2018-03-15/technology-meant-to-make-Bitcoin-money-again-is-going-live-today).

But this design was not short of weaknesses, such as liquidity shortage, as it needed to borrow from the original network.

In the blockchain community, agreeing on a protocol change in the same chain is called soft fork. However, there is an unhappy version called hard fork. While the mining community of Bitcoin were formulating SegWit, a group of miners decided to develop a new code that allowed for a more aggressive block size (8 megabytes). The name was Bitcoin Cash. Since most Bitcoin users decided to stay, the spinoff one needed to build a new chain and hence a new cryptocurrency. The story of Bitcoin Cash and other "altcoins" highlighted the difficulty in reaching a compromise solution in the mining community.[28]

The issue of "soft forks" and "hard forks" originated from the Scalability Trilemma. This problem attracted some academic interests, which formalized the tradeoffs from the perspective of industrial organization. Biais et al. (2018) developed a theory for forking in a proof-of-work blockchain. They analyzed the behavior of miners in a stochastic, game theoretic framework. In their model, there existed a case where a miner anticipated all others to fork, and mined a new branch. Therefore, the rational response was to follow them and develop a new chain. This type of game theoretic modeling was also used to study the stability of distributed computing system as a Byzantine Generals Problem (Lamport et al. 1982). To avoid system failure, members in the system must agree on a concerted strategy. However, some of these actors could be unreliable. The beauty of proof-of-work and transparent system in Bitcoin was to overcome the Byzantine problem.

Abadi and Brunnermeier (2018) modeled the blockchain trilemma in a theoretical framework of coordination game, describing the incentive structure of amongst three parameters: (1) decentralization, (2) information correctness, and (3) cost efficiency. Their model provided an analytical framework characterizing fork behavior as well as comparing DLT and centralized intermediation system. When network externalities are weak, coordination among the blockchain community becomes fragile and the community is susceptible to hard forks.

---

[28] *Wall Street Journal.* December 23, 2017. (https://www.wsj.com/articles/Bitcoin-cash-litecoin-ether-oh-my-whats-with-all-the-Bitcoin-clones-1514037600).

The implication is that online retail platforms might be better suited to a blockchain, as the network could benefit from joining the strong existing network.

In fact, the fundamental belief about information sharing in a DLT framework could also be a risk, as it may propel collusion, defeating the original purpose of decentralization. Cong and He (2019) suggest that generating decentralized consensus in blockchain also inevitably leads to greater observability of the network activity recorded on the blockchain. But the increase in observability actually fosters collusion among sellers. The early promise about the ease of entry and enhanced competition in a DLT may not necessarily be welfare improving. The authors suggested future design should regulate the use of the consensus-generating information for the purpose of collusion.

To quicken the solving process of the longest chain, one proposed approach is service payment. In a generic blockchain, the only reward is the new coin to the new block builder. By offering varying amounts of transaction fees, miners can be motivated to validate the history. In 2016, transaction fees became an emerging phenomenon. Using a game-theoretic framework, Easley, O'Hara, and Basu (2019) analyze the economics of transaction fees (Figure 6.6). They propose that higher transaction fees are induced by long waiting time facing the

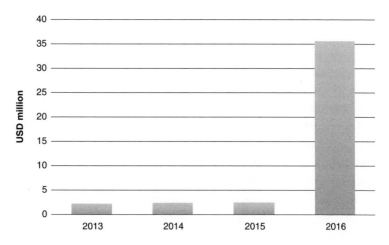

Figure 6.6   Transaction fee of blockchain.
Sources: Blockchain.info; Easley et al. 2019

users. However, with users paying increasing transaction fees, their participation will eventually drop, prolonging the time of chain building. Transaction fees are not a solution to solve the scalability problem.

It appears that the subsequent developments of alternative algorithms have not solved the problem of scalability facing the generic blockchain. Dark et al (2019) believed alternative consensus algorithms, such as byzantine fault tolerance or proof-of-authority, are unlikely to be implemented in widely used public cryptocurrencies because of the centralization needed for proposing and/or validating blocks. The general conclusion is that a sacrifice of decentralization to some degrees is needed. Despite the massive transaction value in the cryptocurrency exchange, the DLT system cannot support the volume of transactions required for running a real economy. It needs another technological breakthrough in order to make cryptocurrency a realistic currency for a country.

6.3 Can Cryptocurrency Replace Money?

6.3.1 Is It a Medium for Payment?

Is cryptocurrency money? Economists typically answer this question religiously, examining the nature of cryptocurrencies using a ruler provided by Jevons (1875). Reports issued by central banks or supranational organizations routinely start with a textbook definition of money with a list of functions money performs in the contemporary context: (1) a medium of exchange; (2) a unit of account; (3) a store of value; and (4) a standard of deferred payment.

In a transaction or exchange, counterparties are willing to accept money because it is a countable and divisible unit that stores value for future use. Therefore, if an item can perform the first three functions, it is a payment currency and is good for cash on delivery. The function of deferred payment describes the ability to create credit, a concept parallel to money supply. It is one step beyond the generic definition of currency and involves an assessment of financial infrastructure. In the fiat money regime, central banks first issue the base money (i.e. the genesis node of "I owe you") before going through the credit creation process. Therefore, it boils down to two questions: (1) Can cryptocurrency be used for payment? (2) Can it be used to extend liability?

The first question is the most important. Medium of exchange or payment is the most basic function of currency. Cash differs from investment on the asset side of a balance sheet. The former is more fungible than the latter. Bank for International Settlements (BIS) described DLT-based digital currencies:

> First, in most cases, these digital currencies are assets with their value determined by supply and demand, similar in concept to commodities such as gold. However, in contrast to commodities, they have zero intrinsic value. Unlike traditional e-money, they are not a liability of any individual or institution, nor are they backed by any authority. As a result, their value relies only on the belief that they might be exchanged for other goods or services, or a certain amount of sovereign currency, at a later point in time.

BIS Committee on Payments and Market Infrastructures, November 2015 (BIS 2015)

The BIS report opined two qualifications for a payment currency: (1) It needs to have "intrinsic value" like commodities; and (2) The value of a currency should come from backing by an authority.

There is an impression that cryptocurrencies offer zero intrinsic value. However, the consumable value generated by gold or silver is not really the basis for pricing their fundamental value. In financial theory, intrinsic value means the present value of expected future cash flows. Sovereign-backed currencies in the form of coins and paper notes do not generate cash flows. There are also saving account deposits in currencies of which the issuing central banks implement zero or negative interest rate policy. Sovereign backing cannot guarantee value (e.g. EM currencies in crisis). As long as it is seen as an asset with a market valuation, the item can perform the store of value function (which could be poor if market pricing is very volatile).

The definition of money is context specific. Currency evolves in accordance with the development of human history. Davies (2002) provides a comprehensive account of different monies from wampum (shell beads) to modern monetary regime. Gold is considered an important monetary reserve because it stores value. But it is not a good medium for payments. Gift cards from Amazon or Starbucks are not legal tender and cannot be used outside their respective stores. But they are payment currencies within the specific network of stores. National currency is officiated administratively by law. But the nature of legal tender is no different from gift cards. If a local currency of an unknown country is not recognizable internationally, it is only acceptable within a country but cannot function as a currency outside the country. Residents in the country may prefer Amazon's gift card than their own currencies.

Likewise, the question of whether cryptocurrency is a medium for payment can only be answered on an ex-post basis. Legal status is not a crucial factor. In fact, Bitcoin or other DLT currency was pointedly motivated by the desire to challenge sovereign power. The status of national currency depends on geographical and regulatory considerations as well as economic factors including price stability and investor orientation. If Bitcoin or Ether becomes increasingly popular, they can be used to denominate underlying assets. They can be used to value debt and equity instruments. Companies can also pay dividends or other payables in cryptocurrencies. The payments can be used to compute discount cash flows, the definition of intrinsic value in the theory of finance.

After a decade of development, Bitcoin is beginning to be accepted by some merchants, although its use is only limited to a dozen of non-mainstream retailing (e.g. Microsoft,[29] KFC Canada[30]). The actual providers of goods and services that claim to accept Bitcoin do not seem to take a currency position on their balance sheets. They require an intermediary to cash out (e.g. Expedia[31]). The reality is that a company financial statement is still denominated in traditional money. A unit of account is a function of money. But this function also requires a certain level of acceptance, which is based on convention or history. Merchants may be willing to accept cryptocurrency as a means of payment as they expect the price to rise. An exchange or trading platform is still required to connect cryptocurrencies to sovereign currency.

---

[29] Microsoft. https://support.microsoft.com/en-us/help/13942/microsoft-account-how-to-use-Bitcoin-to-add-money-to-your-account.

[30] CBC News. January 13, 2018. (https://www.cbc.ca/news/canada/saskatoon/kfc-canada-cryptocurrency-blockchain-Bitcoin-bucket-1.4486698).

[31] Expedia. https://www.expedia.com/Checkout/BitcoinTermsAndConditions.

Investment motive is as important as medium of exchange. Garratt and Wallace (2018) point out that people are willing to hold Bitcoins because they treasure the potential capital gain in the future. There can be multiple equilibria. If this belief collapses due to some stochastic shocks, the Bitcoin mania will cease. However, there also exists a scenario that cryptocurrency defeats sovereign currency. It is too early for policymakers to rule out cryptocurrency. Therefore, cryptocurrency could be viewed as both investment goods and medium of exchanges. At this stage, it is more the former.

Athey et al. (2016) conducted a large-scale empirical study to examine the use of cryptocurrencies. They examined a list of approximately 220,000 entities, took about 78 million Bitcoin addresses, and grouped them into 27 million distinct "entities." Their study found that as of mid-2015, the price of Bitcoin was sensitive to beliefs about the future value and less sensitive to current transaction volume for its own sake.

6.3.2 Can Cryptocurrency Create Credit?

In Economics 102, total money supply is created in a fractional reserve banking system. Central bank issues paper notes and coins as the seed money. The currency in circulation either sits with commercial banks as deposits or is stuffed in people's wallets. At the maximum, a bank can lend a fraction of its deposits and the proceeds become a fraction of deposits in another bank. The recipient bank, in turn, lends out a fraction of this fraction of deposits to the third bank. The fractions are one minus the reserve requirement ratios (RRR) applied to each bank. The reserve sitting with the central banks and the currency in circulation equals the monetary base. The total money supply, typically defined by total deposits held by all commercial banks, is multifold the monetary base.

Blockchain may substitute a part but not the whole of the monetary system because the money creation process is very different. Blockchain is a ledger recorder booking the payment flows amongst parties. The payments are not necessarily borrowing and lending activities. The distributed ledgers may potentially replace the payment booking system of our financial system. The coins may be a candidate to replace the currency issued by central banks as they can fulfil the requirement of medium of exchange, store of value, and unit of accounting. However, the system by itself does not embed mechanism to extend M0 to M2. To make cryptocurrency a board money, it needs an extra layer of infrastructure for credit creation.

Interest rate is an important element in the monetary system as it induces credit creation. It is the price paid to lenders for forgoing present spending. Central banks use it to influence macroeconomic activity. In Bitcoin, the ledgers can record the net balance of all network members and the aggregate balance should be the total amount of coins in circulation. Network members can borrow and lend coins amongst themselves. But there is no single authority to set a benchmark interest rate. Bitcoin network does not identify account payment or receivable information and publish a market interest rate. (The smart contract feature of Ethereum can perform this function.) The interest rate benchmark likely comes from the sovereign currency system. Bitcoin lenders and borrowers likely refer to similar rates of US dollar loans (or other currency), adjusted for expected change in "exchange rate" of Bitcoin against the US dollar.

Some fintech companies launched crypto-backed loans that allowed holders of cryptocurrencies to utilize their assets as collateral for cash in US dollar, euro, or stablecoins. Some lenders offered up to 90% loan-to-value ratio. The interest rate appeared to be akin to normal US dollar loans. Some fintechs explored the use of Secured Automated Lending Technology (SALT) based on the technology of smart contracts.[32] This type of platform facilitated sovereign currency borrowing using blockchain-based assets as collateral. One provider, Youholder, also allowed borrowers to use other cryptocurrencies (e.g. ETH) to back their loans in euro, dollar, and also Bitcoin. Using the language of finance, borrowing BTC using ETH could be expressed as shorting BTC/ETH. Some fintechs seemed to perform like a bank. Celsius Network, for example, claimed to pay interest to members' deposits, using the BitGo Trust Company as a custodian of their crypto wallets.[33] Members could borrow at an interest rate higher than the deposit rates.

---

[32] Salt Lending.com. (https://saltlending.com/).

[33] Celsius Network. (https://www.bitgo.com/clients/client-story-celsius-network).

Technically, a blockchain system does not need a bank. In reality, the blockchain community needs to draw resources from the real world because their ecosystem has not developed to a self-sufficient stage. They interact with the financial system of the real world on two fronts:

1. Fund raising: To develop their systems, companies in the virtual world need financial support from the real world in the form of seed money. Venture capital and workers are still rewarded in sovereign currency.
2. Currency exchange: Buying and selling of cryptocurrencies involves conversions between sovereign currencies and cryptocurrencies. Crypto exchanges or fintech companies receive sovereign currency and maintain bank accounts in formal banking systems.

While the blockchain ecosystem has developed channels to facilitate the credit flows between cryptocurrency and sovereign cash, almost no financial institutions are willing to go out on a limb because of regulatory concern. In some jurisdictions, banks ban the purchase of Bitcoin using their credit card. Regulators are the gatekeeper to limit the exposure of formal financial institutions to crypto assets. In addition, many fintech sites are not available to citizens in some jurisdictions, as they are not licensed to provide financial services in these countries. The real world has established accounting treatment (e.g. US GAAP) for airlines' frequent-flyer programs, valuing the mileages as a liability item. Unless similar treatment is extended to cryptocurrency, there will still be a gap between the formal financial sector and the blockchain economy.

6.4 Regulatory Responses

The rapid development of cryptocurrencies has aroused the interests of governments, financial regulators, and central banks. There are typically two types of responses. On one hand, central banks see cryptocurrencies as a risk. Financial institutions are warned to be cautious about the potential use of cryptocurrencies as a tool for money laundering or terrorist finance. Central banks are also concerned that cryptocurrencies could undermine the effectiveness of monetary policy. Paul Krugman believes cryptocurrency is a bubble and may set the monetary system back 300 years.[34] On the other hand, governments do see the DLT as an opportunity to enhance financial service delivery. Many countries have started to develop their official version of digital currencies. They also explore the opportunity to upgrade payment infrastructure via mobile wallets.

Bitcoin has been perceived as a vehicle in the underground economy and a means to support illegal activities. In 2014, the Financial Action Task Force (FATF) of BIS published an extensive report on digital currency issues, noting that "convertible virtual currencies that can be exchanged for real money or other virtual currencies are potentially vulnerable to money laundering and terrorist financing." It also provided guidance on a risk-based approach to handling virtual currency payments for products and services, aiming to enhance the global consistency and the effectiveness of the Anti-Money Laundering/Counter-Financing of Terrorism (AML/CFT) standards.

Another regulatory response is to develop a central bank's version of digital currencies, i.e. Central Bank Digital Currency (CBDC). Since the money is issued by central banks, CBDC is virtually an electronic version of paper notes and coins. The rationale is to provide a safe and secure digital currency for retail transactions. Currently, electronic transactions via credit or debit cards are still going through the banking system. For CBDC to be meaningful, central banks should aim to develop some electronic tokens that are counterfeit resistant and transferable without going through banks. This was the approach of Riksbank, which explored the development of e-krona in view of declining cash balance (Griffoli et al. 2018).

Many countries develop CBDC for other, different reasons. They include antitrust, risk management, cost efficiency, and financial inclusion (see Table 6.2). In general, policymakers believe digital currency can improve financial inclusion. The idea is that there are still some segments of the population that have no access to (costly) financial services. Digital option can facilitate their transactions. However, in

---

[34] *New York Times*. July 31, 2018. (https://www.nytimes.com/2018/07/31/opinion/transaction-costs-and-tethers-why-im-a-crypto-skeptic.html).

Table 6.2 Rationale for Developing CBDC.

	Anti-monopoly	Operational risks	Cost efficiency	Financial inclusion
Bahamas				X
Canada	X			
China	X	X	X	X
CBCS		X	X	X
ECCB		X	X	X
Ecuador			X	
Norway	X			
Senegal				X
Sweden	X	X		
Tunisia				X
Uruguay			X	X

Source: IMF (Griffoli et al. 2018)

the case of China, the story also concerns public–private competition. Although internet giants like Alibaba and Tencent are considered very successful businesses, there has been some concern about their monopolistic power. Internet business enjoys strong network externalities that support natural monopoly (just like the US dollar). If platform operators begin to levy the users, consumers will have very few alternatives. Given this consideration, CBDC appears to be a legitimate development.

Unfortunately, CBDC unlikely presents any major breakthrough in upgrading our financial architecture. The industry has already tapped the mobile technology quite successfully during the past decade. One example is RFID. Retail payments can be easily done via payWave at the point of purchase, enhancing the speed of card-based or phone-based transactions. Other examples are Alipay, which has replaced the use of cash in China. In the case of WeChat Pay, Tencent can combine the spending pattern with their social media platform. Combined with the application of big data technique, these private sector solutions drive the technological improvement in their service delivery. Regulators can only react to the technological development passively.

From a macroeconomic perspective, CBDC is nothing more than a "save the paper" version of traditional currency. The digital cash will likely be a list of unique serial numbers, similar to the string printed on the paper notes. This development does not introduce any fundamental change to the fiat money regime, i.e. CBDC is still the central bank's liability to the public. In blockchain, money is not created by a central authority. The supply of currency is purely a function of computational power of the network. The concept of CBDC does not close the gap between sovereign and cryptocurrency.

6.5 Implication on Monetary Policy

The economics literature to date has mainly focused on the microeconomic structure of blockchain. Academic economists seem to have little concerns about the impact of cryptocurrencies on the monetary policy and financial stability. In terms of market capitalization, the cryptocurrency market capitalization was about USD 190 billion by the end of 2019. This is less than 5% of the balance sheet of the US Fed (USD 4.1 trillion). As discussed in the previous section, regulators mainly see the cryptocurrency as a potential source of financial instability. Central banks only appreciate the feature of DLT and do not view cryptocurrencies as an alternative medium of exchange and even store of value. The authorities do not accept the view that privately developed cryptocurrency will replace sovereign currencies.

However, there is no reason for policymakers to be complacent. In the digital world, new trends are constantly being executed at lightning speed. Financial regulators may cut the tie between the formal banking system and privately run cryptocurrency. But society may have already accepted cryptocurrency as a common form of payment. If the economy turns out to be cryptonized instead of dollarized, central banks could be marginalized. Monetary policy will be ineffective. The situation will be very similar to the experience of many emerging markets in which local residents prefer foreign rather than local currency. The local central bank cannot use interest rate policy to influence inflation or the exchange rate.

Increasing use of an alien currency also affects the external balance of an economy. Some countries, such as Venezuela[35] and China,[36] cracked down on cryptocurrency exchanges, as they feared the negative consequences to financial stability. While AML/CFT as well as consumer protection are usually the cited reasons for regulatory tightening, the action can also curb capital outflows because cryptocurrency is indeed an efficient method for cross-border payments. This new asset class will risk the external balance of some countries, especially if the economy is vulnerable. In these countries, cryptocurrencies are particularly popular. Local residents are willing to pay a higher price for the coins. The price is virtually the exchange rate against the local currency. Cracking the cryptocurrency exchanges is a form of capital control.

Therefore, central banks need to understand the very nature of cryptocurrency. First, the supply of cryptocurrency is not controlled by a foreign central bank. To deal with an official foreign currency, a local central bank needs to read the monetary policy of another central bank (e.g. US Federal Reserve). This does not apply to cryptocurrency because its "money supply" is based on an algorithm. Actually, the supply function of Bitcoin is easier to predict than the preference of different Federal Open Market Committee (FOMC) or monetary policy committee (MPC) of other central banks. Secondly, cryptocurrency can be regarded as a non-interest-bearing asset. In considering exchange rate management, covered or uncovered interest rate parity does not apply. Thirdly, there is no global authority like the IMF or BIS to regulate international affairs. In blockchain, any change in protocol is decided by consensus of the network members. Cryptocurrency follows a different rule of law.

Fernández-Villaverde and Sanches (2016) analyzed the competition between cryptocurrency and sovereign money. They showed that privately issued money can create problems for monetary policy implementation if a central bank follows a money growth rule. It is crucial for private money issued by profit-maximizing entrepreneurs (or a network

---

[35] Business Insider, March 14, 2017. (https://www.businessinsider.com/venezuela-bitcoin-use-popularity-restrictions-and-crackdown-2017-3).

[36] Bloomberg, November 27, 2019. (https://www.bloomberg.com/news/articles/2019-11-27/all-you-need-to-know-about-china-s-latest-crypto-crackdown).

of them) to be capped (such as Bitcoin) so that its existence still allows a price stability scenario. One important insight from this study is that the competition can help uplift the discipline of fiat money issuers, as they need to ensure the attractiveness of fiat money over cryptocurrencies.

Many central banks adopt an explicit inflation target in controlling money supply. This contrasts the supply of Bitcoin, which is based on proof-of-work as opposed to economic targets. Schilling and Uhlig (2018) characterize this difference as when there exists an inflation target central bank with the presence of Bitcoin issued by a decentralized network. Equilibrium condition is derived through the tradeoff between currency holding for speculation and using for payments. An important message of this study is when a central bank issues money in such a way to have achieved the inflation target of above unity, there are conditions where the value of Bitcoin becomes zero. Under this condition, sovereign currency can compete away cryptocurrency.

To doubters, cryptocurrency plays no role in economics. Fundamentalists believe the idea of a digital token is completely flawed because cryptocurrency does not inherit the features of traditional money. To them, a qualified medium for payments should be one that holds value. It is a matter of trust. Sellers are willing to receive digital tokens when they know they can exchange it for something at least as valuable. However, price volatility of many cryptocurrencies deters acceptance. The general expectation is that the mania of cryptocurrency will eventually vanish. Policymakers can continue to acknowledge the technological aspect of blockchain and appreciate the security feature of DLT. They can continue to assume that the current monetary policy regime remains intact.

The major problem of this assumption is double standard. Both fiat money and cryptocurrency do not carry intrinsic value. The foundation of the US dollar or other G10 currencies is the confidence in the political-economic conditions of the issuing countries. However, this foundation is not unshakable. The trust is based on an assumption that their central banks will maintain price stability. However, history suggests that the policy of many central banks has not been really disciplined. If Bitcoins can coexist with sovereign currency under some conditions as postulated by Schilling and Uhlig (2018), it will gradually substitute sovereign money. With the rise of anti-authoritarianism, public belief in sovereign currency is dissipating.

Network externalities are the foundation of the US dollar. People are willing to hold it because it is highly convertible. It is freely usable in purchasing goods and services or converting into other currencies. Like the US dollar, cryptocurrency is also borderless and global. The power of network externalities can also apply to cryptocurrency. The more people use it, the more it will gain acceptance. Economists can rule out cryptocurrency as money based on some criteria from a textbook. But the real world can ride roughshod over the economists' verdict.

When cryptocurrency becomes a global standard, the law and order of the international monetary regime will be redefined. Global monetary affairs will witness a power shift. Currently, the stablecoin still needs to promote itself by pegging with a sovereign currency. In the future, central banks may need to build a cryptocurrency reserve to support fiat money. Banks and other financial institutions will rediscover their value proposition. First movers in the crypto community will reap the benefits and capture the value added. Fintech would provide a whole new way to organize blockchain-based lending, depositing, and investing. The impact of Satoshi Nakamoto's paper is no less than the Nixon shock.

Chapter 7

Foreign Reserves Go Digital

7.1 From Zhou to Carney

Mark Carney, governor of the Bank of England, commented on the international monetary system at the Jackson Hole Symposium on August 23, 2019:[1]

> Transitions between global reserve currencies are rare events given the strong complementarities between the international functions of money, which serve to reinforce the position of the dominant currency. And the most likely candidate for true reserve currency status, the Renminbi (RMB), has a long way to go before it is ready to assume the mantle.

---

[1] Carney, M. (2019). The growing challenges for monetary policy in the current international monetary and financial system. Speech at the Jackson Hole Symposium (August 23, 2019).

Mr. Carney's comment is a fair assessment of the state of global currency affairs. When the global financial crisis (GFC) hit the world a decade ago, governor of the People's Bank of China (PBOC), Zhou Xiaochuan, expressed a deep concern about the inherent weaknesses brought by the dollar-based international monetary system. A decade is over. The global position of the US dollar remains untouched despite a series of quantitative easing by the Fed. Even after two decades since its inception, the euro still has a sizeable gap against the dollar position in the global foreign reserve system. Almost no central bank pegs their currency with the Japanese yen. Only 1.9% of SWIFT global payments were in the Chinese yuan in December 2019, falling from the peak of 2.3% in 2015.

Mr. Carney offered a more important piece of insight, "History teaches that the transition to a new global reserve currency may not proceed smoothly. . . . Technology has the potential to disrupt the network externalities that prevent the incumbent global reserve currency from being displaced." The past few years have clearly seen a chain of disruptions: nationalism, populism, nativism, and protectionism. All of them are reshaping the political-economic order of global trade.[2] Changes in social values began to question the authority of sovereign currency. The two world wars introduced a shock that was big enough to cause the global shift from the pound to the US dollar. The US–China trade war could also be an onset of another reserve currency regime.

Interestingly, this regime shift would be a solution for the Triffin dilemma. De-dollarization can end the problem of the global saving glut. A new regime is needed to align the US' ability to print money with their purchasing power. This regime needs to reduce the obsession of net exporting countries to over-recycle their foreign earnings to US dollars. At present, the power of network externalities is too strong. The hurdle for another currency to challenge the incumbent is too high. Neither the euro, the yen, nor the yuan is sufficient to break the feedback loop of the dollar recycling process. A quantum jump is required for an alternative scenario.

---

[2] Fromen, M. (2019). Beyond populist disruption, what now for global free trade? Contribution to World Economic Forum (January 10). (https://www.weforum.org/agenda/2019/01/the-future-of-free-trade).

Blockchain technology represents an idiosyncratic shock that can shake the global reserve system. It represents a new way to define money supply. Well-designed cryptocurrencies can potentially enable peer-to-peer (P2P) transactions without the presence of a trusted intermediary. Currently, the global payment system relies on our trust to the central banks. Sovereignty defines their capacity to supply medium for exchanges but the US Fed is the ultimate supplier of reserve currency. The trade war exposes the weakness of this system. China is expected to move away from the dollar-centric regime. Cryptocurrency provides a politically neutral medium to handle the transition.

Naturally, we will ask whether cryptocurrency will take over the US dollar and become a global reserve currency one day. Mr. Carney also agrees that digital currency can potentially rival global reserve currency. His proposal is to develop a new synthetic hegemonic currency (SHC) perhaps through a network of central bank digital currencies (CBDC). Meanwhile, Facebook's initiation of Libra acknowledges the importance of the legacy system, as the design is to peg with a basket of sovereign currencies. Stablecoins appear to be the starting point in the current monetary revolution.

This chapter will begin with a discussion about the nature of global reserve currency. While there exists a list of qualifications adopted by the IMF, a new angle is needed to transform the dollar-centric regime in the digital age. Is the world willing to let the private sector take the helm? Besides CBDC or the IMF's SDR, will the global monetary system accept a non-sovereign reserve? Our conclusion is that cryptocurrency is also a qualified reserve asset. It has all the technical features as a medium of exchange. Legal status is a political rather than an economic issue. The same network externalities that support the dollar can also potentially support cryptocurrency, particularly in the digital world.

7.2 Reserve Currency Based on Liquidity

Global reserve currency is broadly understood as major currencies held by most central banks as part of their foreign exchange reserve. What are the major currencies? They can be any G10 currency heavily traded in the global FX market. But to be called "global," the policymaking circle demands for some sort of accreditation. The five currencies, USD, EUR, JPY, CNY, and GBP, included in the IMF SDR basket can be regarded as global reserve currencies (Figure 7.1). The IMF defines the SDR as "an international reserve asset created by the IMF in 1969 to supplement its member countries' official reserves. . . . The SDR is neither a currency nor a claim on the IMF. Rather, it is a potential claim on the freely usable currencies of IMF members. SDRs can be exchanged for these currencies." The IMF is not the issuing authority of the currency. Holders of the SDRs own the reserve assets.

In the context of balance of payments (BOP), a country holds reserve assets to meet external obligations. According to the World Bank's Reserves Advisory & Management Partnership (RAMP) survey in 2018, 84% of central bank reserve managers state that "self-insurance against potential external shocks" is the most relevant motive for holding foreign exchange reserves, followed by "the need to conduct foreign exchange policy (66%)" (Figure 7.2).[3] Given this precautionary motive,

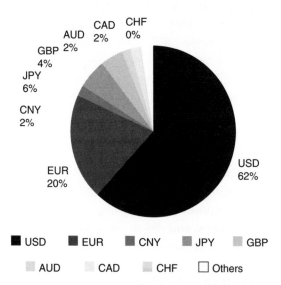

Figure 7.1   Allocated foreign reserves by currency for Q32019.
Source: IMF

[3] World Bank (2019). Inaugural RAMP Survey on the Reserve Management Practices of Central Banks Results and Observations.

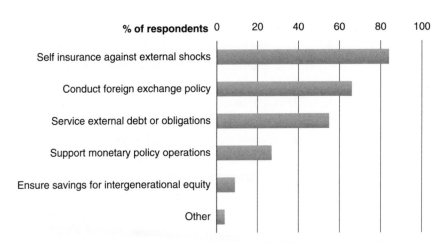

Figure 7.2 RAMP survey 2018—Motives for holding foreign reserves.
Source: World Bank

reserve holding is a function of market volatility. Although reserve adequacy is determined by a list of factors such as exchange rate regime or trade exposure, risk-averse central banks will tend to hold more reserves than the risk taker. They will also demand more safe assets, notably US government securities, so as to mitigate the risk of capital outflows, especially when the financial market is full of risk-off sentiment.

According to IMF's Balance of Payments and International Investment Position Manual Sixth Edition (BPM6), "reserve assets are those external assets that are readily available to and controlled by monetary authorities for meeting balance of payments financing needs, for intervention in exchange markets to affect the currency exchange rate, and for other related purposes (such as maintaining confidence in the currency and the economy, and serving as a basis for foreign borrowing)." Therefore, liquidity and convertibility are the major considerations in choosing reserve currency. The external assets have to be "readily available." The assets should be widely accepted by the counterparty and supported by an international payment system. The assets have to have the market depth, as reserve managers need to sell and buy sizeable amounts swiftly.

The RAMP survey also indicates that 97% and 95% of 99 central banks consider safety and liquidity, respectively, as the highly relevant investment principles (Figure 7.3). Only 37% of the respondents stated investment returns as an important objective in their practice. Safety requires convertibility and market liquidity. IMF defines a set of liquid instruments as qualified reserve assets, namely, gold, SDR holdings, reserve position in the IMF, currency and deposits, securities (including debt and equity securities), financial derivatives, and other claims (loans and other financial instruments). Non-liquid currencies or securities cannot perform the basic function of reserve assets.

IMF provides a technical elaboration about convertibility in BPM6: "Furthermore to be liquid, reserve assets must be denominated and settled in convertible foreign currencies, that is, currencies that are freely usable for settlements of international transactions." The term "freely usable" has been the focal point in the recent years during the debate about the inclusion of the RMB in the SDR.[4] All five currencies in the SDR basket are convertible as they are "freely usable." BPM6 also states that economies may hold assets denominated in the currency of a neighboring economy due to its trade exposures to their neighbor.

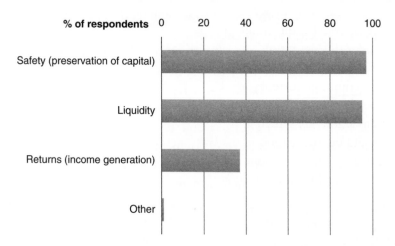

Figure 7.3   RAMP Survey 2018—Investment principles.
Source: World Bank

---

[4]IMF (2015). Selected Decisions and Selected Documents of the IMF, Fortieth Issue—Review of the Method of Valuation of the SDR—Freely Usable Currency—Renminbi, updated November 30, 2015.

These assets should be excluded from reserve assets if the currency does not meet the definition of a convertible foreign currency.

The five currencies included in the SDR basket are qualified because they are liquid and convertible. In reality, reserve currency is not limited to those included in the SDR basket. Central banks and monetary authorities also invest in Australian dollars, Canadian dollars, and Swiss francs. These three currencies are amongst the top eight choices in central banks' allocation, according to IMF COFER data (as of Q3 2019). The dollar alone constitutes more than 60% in central banks' reserve, followed by the euro's 20%. Needless to say, central banks will prefer assets issued by advanced economies. Given the active marketing by the Chinese government since 2009, the share of the yuan has risen rapidly within a few years. As a developing country, China always wants some international recognition. They consider the reserve currency status a national achievement.

When policymakers talk about reserve currency, the definition of money is never ambiguous. BPM6 (3.95–3.96) states that:

> Domestic currency is that which is legal tender in the economy and issued by the monetary authority for that economy. . . . Under this definition, an economy that uses as its legal tender a currency issued by a monetary authority of another economy or of a common currency area to which it does not belong should classify the currency as a foreign currency, even if domestic transactions are settled in this currency. . . . The term "currency" should be understood in the broad sense (i.e., currency includes not only banknotes and coins but all means of payments issued by financial institutions in an economic territory).

Under this definition, reserve currency has to be issued by a sovereign authority. This requirement is consistent with the BOP system as cross-border payment flows are country-based. The system only values national currencies. It is a game between countries that is supposed to be well-defined geographically. Gold and precious metals are permissible only because of legacy.

It is important to note that this sovereign requirement applies to currency denomination, not the issuers of the financial instruments. Denomination refers to the unit of measurement. The IMF COFER data do not distinguish the nationality of the financial instruments. Dollar-denominated bonds issued by Sinopec are dollar assets. The Dim Sum bond issued by McDonald was an RMB-denominated paper. This concept of unit of measurements excludes many options. Reserve has to be expressed in value. If a foreign central bank holds an Australian mine with million tons of iron ore reserve, it is expressed in AUD, not in tons.

With capital account liberalization, many countries need to maintain sufficient reserve for the sake of exchange rate stabilization. For countries that peg or anchor their currencies to the US dollar, they must hold a higher proportion of USD-denominated reserve assets. According to the IMF's Annual Report on Exchange Arrangements and Exchange Restrictions (AREAER), there were still 59% of member countries maintaining either hard or soft peg with other currencies, more than the number of central banks adopting a floating regime (see Table 7.1). If many countries were to allow for a free-floating regime, demand for foreign reserve should have been much less.

Table 7.1 Exchange rate arrangements 2010 and 2018.

% of IMF members	2010	2018
Hard peg	13.2	12.5
– No separate legal tender	6.3	6.8
– Currency board	6.9	5.7
Soft peg	39.7	46.4
– Conventional peg	23.3	22.4
– Stabilized arrangement	12.7	14.1
– Crawling peg	1.6	1.6
– Crawl-like arrangement	1.1	7.8
– Pegged exchange rate within horizontal bands	1.1	0.5
Floating	36.0	34.4
– Free floating	15.9	16.1
– Other floating	20.1	18.2
Other exchange rate arrangement	11.1	6.4

Source: IMF AREAER database

The major problem of the global reserve regime stems from high concentration on the US dollar and to a certain extent, the euro. Balance sheet expansion of the Fed and ECB floods the global economy with massive amounts of excessive liquidity in the form of foreign reserve (Figure 7.4). The asset side of their balance sheet is primarily government and agency debts in the United States and Europe (Figure 7.5). The supply of these reserve assets is driven by their monetary and fiscal policy. They are not incentivized to look after the global system collectively. This problem is more pronounced in the era of unilateralism. China hoards dollar assets in their foreign reserve because they want to stabilize the yuan's exchange rate against the US dollar. But the PBOC can only take the decision of the FOMC passively. Some other economies simply peg their currencies with the greenback and abandon their own monetary policy (e.g. Hong Kong), resulting in a possible mismatch between their macroeconomic profile and monetary policy direction.

Since the US dollar is a base currency in the exchange rate market, the Fed is virtually a global central bank. As Rogoff (2001) pointed out, "Absent a global government, it would be difficult to establish adequate checks and balances on a global central bank. The US Federal Reserve is technically independent, but it is also fundamentally a creature of

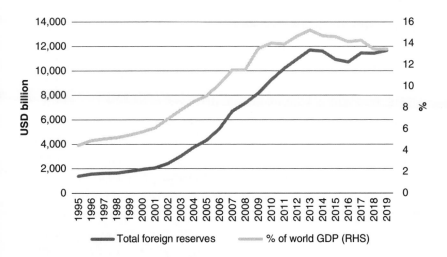

Figure 7.4 Global foreign reserve over time.
Source: IMF

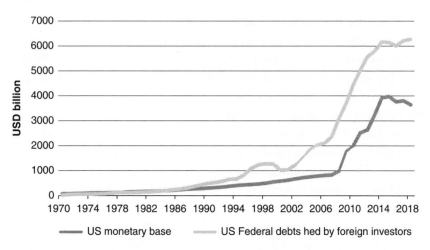

Figure 7.5   Foreign holding of US government debts vs. US monetary base.

Source: FRED

Congress, one that could in principle be dissolved at short notice." The mandate of the Fed is to look after price stability of the United States itself. The most the Fed can do is to consider some "requests" from the White House, obviously not from the State Council of China. When the Fed wants to boost inflation by massive injection, it may help change inflation expectation or stop property prices from falling further. But the spillover effect of this US-centric decision fuels the property bubbles elsewhere. Expressed in local currency, the real value of the foreign reserve holding will have dropped.

The question is why many countries are so addicted to US dollar assets, in particular US government securities, even though the nominal return continues to beat the record low? It is because the US treasuries are the most liquid instrument. Market depth is the biggest advantage of US dollar assets. This advantage was artificially created in Bretton Woods, further extended through the network externalities. The US was not only a winner of World War II but also the currency advantage. It was granted the license as a bank for gold. The war was a stochastic event (although under our theory of globalization cycle, it could be predictable). It helped overcome the threshold level of network advantage. After the US dollar gained a significant share, its dominance was hard to break.

However, the outcome today may be suboptimal as network externalities imply multiple equilibria (Meissner and Oomes 2008). If many countries opt out from the US dollar, its network advantage and also liquidity advantage would dissipate rapidly. If deglobalization and rising populism signals a forthcoming shift of the geopolitical regime, just as World War II, the change would sufficiently offset the effect of network externalities. The trade war is a tip of the iceberg. It highlights a tension between two sovereign nations. The currency world will not be immune from the subtle geopolitical evolution.

More countries have increased their yuan holding as their foreign reserve. Reportedly, China signed an oil importing deal of USD 400 billion with Iran using the yuan as the payment currency.[5] Russia, another major oil supplier, was cited to hold 14% of its reserve in the RMB.[6] Using the yuan in the commodity trade has been the major strategy in the RMB internationalization. With China pushing closer economic and cultural ties with Belt and Road countries, it is reasonable to expect a rising penetration of yuan payment in Eurasia in the future. In fact, as a supplier of the second-largest reserve currencies, the ECB has also included CNY in its total reserve holding (Figure 7.6).[7] However, the size is small.

Can China's Belt and Road crack the network advantage of the US dollar in the currency market? The answer is unlikely. Even with a formal institutional arrangement, the euro cannot rival the greenback. Ilzetzhi et al. (2017) conducted a comprehensive review of the exchange rate system of 194 countries over the period 1946–2016. Their conclusion is that the use of the US dollar remained far wider in recent years than 70 years ago, due in part to the demand for safe assets by emerging economies. The Chinese currency will be used more frequently in other countries. Sovereign wealth funds and central bank reserve managers

---

[5] *Telegraph*. September 20, 2019. (https://www.telegraph.co.uk/business/2019/09/20/chinas-400bn-oil-deal-iran-major-step-cold-war-could-derail/).

[6] Bloomberg. January 9, 2019. (https://www.bloomberg.com/news/articles/2019-01-09/russia-boosted-yuan-euro-holdings-as-it-dumped-dollars-in-2018).

[7] Port, E. (2019). ECB foreign reserves management. Presentation at the 13th ECB Central Banking Seminar, July 1, 2019.

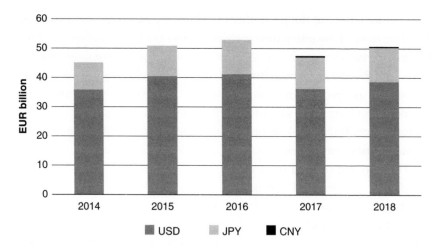

Figure 7.6 Foreign reserve of ECB.
Source: ECB

will add China Government Bonds or Policy Financial Bonds to their portfolio. The yuan may be an alternative to other currencies such as the yen, the Canadian, or the Australian dollar. But the Chinese yuan is still something "nice to have" in their currency portfolio, rather than the base currency in the eyes of global asset managers.

7.3 The Potential Role of Cryptocurrency in Global Reserving

As discussed in the previous chapter, Blockchain technology has laid the foundation for cryptocurrency as a new form of money. Some merchants have started to accept it for payments. Cryptocurrency will possibly become a form of money for cross-border payments (not only in the underground economy). It would be a candidate currency in foreign reserve management. If the world begins to acknowledge the status of the yuan because of the growing economic power of China and allows it to challenge the prevailing regime, cryptocurrency should also be qualified to join the league as the size of digital economy is also expanding.

For cryptocurrency to become an acceptable reserve asset, they need to overcome a number of hurdles. Under BPM6, the requirement of legal tender rules out the possibility of using cryptocurrency as a form of denomination. This restriction sounds natural because the whole BOP framework is sovereign based. National currencies are issued by central banks, not by the private sector. The IMF acknowledges the historical role of gold as a proper form of reserve assets. However, other commodities like copper or soybeans are not legal tender. Fixed-income investors (including central banks) wanting to gain exposure to iron ore or oil invest in proxy currencies, like Australian or Canadian dollars.

The concept of legal tender does not have a long history. The Bank of England was granted the power to control over issuing banknotes after the Bank Charter Act 1844. Prior to this Act, commercial banks in Britain and Ireland were able to issue their own banknotes. Money printed by provincial banking companies were widely circulated.[8] Likewise, the US National Banking Act of 1863 paved the way for the Federal Reserve Act in 1913, which created a league of 12 regional Federal Reserve Banks jointly responsible for managing money supply, supervising commercial banks, and serving as a lender of last resort. These events shaped the one-country-one-currency regime. The era of sovereign money was originally motivated by the government's desire to regulate the banking sector and to control private money.

Eichengreen (2019) suggested the economic rationale behind a single currency regime within a country. He pointed out that "the argument for government monopoly of money issuance must rest on the economic efficiency of a currency that is both uniform (because there is only one issuer) and stable." The efficiency gain is driven by lowering information cost. By using fewer recognizable currencies or means of payment, the society can save a lot on verification. He reckoned digital currency stood against this trend toward uniformity and was not a good candidate in terms of information efficiency. The unstable price of Bitcoin and other cryptocurrencies is seen as the cause of information inefficiency. Based on this logic, the central bank's backing remains essential to the future of digital currency.

---

[8] This tradition continues to inherit in an ex-British colony. HSBC, Standard Chartered, and Bank of China (Hong Kong) are still issuing the Hong Kong dollar notes.

However, this argument is questionable from a dynamic perspective. Information advantage can be built. Government background is not an exclusive license of information efficiency. Sovereign-based US dollar is globally recognizable; so are private-sector payment platforms like Visa and Mastercard. The two credit card companies often propagate the concept of recognition by filming their TV ad in a hotel in a third-world country. Trust can be built. Digital economy allows faster recognition of a new form of payment. Within a decade, Alipay and WeChat have turned China into a cashless society. Both were developed by entrepreneurs. The economics of network externalities is faster in the digital network. The globalized world is more prepared to accept new means of payment provided that they can illustrate its counterfeiting feature and remain free from fraud.

Due to network externalities, currency having information advantage must be a liquid instrument. The liquidity and convertibility requirement under BPM6 is a data reporting standard. This type of rule-based standard has its own limitations; for example, it only counts liquid assets held outside its jurisdiction. Foreign currency assets held within the national border are ruled out. The reality is that central banks are free to invest their assets subject to local regulatory approval, not the IMF. Reserve managers can hold real estate, gold, or cryptocurrency. They can even acquire Bitcoin mining companies. If there exists a liquid, market-accepted cryptocurrency that allows a country to meet their external obligations, holding reserve assets denominated and settled in the cryptocurrency is justifiable from an economic standard point.

In 1944, world leaders were willing to test out the gold exchange standard. By crowning the US dollar, it took only a decade for the non-gold reserves to take off (Figure 7.7). The same world should also stay open to any new idea that can fix the problem of the dollar centric system. At present, cryptocurrency is ready to take off in the near term unless the following issues are addressed:

1. Scarcity of supply: By the quantity theory of money, the value of fiat currency will continue to drop if central banks supply money excessively. Fiat money is inflationary, often resulting in financial bubbles. In contrast, finite money supply is deflationary, as price needs to adjust downward in economic expansion. Just like gold or oil

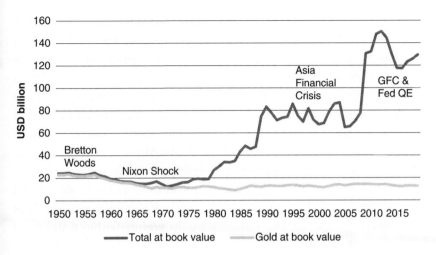

Figure 7.7 US non-gold reserves.

Source: FRED

reserves, the design of Bitcoin is to cap the total supply to 21 million coins. It is a finite currency. The downside is that people will hoard the coins instead of lending out. That is why economists are worried about deflation. For a cryptocurrency to function, its supply should be in line with the pace of economic expansion.

2. Counterfeit resistance: The development of blockchain is motivated by the desire to design a payment system that can avoid double spending, i.e. counterfeit. In terms of security, Bitcoin relies on a proof-of-work system. Once a transaction is booked, it is widely distributed to network participants. The record cannot be easily altered. In Bitcoin, SHA-256 increases the cost of duplication. This security feature facilitates P2P transactions even without a trusted third party. The downside is that the security feature slows the money supply, resulting in the scalability constraint that hinders economic growth.

3. Equal opportunity: The boom of cryptocurrency mining coincides with growing populism in global politics. Anyone who has access to a computational network can mine cryptocurrency. The idea is to replicate the era of gold mining in the digital era. Everyone who is willing to spend time and effort would be rewarded. In reality, however, mining of cryptocurrency requires expensive computational

and electricity resources, attracting criticism from environmentalists. Some researchers estimate that Bitcoin mining takes more energy than mining gold, generating about as much CO_2 over 30 months as 1 million vehicles in the same period.[9]

4. Non-sovereign: Cryptocurrency is a digital representation of value that is not issued by a central bank or a licensed authority. In theory, like gold, its global acceptance should not be subject to political consideration. It is not subject to restrictions imposed by the authority. Anyone can use a cryptocurrency for payments domestically, although some governments, like China, ban its usage on the basis of financial instability (this is also to uphold the status of legal tender). The "freedom" in the network currency without sovereign influence enhances global portability. A downside is that the non-sovereign status requires substantial boosting in order to gain user confidence, either by a government or a prominent private organization, as in the case of CBDC and Libra, respectively.

In the nineteenth century, the Bank of England was granted the exclusive right to print money. Interestingly, 170 years later, Governor Mark Carney became the first top-notch official who sees the potential of a digital alternative. Specifically, a report of the Joint Cryptoasset Taskforce (HM Treasury, Financial Conduct Authority, and Bank of England) proposed that the Bank of England would work towards enabling the renewed Real-time Gross Settlement (RTGS) service to be capable of interfacing with innovative payment platforms, including those based on distributed ledger technology.[10] In general, given the increasing adoption of cryptocurrency as an alternative asset class, the tone in the policymaking circle recently seems to be more open to the future scenario. Dabrowski and Janikowski (2018) concluded that "Policy makers and regulators should not ignore virtual currencies, nor should they attempt to ban them. Both extreme approaches are incorrect."

---

[9] Nature Research. November 6, 2018. (https://www.nature.com/articles/d41586-018-07283-3).

[10] Bank of England. Publication of the Cryptoassets Taskforce report. October 29, 2018.

With the rising popularity of digital means of payments (including WeChat Pay, Alipay), central banks are under pressure to go digital. Adrian and Griffoli (2019) and Bech and Garratt (2017) developed the Money Tree and Money Flower, respectively, to categorize different forms of payments. The former study attached four attributes to different means of payments: type (a claim or an object), value (fixed or variable for claim; unit of value or other for object), backstops (government or private related fixed payment under claim), and technology (centralized or decentralized). The latter considered issuer (central bank or other), form (digital or physical), accessibility (widely or restricted), and technology (token- or account-based). Interestingly, under both analytical frameworks, private digital tokens (e.g. Bitcoin) and CBDC perform similar functions.

After the discussion in the past few years, the central bank community eventually accelerated the development of CBDC. In January 2020, the Bank of Canada, Bank of England, Bank of Japan, the European Central Bank, Sveriges Riksbank, and the Swiss National Bank, together with the BIS have created a group to share their experience in developing CBDC in their home countries.[11] On the other hand, China continues to develop its Digital Currency/Electronic Payments (DC/EP) on their own. The PBOC established the Digital Currency Research Institute in 2017. It is expected that China will launch a digital form of physical cash (M0) very soon. As opposed to account-based debit via WeChat Pay or AliPay, the PBOC version would likely be an electronic form of cash rather than a new cryptocurrency.[12] The e-cash can function in rural areas or even airplanes, as money can still be transferred without the internet.

The major difference between CBDC and cryptocurrency is the issuing entity. In the latter case, there is no central authority, just like shell beads or gold. Fiat currency is a portable piece of trust. The remaining question is to whom we trust. The core belief of many economists is the government. But the very nature of Blockchain currency is

---

[11] Bank of England, Press release. January 21, 2010.

[12] Bloomberg. September 10, 2019. (https://www.bloomberg.com/news/articles/2019-09-10/why-china-s-rushing-to-mint-its-own-digital-currency-quicktake).

to build the trust through network consensus, not the authority. Given some time, the technology will eventually generate a digital version of this trust through a proof-of-work or a proof-of-stake technique (see Chapter 6). A new form of cryptocurrency would also gain global traction rapidly and would likely become a popular medium of exchange. Network externalities and hence liquidity improvement would help stabilize the new currency, pushing the global currency mix into a new equilibrium, as suggested by Meissner and Oomes (2008).

7.4 Implication of the Libra Project

On the back of global digitization, social media has become a powerful tool that exerts great influence on the way people interact, the way companies conduct business, and the way politicians run their election campaigns. It is a platform reaching those who can use a finger to swipe the screen, share information, deliver messages, and make payments. From e-commerce giants to small businesses, many industry players have already integrated social media into their global marketplace. According to a study by McKinsey (2019), social recommendations motivated an average of 26% of purchases across 30 product categories, and consumers made 10% more purchases on the back of social-media recommendations in 2014 than they had in the previous year. The influence of social media continues to grow after their studies.

As the leading social media with active users approaching 2.5 billion, Facebook proposed a stablecoin named Libra in May 2019. According to the whitepaper, the Geneva-based Libra Association will serve as an independent agency to manage a backing reserve and the reserve consists of a basket of major currencies. This is an appealing feature that can help reduce price volatility of the coin.

The announcement triggered a slew of regulatory concern. In October 2019, Facebook CEO Mark Zuckerberg pitched the project of Libra at the US Congress Financial Service Committee. The reply from Chairwoman Maxine Waters was, "With all of these problems I have outlined, and given the company's size and reach, it should be clear why we have serious concerns about your plans to establish a global digital currency that would challenge the U.S. dollar." Meanwhile, many high-profile companies that were initially interested in the Libra project pulled out (such as eBay, Visa, and Mastercard), clouding the future of Facebook's currency.

The remark of Ms. Waters has brought about a very important conclusion. Developing a currency through a social media giant can become a prominent rival to the US dollar. The rise of instant messaging social networking was one of the most important digital evolutions in the past decade. Email became obsolete. Post offices work mainly for Christmas. The top-ten social media platforms have more than 10 billion subscribers, more than the total population of the world (Figure 7.8). The platforms continue to capture all kinds of behavioral data. Embedding social media with marketing and payment has become an attractive value proposition in the e-commerce community.

Network externalities support the market value of social media, in the same way they sustain the franchise value of the US dollar. It is reasonable to expect all households, from advanced to underdeveloped countries, to be connected to social media of some form very soon. They receive and disseminate information. They can make buy/sell decisions and complete the transaction process electronically. In fact, 823 million Chinese people used WeChat to transfer their red packet gift money

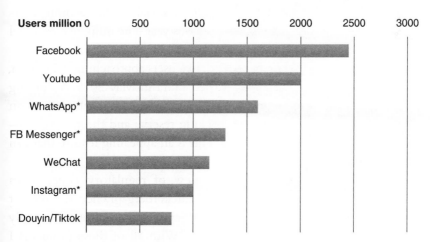

Figure 7.8   Social media by active users, January 2020.

*Estimates only. No published data available for January 2020.

Source: Data from Kepios analysis (https://datareportal.com/social-media-users)

during the Lunar New Year in 2019.[13] Needless to say, the social media platform is an ideal testbed to pilot digital currencies.

The development in the online gaming industry offers some insight of how social media currency can evolve. The online gaming market was estimated to have reached USD 100 billion by 2018. Many tech giants earn multibillion dollars from the market (see Figure 7.9). Different from the business model that relies on generic digital marketing, game providers receive direct consumer spending as players upgrade their superior weapons or access to other advantages in their competitions in addition to the fee received from player initial subscription. For instance, an online game called Fortnite reportedly earned revenue of USD 2.4 billion in 2018, the highest of any game. The game had more than 200 million players worldwide. While it was freely downloaded, Fortnite sold in-game "skins" and emotes via micro transactions. It also

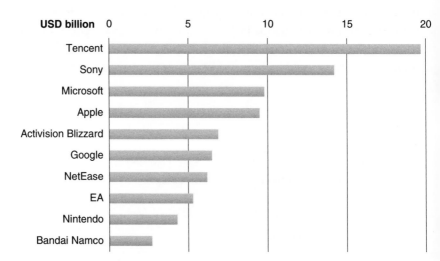

Figure 7.9 Top 10 listed companies of online game revenue 2018.
Source: Data from Newzoo 2019 Global Games Market Report

---

[13] The Paper (澎湃新闻). February 11, 2019. (https://www.thepaper.cn/newsDetail_forward_2968788).

upgraded players' experience through offering "Battle Pass." Within the virtual world, there is already a micro currency system.[14]

Governments are cautious about the growing influence of social media. For health reasons, China limited the access to the hugely successful online game Honor of Kings to one hour a day for children aged under 12 and two hours for children between 12 and 18.[15] For other reasons, the US government expressed its concern about Facebook's launching of Libra.[16] Ms. Lael Brainard, chair of the Committees on Financial Stability of the US Federal Reserve, said Libra needed to address three broad areas before it can be launched: (1) anti-money laundering, (2) consumer protection, and (3) the types of financial transaction being undertaken by each partner.[17] These regulatory actions only revealed one thing: Libra can disrupt the current economic system, including the monetary and foreign reserve regime.

Globally, potential integration between e-commerce and social media may form a digital economy with a size bigger than many countries. If e-commerce giants, be they Amazon, Alibaba, Uber, or Didi, begin to accept cryptocurrency, the volume of digital tokens transacted on their platform could be huge. In-house or third-party coin exchanges could act as intermediaries to convert virtual currencies into fiat money. Once token users reach a critical mass, more buyers and sellers would maintain a balance of cryptocurrency to meet daily transactions. Digital tokens would take a position in the balance sheet and be recognized by the accounting body. Cryptocurrency circulated in the global and private operator would be a foreign currency, no different from the currency issued by other sovereign entities.

There are two options for central banks. The tendency is that they would regulate or even ban the use of the private sector option and

---

[14] *Telegraph*. January 17, 2019. (https://www.telegraph.co.uk/gaming/news/fortnite-earned-annual-revenue-game-history-2018/).

[15] BBC News. July 7, 2017. (https://www.bbc.com/news/business-40516125).

[16] BBC News. April 4, 2018. (https://www.bbc.com/news/technology-43649018).

[17] Reuters. December 18, 2019. (https://www.reuters.com/article/us-usa-fed-brainard/feds-brainard-facebooks-libra-faces-core-set-of-regulatory-hurdles-idUSKBN1YM12L).

launch their sovereign CBDCs. Another option is to accept the reality and recognize the status of cryptocurrency. There are many possibilities as to how the situation will evolve. Given the economics of network externalities, first-mover advantage will likely dictate the final outcome. Ultimately, the global economy will be dominated by a working currency as a principal medium of exchange. Given the growing voice of reforming the international monetary system, the global currency regime will only become more digital.

Chapter 8

The Endgame

8.1 The Trade War as the Perfect Shock

When Donald Trump took over the White House as the US president in the first week of January 2017, he announced that he would pick Robert Lighthizer as the US Trade Representative (USTR). Lighthizer was deputy USTR under former US president Ronald Reagan. After the appointment, Lighthizer took charge of the trade war with China. He used the same trade tools the administration used previously, notably "Section 301" tariffs to combat a tide of imports of steel and vehicles from Japan in the 1980s. The US also struck the Plaza Accord currency deal with Japan and West Germany, based on a belief that weak currencies of other countries were the culprit behind the loss of US international competitiveness. However, the effort was proven to be useless. The US has continued to run trade deficits to the present day.

History clearly suggests that trade barriers, as well as currency agreements, cannot address the trade imbalance in the US. Shortly after the worst trade deficits, it experienced the worst economic recession, the global financial crisis (GFC), a financial phenomenon due to global saving glut, as Bernanke put it. It was a problem of the dollar dominance, a structural deficiency inherited from its "exorbitant privilege." After the Nixon shock, the fiat money regime gave a passport to the US for indiscipline spending, fueled by unsatiated foreign demand for US dollar assets. Half a century ago, Professor Triffin warned about the consequence of this curse. Central bankers of other countries have also cried for reform of the international monetary system for many decades. The world has experienced crisis after crisis: oil shocks, stock market clashes, and trade wars. The currency arrangement continues to dictate the fate of the global economy.

Well, the US should take no blame. Shortly after the war, it took up the responsibility to tie its currency with gold. The atmosphere after the victory favored a one-world approach. The rise of corporate America, Japanese car makers, and Germany's machinery reconstructed the Western economy rapidly. Four decades ago, the open door policy of China pushed globalization to an unprecedented level. Several hundred million workers helped the country accumulate multitrillion dollars of foreign currency reserve after its entry into the WTO. China has been looking for a venue to recycle its earnings and saving. The wall of money is circulating around the clock in London, Dubai, Hong Kong, Tokyo, and New York. Network externalities of the dollar are too strong to crack. Dollarization is a symbol of globalization.

China holds the largest stakes in terms of foreign currency reserve. On the issue of reforming the international monetary system, it has been vocal. China can take up the responsibility to tackle the Triffin dilemma, just as the US did in Bretton Woods in 1944. China is diversifying its foreign reserve. It allows the exchange rate to move more flexibly against the dollar. It has signed a list of currency swap agreements with other central banks. It is opening the financial market and allows foreign investors and central banks to buy and sell onshore bonds and equity. It is also developing its digital currency.

But the aforementioned actions are not sufficient. Even if these efforts may place the Chinese yuan as a small share of central banks' reserve portfolio, the monopolistic position of the US dollar will likely be untouched. Despite the concerted efforts of the EU members, the EUR has yet to gain major share in global reserves outside the Atlantic. Japan has also attempted to internalize its currency. Almost no other central bank regards yen as an anchor currency.

Fairly speaking, the leading position of the British pound in the nineteenth century and the US dollar in the last century were primarily a result of political shocks. It is clear that market force alone cannot crack the incumbent position of the US dollar. The world will continue to live with the global saving glut. A strong and exogenous force is needed to bring a material change and hence transform the architecture of international monetary regime.

8.2 Libra or RMB, Which Is the Designated One?

Blockchain technology represents a perfect shock to spur a transformation. The payment system is based on proof-of-work or proof-of-stake. It does not require a market maker to issue the numeraire currency. Cryptocurrency is neutral, independent, and apolitical. Cryptocurrency can be used as a third-party currency for denominating international trade settlement and payment currency. In the past, countries running trade surplus prefer dollar instruments. With cryptocurrency, international balance becomes more "balanced." Using a non-sovereign currency can end the loop of factor dollar recycling. Bitcoin frenzy was partly a response to the lack of trust in sovereign money. The rise of populism calls for an end to the regime solely governed by central banks. As globalization is challenged, so is dollarization. The global economy calls for a whole new payment system in the digital era.

Is Libra the change we have been expecting? Unlikely, but it is the one preparing the way. The problem of Libra is governance. Having reserve assets to back this stablecoin is a good transition to establish the new currency. But it remains difficult to entrust a private sector company that does not enjoy a risk-free status. Although the very nature of blockchain does not need an underwriter or an intermediary, having one can help bridge the convertibility between the legacy and digital regime. To end dollar recycling, the reserve should be looked after by an independent agency with unquestionable access to central banks in the existing system in order to ensure convertibility in the transitioning phase.

Ideally, institutions like the IMF, BIS, or the World Bank can take up this role. They can initiate the development of an official cryptocurrency for world use. I call it World Cryptocurrency (WCC). With digital technology advancing exponentially, a reasonable assumption is that the blockchain technology will ultimately overcome the technical barriers, notably scalability. Unlike central bank digital currency (CBDC) or electronic cash, this new currency should not be issued by a central bank. It is a non-sovereign currency to support the issue of sovereign currency, ultimately.

The WCC is not a collection of CBDCs, i.e. electronic M0 of different countries. Cryptography remains the core technology to generate money supply. To address the global saving gluts, the current state of the fiat money regime needs to end. Like gold, the supply of this cryptocurrency should not be generated by individual central banks. The creation of the crypto monetary base should be based on blockchain, smart contracts, or further refined technology that can overcome the scalability issue. Proof-of-work or proof-of-stake remains the underlying process to generate the monetary base.

The value of WCC should be market-determined and reflect the level of purchasing power in the global market. While governments of individual countries can decide on its respective exchange rate regime (and monetary policy), it requires a period of stabilization. Policymakers can draw on the experience of previous regime shifts. The first one was the beginning of the Bretton Woods regime in which the US dollar was fixed at USD 35 per ounce.

Another was the formation of the EUR, which required a conversion between individual currencies of Economic and Monetary Union (EMU) members. The goal was to minimize any disruption to the global financial system and ensure smooth transition to the new currency era. In the case of WCC, after setting a set of baseline exchange rates with the basket currencies (USD, EUR, JPY, CNY, and GBP), the conversion rates with individual currencies should be flexible.

Rather than relying on private sector coin exchanges, the independent agency issuing the WCC can ensure convertibility with sovereign currencies through its swap arrangement with central banks. To promote the penetration and to ensure compatibility, it is still important for this agency to engage the private sector from global financial institutions (major banks and asset managers), payment companies (Visa, Mastercard, JCB, and UnionPay), e-commerce giants (like Amazon and Alibaba) and social media providers (like Facebook, WeChat, Line).

The new currency unit can be used to denominate different financial instruments, including government bonds. Once the world adopts the cryptocurrency as the new standard, many governments and the private sector can use it to denominate their balance sheet positions. A new class of safe assets will be available other than UST, Bund, or JGB.

8.3 What Can China Do?

As a victim of Trump's unilateralism and the world's largest holder of foreign currency reserve, China has an immediate interest in pushing for a digital transformation of the global monetary regime:

- First, China could actively participate in the development of the WCC. The Chinese government always cares about their sovereignty. But this solution does not undermine their concern. As China also wants to promote the use of the RMB, a connection with the WCC can enhance yuan's international circulation. Once the WCC is established, the international payment system can support CNY–WCC convertibility. The international cryptocurrency will be the base reserve governing the total money supply in different economies, including China.

- Second, China could help develop convertibility of the yuan with the world currency, just as it does with other foreign currencies in the process of RMB internationalization. In the past few years, the China Foreign Exchange Trade System (CFETS) began to expand the list of currencies available for conversion. The list can also include the WCC. As an important member of the IMF, the PBOC should have an ability to swap arrangements with the agency for CNY and WCC. The PBOC can also denominate its foreign currency reserve of USD 3.1 trillion in the WCC.

- Third, China would be able to accelerate a de-dollarization process by encouraging its importers and exporters to use the WCC. With the network advantage of the USD, it is a chicken-and-egg process. Based on the experience of RMB internationalization, exporters are still not willing to use the yuan, as they need the USD funds to finance their imports of materials and parts. Overseas suppliers are not willing to receive the yuan, as the proceeds do not have sufficient usage. The key is to develop the investment aspect of the RMB, which requires capital market liberalization in the onshore market. Foreign recipients can recycle their proceeds to financial instruments such as the China Government Bond. The same logic of the yuan-cycling process applies to WCC.

- Fourth, China could issue more government securities denominated in the WCC, similar to its issuance denominated in Special Drawing Right (SDR) in the offshore market. Regular issuance of such would help develop a base curve with China's sovereign credit. In 2016, the World Bank issued a 3-year "Mulan Bond" of SDR 300 million in China, using the RMB as a settlement currency.[1] With the availability of the WCC, money raised by bond issuance could be settled in the cryptocurrency, which can be used to support currency conversion in the crypto-money market. Foreign holders of WCC could tap the depth of China's onshore bond market, currently equivalent to a year of China's GDP (Q1 2020: CNY 103 trillion of which CNY 2.3 trillion was held by foreign institutional investors). China's capital market could contribute to the reform of global monetary regime.

One may argue that China (and other countries) could have kicked off the de-dollarization process by using the IMF's SDR proactively, even without the WCC. The IMF itself has attempted to promote SDR but has not been successful (Ocampo 2019). The current setup of SDR remains a sovereign-based system. Here, the proposal is to revamp this existing regime. Cryptographic technology offers an opportunity to

---

[1] *China Daily*. September 1, 2016. (http://www.chinadaily.com.cn/business/2016-09/01/content_26666069.htm).

extend gold standard in a virtual form, as several applications of block-chain in the past decade have proved that cryptocurrency is a viable form of payment.

The agency issuing WCC will serve as an administrator guiding this innovation, performing a function similar to the IMF or the World Bank. It will also oversee the AML/CTF aspects of the cryptocurrency. Since all transactions can be tracked, the shift from a fiat money regime to the digital one should make the financial system cleaner and safer.

Bernanke (2015) puts the role of USD dominance in global trade imbalance in an accurate language, "US finances its trade deficit in large part through the risk premium it earns from issuing safe liabilities and investing in risky assets." Currently, it is estimated that at least 50% or more of US dollar currency notes are circulated offshore in 2016 (Judson 2017). Foreign holdings of US government securities reached USD 6.7 trillion at the end of 2019, roughly one-third of US government debts.

The WCC proposal here could be a solution to address the global imbalance. If China shifts its foreign reserve holding from the dollar to WCC, herd behavior will likely follow and reduce their dollar exposure. The dollar will weaken as foreign central banks and the market sell the greenback. Unless the Fed desterilizes, foreign withdrawal will likely push the interest rate higher. Weaker currency and tightened monetary conditions will reduce US imports and help restore the trade balance. Obviously, advocates of the dollar standard (including Mr. Bernanke) would cite the efficiency loss as a result of the shift, as the global economy needs to search for a new equilibrium state, which may not be globally optimal. However, there is no evidence that the WCC regime is less efficient. The same network externalities applied to the dollar can also apply to a new global standard.

However, solving the Triffin dilemma only addresses one deficiency of the international monetary system. If the fiat money regime is replaced with our proposed cryptocurrency regime, the global economy will virtually become a currency union because the cryptocurrency base governs the total money supply expressed in WCC terms. The experience of the eurozone suggested that countries continued to register current account deficits and fiscal deficits even under the absolute authorities of a single central bank. For the WCC regime to be sustainable, the new system needs to coordinate with the fiscal discipline of the member economies (similar to EU's Six-Pack agreement). An official cryptocurrency for the world could potentially break dollar recycling. The Fed would still need to commit to an inflation target so that it can manage its balance sheet responsibly.

In addition, economic measure is not a solution to the end of populism, unilateralism, and protectionism. Politicians may still prefer to use import tariffs and other trade barriers, which are more visible and appealing to voters. Economic policy is often not a function of economics but politics. The currency solution proposed here can only right the wrong done to the global monetary system, addressing the moral hazard problem caused by the money printing monopoly. If the US decides to back off from its trade ties with China, or continue to raise national debts in an uncontrollable fashion, the world economic outlook will continue to be structurally uncertain.

Will the WCC end the trade war? Maybe the Marvel heroes can answer. Given the Triffin dilemma, the status of global reserve currency — let's call it the "Infinity Stones" now — should be handed to the right side. Thanos flagged the "Infinity War" and wanted to make the "universe great again." He thought he was the designated one. In the Endgame, he snapped his fingers, saying "I am . . . inevitable." Half of the population could have disappeared. Thanks to new technology, not blockchain, but Tony Stark's nanotechnology, the stones fell into his right hand. He righted the wrong. He said, "And I . . . am . . . Iron Man!" With that being said, he ended the battle.

The Avengers searched for the Infinity Stones. The world economy in digital time also needs to find a new global reserve currency.

Bibliography

Abadi, J. and Brunnermeier, M.K. (2018). Blockchain economics. NBER Working Paper, 25407 (December).

Adler, G. and Osorio Buitron, C. (2017). Tipping the scale? The workings of monetary policy through trade (June). IMF Working Paper. WP/17/142.

Adrian, T. and Griffoli, T.M. (2019). The rise of digital money. IMF FinTech Notes No.19/001.

Ahir, H., Bloom, N., and Furceri, D. (2019). New index tracks trade uncertainty across the globe. IMF Blog (September 9). (https://blogs.imf.org/2019/09/09/new-index-tracks-trade-uncertainty-across-the-globe/).

Alesina, A., Barro, R.J., and Tenreyro, S. (2002). Optimal currency areas. NBER Working Paper, 9072 (July).

Aliber, R.Z. and Kindleberger, C.P. (2015). *Manias, Panics, and Crashes: A History of Financial Crises.* Basingstoke: Palgrave Macmillan. doi: 10.1007/978-1-137-52574-1.

ANZ Research (2019). China Insight, October 11.

Athey, S., Parashkevov, I., Sarukkai, V., and Xia, J. (2016). Bitcoin pricing, adoption, and usage: Theory and evidence. (August). Stanford University Graduate School of Business Research Paper No. 16-42.

Authers, J. (2019). China may have miscalculated trump's weak spot. Bloomberg Opinion (May 14, 2019).

Autor, D.H., Dorn, D., and Hanson, G. (2016). The China shock: Learning from labor market adjustment to large changes in trade. NBER Working Paper, 21906 (January).

Bairoch, P. (1993). *Economics and World History*. London: Harvester-Wheatsheaf.

Bairoch, P. and Burke, S. (1989). European trade policy, 1815–1914. In P. Mathias & S. Pollard (eds.), *The Cambridge Economic History of Europe from the Decline of the Roman Empire*, Cambridge: Cambridge University Press, pp. 1–160. doi:10.1017/CHOL9780521225045.002.

Bairoch, P. and Kozul-Wright, R. (1996). Globalization myths: Some historical reflections on integration, industrialization and growth in the world economy. Discussion Papers 113. United Nations Conference on Trade and Development.

Baldwin, R.E. and Martin, P. (1999). Two waves of globalization: Superficial similarities, fundamental differences. NBER Working Paper, 6904 (January).

Bank of America / Merrill Lynch. (2019). The 5G chip primer: from faster consumer to smarter enterprise. Equity research report (March 3).

Barro, R. (2016). Economic growth and convergence, applied to China. *China & World Economy*, 24: 5-19. doi: 10.1111/cwe.12172.

Bayoumi, T., Lee, J., and Jayanthi, S. (2005). New rates from new weights. IMF Working Paper. WP/05/99 (May).

Bech, M. and Garratt, R. (2017). *Central bank cryptocurrencies, BIS Quarterly Review*, September.

Bernanke, B. (2005). The global saving glut and the US current account deficit. Speech presented at the Homer Jones Lecture, St. Louis, Missouri, on April 14.

Bernanke, B. (2015). Federal Reserve policy in an international context. Speech presented at the 16th Jacques Polak Annual Research Conference November 5-6 hosted by the IMF.

Biais, B., Bisière, C., Bouvard, M., and Casamatta, C. (2018). The blockchain folk theorem. Toulouse School of Economics. Working Paper 17-817 (January 5).

BIS (2015). Digital Currencies. CPMI Papers 137 (https://www.bis.org/cpmi/publ/d137.htm).

BIS (2017), Understanding Globalization. BIS Annual Economic Report (June).

Bloom, D.E., McKenna, M., and Prettner, K. (2018). Demography, unemployment, automation, and digitalization: Implications for the creation of (decent) jobs, 2010–2030. NBER Working Paper, 24835 (July).

Bordo, M.D. and McCauley, R.N. (2017). Triffin: dilemma or myth. BIS Working Paper, 684. (December).

Bordo, M.D. and Rockoff, H. (1996). The gold standard as a "good housekeeping seal of approval." *Journal of Economic History*, 56 (2): 389–428. Papers Presented at the Fifty-Fifth Annual Meeting of the Economic History Association (June).

Bordo, M.D. and Schwartz, A. (1997). Monetary policy regimes and economic performance: The historical record. NBER Working Paper, 6201.

Borio, C. and Disyatat, P. (2015). Capital flows and the current account: Taking financing seriously. BIS Working Paper No. 525 (October).

Bown, C.P. (2019). US–China trade war: The guns of August. Peterson Institute for International Economics (September 20).

Broner, F. and Ventura, J. (2016). Rethinking the effects of financial globalization. *The Quarterly Journal of Economics* 131 (3): 1497–1542 (August). https://doi.org/10.1093/qje/qjw010.

Bullmann, D., Klemm, J., and Pinna, A. (2019). In search for stability in crypto-assets: Are stablecoins the solution? ECB Occasional Working Paper, 230 (August).

Calomiris, C.W. (2007). Bank failures in theory and history: The Great Depression and other "contagious" events. NBER Working Paper. 13597 (November).

Catão, L. and Terrones, M. (2016). Financial de-dollarization: A global perspective and the Peruvian experience, IMF Working Paper 16/97 (April).

Cavallo, A., Gopinath, G., Neiman, B., and Tang, J. (2019). Tariff passthrough at the border and at the store: Evidence from US trade policy. Becker Friedman Institute Working Paper (October 16).

Chiu, J. and Koeppl, T.V. (2018). Blockchain-based settlement for asset trading (May 1). http://dx.doi.org/10.2139/ssrn.3203917.

Clark, G. (2005). The British Industrial Revolution, 1760-1860. Course reading. (http://faculty.econ.ucdavis.edu/faculty/gclark/ecn110b/readings/ecn110b-chapter2-2005.pdf).

Clausen, J.R. and Kandil, M. (2005). On cyclicality in the current and financial accounts: Evidence from nine industrial countries, IMF Working Paper. 05/56 (March).

Cong, L.W. and He, Z. (2019). Blockchain disruption and smart contracts. *The Review of Financial Studies*, 32 (5) May: 1754–1797. https://doi .org/10.1093/rfs/hhz007

Cooper, R. (2005). Living with global imbalances: A contrarian View. Institute of International Economics. *Policy Briefs PB05-3.* (November).

Dabrowski, M. and Janikowski, L. (2018). Virtual currencies and central banks monetary policy: Challenges ahead. European Parliament *Monetary Dialogue* July 2018.

Dark, C., Emery, D., Ma, J., and Noone, C. (*2019*). Cryptocurrency: Ten years on. *Reserve Bank of Australia Bulletin.* June 2019.

Das, M. and N'Diaye, P. (2013). Chronicle of a decline foretold: Has China reached the Lewis Turning Point? IMF Working Paper. WP/13/26. (January).

Das, S. (2019). China's evolving exchange rate regime. IMF Working Paper WP/19/50 (March)

Daunton, M. (2005). Britain and globalization since 1850: I. Creating a global order, 1850-1914. *Transactions of the Royal Historical Society,* 16 (November), 1-38.

David, A., Sobolewski, M., Vaccari, L., and Pignatelli, F. (2019). Blockchain for digital government. Office of the European Union. doi: 10.2760/942739 (online).

Davies, G. (2002). *A History of Money: From Ancient Times to the Present Day.* Cardiff: University of Wales Press.

Drinot, P. and Knight, A. (2014). *The Great Depression in Latin America.* Durham and London: Duke University Press Books.

Easley, D., O'Hara, M., and Basu, S. (2019). From mining to markets: The evolution of bitcoin transaction fees. *Journal of Financial Economics* 134(1): 91–109.

Economist, The (2014). https://www.economist.com/news/essays/ 21600451-finance-not-merely-prone-crises-it-shaped-them-five-hist orical-crises-show-how-aspects-today-s-fina.

Edwards, S. (2005). Is the US current account deficit sustainable? And if not, how costly is adjustment likely to be? NBER Working Paper, 11541. (August).

Eichengreen, B. (2011). *Exorbitant Privilege: The Rise and Fall of the Dollar and the Future of the International Monetary System.* Oxford: Oxford University Press (January). ISBN-10: 0199753784.

Eichengreen, B. (2019). From commodity to fiat and now to crypto: What does history tell us? NBER Working Paper, 25426 (January).

Eichengreen, B. and Flandreau, M., (2008). The rise and fall of the dollar, or when did the dollar replace sterling as the leading international currency? NBER Working Paper, 14154 (July).

Eichengreen, B., Mehl, A., and Chitu, L. (2017). Mars or Mercury? The geopolitics of international currency choice. NBER Working Paper, 24145 (December).

Elwell, C.K. (2011). Brief History of the Gold Standard in the United States. Congressional Research Service 7-5700 (June 23). https://fas.org/sgp/crs/misc/R41887.pdf.

European Commission (2011). The Fiscal Compact—Taking Stock. (February 22). (https://ec.europa.eu/info/publications/fiscal-compact-taking-stock_en).

Federal Reserve (1989). The international gold standard and U.S. monetary policy from World War I to the new deal. *Federal Reserve Bulletin,* 75 (6) (June).

Fehl, C. and Thimm, J. (2019). Saving multilateralism in times of Trump: What can Europe do? [Blog post]. Peace Research Institute Frankfurt Blog (March 21).

Feldstein, M. and Horioka, C. (1980). Domestic saving and international capital flows. *Economic Journal,* 90 (358): 314–329.

Fergusson, I.F. (2007). The World Trade Organization: Background and Issues. CRS Report for Congress. Order code 98-928. (May 9).

Fernández-Villaverde, J. and Sanches, D. (2016). Can currency competition work? NBER Working Paper, 22157 (April).

Frankel, J. (2012). Internationalization of the RMB and historical precedents. *Journal of Economic Integration,* 27(3): 329-365.

Frankel, J. (2015). The Plaza Accord, 30 years later. NBER Working Paper 21813 (December).

Furceri, D., Loungani, P. and Ostry, J. (2018). The aggregate and distributional effects of financial globalization: Evidence from macro and sectoral data. IMF Working Paper. WP/18/83 (April).

Garratt, R. and Wallace, N. (2018) Bitcoin 1, Bitcoin 2, ... An experiment in privately issued outside monies. Economic Inquiry (March) (https://doi.org/10.1111/ecin.12569).

Ghosh, A. and Ramakrishnan, U. (2006). Do current account deficits matter? *IMF Finance and Development 43* (43 (4) (December).

Ghosh, A. and Ramakrishnan, U. (2017). Current account deficits: Is there a problem? *IMF Finance and Development (November)*.

Glick, R. and Rose, A. (2016). Currency unions and trade: A post-EMU reassessment. *European Economic Review*, 87, issue C: 78–91.

Goetzmann, W. and Ukhov, A. (2005). British investment overseas 1970–1913: A modern portfolio theory approach. NBER Working Paper, 11266 (April).

Gowrisankaran, G. and Stavins, J. (2004). Network externalities and technology adoption: Lessons From electronic payments. *The RAND Journal of Economics* 35 (2): 260–276.

Griffoli, T.M., Martinez Peria, M.S., Agur, I., Ari, A., Kiff, J., Popescu, A., and Rochon, C. (2018). *Casting light on Central Bank Digital Currencies*. IMF Staff Discussion Notes 18/08.

Hale, G., Hobijn, B., Nechio, F., and Wilson, D. (2019). Inflationary effects of trade disputes with China. *Federal Reserve Bank of San Francisco Economic Letter* (February 15).

Haltmaier, J. (2014). Cyclically adjusted current account balances. FRB International Finance Discussion Paper No. 1126. (December 4).

He, D. and McCauley, R.N. (2012). Eurodollar banking and currency internationalization. *BIS Quarterly Review (June)*.

Hirsh, M. (2016). Why the new nationalists are taking over. *Politico Magazine* (June 27).

IHS Markit (2017). *The 5G economy: How 5G technology contribute to the global economy*. January 2017. (https://cdn.ihs.com/www/pdf/IHS-Technology-5G-Economic-Impact-Study.pdf).

Ilzetzki, E., Reinhart, C.M., and Rogoff, K.S. (2017). Exchange arrangements entering the 21st century: Which anchor will hold? NBER Working Paper 23134.

Ito, T., Koibuchi, S., Sato, K., and Shimizu, J. (2019). Growing use of local currencies in Japanese trade with Asian countries: A new puzzle of invoicing currency choice (June). (https://voxeu.org/article/growing-use-local-currencies-japanese-trade-within-asia).

Japan Ministry of Finance (1999). Internationalization of the Yen for the 21st Century—Japan's Response to Changes in Global Economic and Financial Environments.April 20, 1999. (https://www.mof.go.jp/english/about_mof/councils/customs_foreign_exchange/e1b064a.htm).

Jaumotte, F., Lall, S. and Papageorgiou, C. (2013). Rising income inequality: Technology, or trade and financial globalization? IMF Working Paper. WP/08/185 (July).

Jevons, W.S. (1875). *Money and the Mechanism of Exchange*. NY: Cornell University Library (republished August 10, 2009).

Johnston, B. and Sundararajan, V. (1991). Sequencing Financial Sector Reforms. IMF (March). http://dx.doi.org/10.5089/9781557757791. 071.

Judson, R. (2017). The death of cash? Not so fast: Demand for U.S. currency at home and abroad, 1990–2016. International Cash Conference 2017—War on Cash: Is there a Future for Cash? April 25-27, 2017.

Kamber, G. and Mohanty, M.S. (2018). Do interest rates play a major role in monetary policy transmission in China? BIS Working Paper 714 (April).

Kang, K.Y. and Lee, S.D. (2019). *Money, Cryptocurrency, and Monetary Policy* (March 23). http://dx.doi.org/10.2139/ssrn.3303595.

Katz, M.L., and Shapiro, C. (1986). Technology adoption in the presence of network externalities. *Journal of Political Economy*, 94 (4): 822–841.

Kawai, M. and Pontines, V. (2015). Is there really a renminbi bloc in Asia? A modified Frankel–Wei approach. *Journal of International Money and Finance*, 62. (December).

Keynes, J.M. (1919). *The Economic Consequences of the Peace*. London: Macmillan, p. 279. Retrieved June 2, 2016—via Internet Archive.

Kose, M.A., Prasad, E.S. and Taylor, A.D. (2009). Thresholds in the process of international financial integration. NBER Working Paper, 14916 (April).

Kraemer, K., Linden, G. and Dedrick, J. (2011). Capturing value in global networks: Apple's iPad and iPhone. UC Irvine Working Paper (July). (http://pcic.merage.uci.edu/papers/2011/Value_iPad_iPhone.pdf).

Lamport, L., Shostak, R. and Pease, M. (1982). The Byzantine generals problem. *ACM Transactions on Programming Languages and Systems*, 4 (3): 382–401.

Lindert, P. (1967). *Key currencies and the gold exchange standard 1900–1913*. Unpublished Ph.D. dissertation, Cornell University (February).

Lindert, P. (1969). *Key Currencies and Gold, 1900–1913* (Princeton Studies in International Finance 24). Princeton, NJ: Princeton University.

Liu, M. (2015). *The China Dream: Great Power Thinking and Strategic Posture in the Post-American Era.* CN Times Beijing Media Time United Publishing Company Limited

Marr, B. (2018). What is Industry 4.0? Here's a super easy explanation for anyone. *Forbes*, (September 2).

Mathias, P. and Pollar, S. (1989). *The Industrial Economies: The Development of Economic and Social Policies.* Cambridge: Cambridge University Press.

McKinnon, R. (1990). The exchange rate and the trade balance. *Open Economies Review*, 1 (1): 17–37.

McKinsey (2017). Digital China: Powering the Economy to Global Competitiveness.

McKinsey (2019). *China Digital Consumer Trends 2019.* (September).

McKinsey Global Institute (2016). *Digital globalization: The new era of global flows.* (February).

Mead, W. R. (1999). The Jacksonian tradition and American foreign policy. *The National Interest*, Vol. 58, Winter.

Meng, G. (2019). China's Belt and Road Initiative and RMB Internationalization (https://doi.org/10.1142/11230) (November).

Mauro, P., Sussman, N., and Yafeh, Y. (2002). Emerging market spreads: Then versus now. *The Quarterly Journal of Economics*, 117 (2): 695–733.

Meissner, C.M. and Oomes, N. (2008). Why do countries peg the way they peg? The determinants of anchor currency choice. IMF Working Paper (May).

Mercator Institute of China Studies (2019). Networking the "Belt and Road" – The future is digital. BRI Tracker. (August 28).

Mitchener, K.J. and Weidenmier, M.D. (2007). The Baring crisis and the great Latin American meltdown. NBER Working Paper 13403 (September).

Mundell, R.A. (1961). A theory of optimum currency areas. *American Economic Review*, 51 (4): 657–665 (September).

Nabar, M. and Tovar, C. (2017). Renminbi internationalization. Chapter 9 in R. Lam, M. Rodlauer, and A. Schipke (eds). *Modernizing China: Investing in Soft Infrastructure.* Washington, DC: International Monetary Fund.

Nakamoto, S. (2008). Bitcoin: A peer-to-peer electronic cash system. (https://bitcoin.org/bitcoin.pdf).

Nsouli, S.M. (2006). Petrodollar recycling and global Imbalances. Presentation at the CESifo's International Spring Conference. March 23-24.

Obstfeld, M. and Rogoff, K. (2005). Global current account imbalances and exchange rate adjustments. *Brookings Papers on Economic Activity* (January).

Obstfeld, M. and Rogoff, K. (2009). Global imbalances and the financial crisis: Products of common causes. CEPR Discussion Papers 7606.

Ocampo, J.A. (2019). Time for a true global currency. Project Syndicate (April 5).

Owyang, M.T. and Shell, H.G. (2017). *China's Economic Data: An Accurate Reflection, or Just Smoke and Mirrors? The Regional Economist, 2nd Quarter.* Federal Reserve Bank St. Louis.

Park, H.S. (2016). China's RMB internationalization strategy: Its rationale, state of play, prospects and implications (August). M-RCBG Associate Working Paper No. 63.

Pinto, L. (2018). Sustaining the GCC currency pegs: The need for collaboration. Brookings Doha Centre (February 19).

Redding, S., Amiti, M., and Weinstein, D. (2019). Who's paying for the US tariffs? A longer-term perspective. Centre for Economic Policy Research. Discussion Paper 6741-1576864082. (December 20).

Reinhart, C.M. and Rogoff, K.S. (2009). *This Time It's Different: Eight Centuries of Financial Folly.* Princeton: Princeton University Press.

Rodrik, D. (2017). Populism and the economics of globalization. Working Paper 23559 (July).

Rogoff, K. (2001). Why not a global currency? *American Economic Review,* 91(2): 243–247.

Rowley, R., Bichler, S., and Nitzan, J. (1989). The Armadollar-Petrodollar Coalition and the Middle East. EconStor Preprints, ZBW— Leibniz Information Centre for Economics.

Russel, D. and Berger, B. (2019). Navigating the Belt and Road Initiative. Asia Society Policy Institute (June).

Ryan, J. and Loughlin, J. (2018). Lessons from historical monetary unions - is the European monetary union making the same mistakes? *International Economics and Economic Policy,* 15: 709-725.

Saad, M., Spaulding, J., Njilla, L., Kamhoua, C., Shetty, S., Nyang, D., and Mohaisen, A. (2019). Exploring the attack surface of blockchain: A systematic overview. (https://arxiv.org/abs/1904.03487).

Sabet, S. (2016). Key ingredients of opposition to free trade? Prejudice and nationalism. *Washington Post,* August 22, 2016.

Sachs, J. D. (2018). The dangers of Trump's unilateralist international economic policies. *Capitalism and Society*, 13: (2) (December 19).

Schilling, L. and Uhlig, H. (2018). Some simple Bitcoin economics (April). NBER Working Paper 24483.

Shirai, S. (2017). Tokyo as a leading global financial center: The vision under the spotlight again. ADBI Working Paper 758 (July).

Spicer, J. (2017). Special Report: How the Federal Reserve serves U.S. foreign intelligence. Reuters (June 26, 2017). (https://www.reuters.com/article/us-fed-accounts-intelligence-specialrepo/special-report-how-the-federal-reserve-serves-u-s-foreign-intelligence-idUSKBN19H198).

Tago, A. (2017). Multilateralism, bilateralism, and unilateralism in foreign policy. *Oxford Research Encyclopedia Politics* (March). (doi: 10.1093/acrefore/9780190228637.013.449).

Taylor, A.M. (1996). International capital mobility in history: The saving-investment relationship. NBER Working Paper 5743 (September).

Triffin, R. (1960). *Gold and the Dollar Crisis: The Future of Convertibility*. New Haven, CT: Yale University Press.

Windsor, C., Halperin, D. (2018). RMB Internationalization: Where to Next? *Reserve Bank of Australia Bulletin* (September).

Volosovych, V. (2011). Measuring financial market integration over the long run: Is there a U-shape? *Journal of International Money and Finance*, 30 (7): 1535–1561.

World Bank (2012). *China 2030: Building a Modern, Harmonious, and Creative Society*. (https://www.worldbank.org/en/news/feature/2012/02/27/china-2030-executive-summary).

World Economic Forum website. A brief history of globalization. (January 17, 2019). (https://www.weforum.org/agenda/2019/01/how-globalization-4-0-fits-into-the-history-of-globalization/).

Yehoue, E.B. (2004). Currency bloc formation as a dynamic process based on trade network externalities. IMF Working Paper WP/04/22 (November).

Yueh, L. (2018). A quick review of 250 years of economic theory about tariffs. *Harvard Business Review* (July 26). (https://hbr.org/2018/07/a-quick-review-of-250-years-of-economic-theory-about-tariffs).

Zevin, R. (1992). Are world financial markets more open? If so, why and with what effects? In Banuri, T. and Schor, J.B. (eds.), *Financial Openness and National Autonomy*. Oxford: Clarendon Press, pp. 43–83.

Zhang, L. (2016). Rebalancing in China—Progress and prospects. IMF Working Paper. WP/16/183 (September).

Zhang, L., and Chen, S. (2019). China's digital economy: Opportunities and risks. IMF Working Paper. WP/19/16 (January).

Zhang, Y., Shao, T., and Dong, Q. (2018). Reassessing the Lewis Turning Point in China: Evidence from 70,000 rural households. *China & World Economy*. (https://doi.org/10.1111/cwe.12226).

Index